IRENAEUS'S *DEMONSTRATION OF THE APOSTOLIC PREACHING*

The theology of Irenaeus, and the *Demonstration of the Apostolic Preaching* in particular, is pivotal in showing the way in which the fathers of the church interpreted scripture and distilled doctrine. The Demonstration is an important hinge showing how the doctrine of the fourth century with its definitive councils and definitions of faith, opens out from the New Testament apostolic and evangelical witness.

Presenting the full translation of the *Demonstration of Irenaeus* by Dean Armitage Robinson, this book offers a detailed theological commentary by Canon Iain MacKenzie on this foundational doctrinal text. MacKenzie sets out the main theological themes throughout Irenaeus's work, and explores his method of systematic theology, Athanasius's dependence on Irenaeus, and Irenaeus's influence on doctrine in the fourth century – particularly the works of Athanasius, Basil of Caesarea, Gregory of Nazianzus and Gregory of Nyssa. Highlighting the importance of this second century theologian for theology today, this commentary and theological interpretation offers an incentive to study Irenaeus in the wider development of Christian doctrine as a cardinal figure in the appreciation of systematic theology.

I0880085

Irenaeus's *Demonstration of the Apostolic Preaching*

A theological commentary and translation

IAIN M. MACKENZIE
Canon Residentiary of Worcester, UK

with
THE TRANSLATION OF THE TEXT OF THE *DEMONSTRATION* BY
J. ARMITAGE ROBINSON

Routledge
Taylor & Francis Group
LONDON AND NEW YORK

First published 2002 by Ashgate Publishing

Reissued 2018 by Routledge
2 Park Square, Milton Park, Abingdon, Oxon OX14 4RN
711 Third Avenue, New York, NY 10017, USA

Routledge is an imprint of the Taylor & Francis Group, an informa business

Copyright © Iain M. MacKenzie 2002

The author has asserted his moral right under the Copyright, Designs and Patents Act, 1988, to be identified as the author of this work.

All rights reserved. No part of this book may be reprinted or reproduced or utilised in any form or by any electronic, mechanical, or other means, now known or hereafter invented, including photocopying and recording, or in any information storage or retrieval system, without permission in writing from the publishers.

Notice:
Product or corporate names may be trademarks or registered trademarks, and are used only for identification and explanation without intent to infringe.

Publisher's Note
The publisher has gone to great lengths to ensure the quality of this reprint but points out that some imperfections in the original copies may be apparent.

Disclaimer
The publisher has made every effort to trace copyright holders and welcomes correspondence from those they have been unable to contact.

Typeset in Times by Manton Typesetters, Louth, Lincolnshire, UK.

A Library of Congress record exists under LC control number: 2002024891

ISBN 13: 978-1-138-71777-0 (hbk)
ISBN 13: 978-1-138-71776-3 (pbk)
ISBN 13: 978-1-315-19621-3 (ebk)

Contents

Acknowledgements

I am grateful that I have been permitted to use the text of the translation of Irenaeus's *Demonstration of the Apostolic Preaching* by J. Armitage Robinson, formerly Dean of Wells. Permission to do so has been granted generously and readily by Edward Robinson, Esq., the late Dean's nephew, in whom the rights of the text of the translation are vested and with whom they remain.

The translation of Irenaeus's *Adversus Haereses* which I have used in quoting excerpts is that of the Edinburgh edition of 1885. Occasionally I have revised the translation. All the references throughout this commentary to this work are therefore to the numeration of its constituent books and chapters found in that edition. I have used these excerpts in places throughout the commentary for the immediate convenience of the reader, but in other instances merely have referred in the notes at the end of each section to the relevant passages in *Adversus Haereses* for comparison. I have also quoted other fathers' works from this same translated edition of the Ante-Nicene Fathers and from the nineteenth-century translation of the Select Library of Nicene and Post-Nicene Fathers.

I am indebted in no small measure to Mrs Winifred Young for so readily undertaking to proofread this work and for so diligently accomplishing the task, and to Mrs Jan Barnes, the Cathedral Co-ordinator of Worcester Cathedral for her equally diligent work in typing out the text of the translation by J. Armitage Robinson of the *Demonstration*. To both ladies go my thanks.

The Demonstration of the Apostolic Preaching

1 Knowing, my beloved Marcianus, your desire to walk in godliness, which alone leads man to life eternal, I rejoice with you and make my prayer that you may preserve your faith entire and so be pleasing to God who made you. Would that it were possible for us to be always together, to help each other and to lighten the labour of our earthly life by continual discourse together on the things that profit. But, since at this present time we are parted from one another in the body, yet according to our power we will not fail to speak with you a little by writing, and to show forth in brief the preaching of the truth for the confirmation of your faith. We send you as it were a manual of essentials, that by little you may attain to much, learning in short space all the members of the body of the truth, and receiving in brief the demonstration of the things of God. So shall it be fruitful to your own salvation, and you shall put to shame all who inculcate falsehood, and bring with all confidence our sound and pure teaching to everyone who desires to understand it. For one is the way leading upwards for all who see, lightened with heavenly light: but many and dark and contrary are the ways of them that see not. This way leads to the kingdom of heaven, uniting man to God: but those ways bring down to death, separating man from God. Wherefore it is needful for you and for all who care for their own salvation to make your course unswerving, firm and sure by means of faith, that you falter not, nor be retarded and detained in material desires, nor turn aside and wander from the right.

2 Now, since man is a living being compounded of soul and flesh, he must needs exist by both of these: and, whereas from both of them offences come, purity of the flesh is the restraining abstinence from all shameful things and all unrighteous deeds, and purity of the soul is the keeping faith towards God entire, neither adding thereto nor diminishing therefrom. For godliness is obscured and dulled by the soiling and the staining of the flesh, and is broken and polluted and no more entire, if falsehood enter into the soul: but it will keep itself in its beauty and its measure, when truth is constant in the soul and purity in the flesh. For what profit is it to know the truth in words, and to pollute the flesh and perform the works of evil? Or what profit can purity of the flesh bring, if truth be not in the soul? For these rejoice with one another, and are united and allied to bring man face to face with God. Wherefore the Holy Spirit says by David: *Blessed is the man who hath not walked in the counsel of the ungodly*: that is, the counsel of the nations which know not God: for those are ungodly who worship not the God that truly is. And therefore the Word says to Moses: *I am He that is*: but they that worship not the God that is, these are the ungodly. *And hath not stood in the way of sinners*: but sinners are

those who have the knowledge of God and keep not His commandments; that is, disdainful scorners. *And hath not sat in the seat of the pestilential*: now the pestilential are those who by wicked and perverse doctrines corrupt not themselves only, but others also. For the seat is a symbol of teaching. Such then are all heretics: they sit in the seats of the pestilential, and those are corrupted who receive the venom of their doctrine.

3 Now, that we may not suffer ought of this kind, we must needs hold the rule of the faith without deviation, and do the commandments of God, believing in God and fearing Him as Lord and loving Him as Father. Now this doing is produced by faith: for Isaiah says: *If ye believe not, neither shall ye understand.* And faith is produced by the truth; for faith rests on things that truly are. For in things that are, as they are, we believe; and believing in things that are, as they ever are, we keep firm our confidence in them. Since then faith is the perpetuation of our salvation, we must needs bestow much pains on the maintenance thereof, in order that we may have a true comprehension of the things that are. Now faith occasions this for us; even as the Elders, the disciples of the Apostles, have handed down to us. First of all it bids us bear in mind that we have received baptism for the remission of sins, in the name of God the Father, and in the name of Jesus Christ, the Son of God, who was incarnate and died and rose again, and in the Holy Spirit of God. And that this baptism is the seal of eternal life, and is the new birth unto God, that we should no longer be the sons of mortal men, but of the eternal and perpetual God; and that what is everlasting and continuing is made God; and is over all things that are made, and all things are put under Him; and all the things that are put under Him are made His own; for God is not ruler and Lord over the things of another, but over His own; and all things are God's; and therefore God is Almighty, and all things are of God.

4 For it is necessary that things that are made should have the beginning of their making from some great cause; and the beginning of all things is God. For He Himself was not made by any, and by Him all things were made. And therefore it is right first of all to believe that there is One God, the Father, who made and fashioned all things, and made what was not that it should be, and who, containing all things, alone is uncontained. Now among all things is this world of ours, and in the world is man: so then this world also was formed by God.

5 Thus then there is shown forth One God, the Father, not made, invisible, creator of all things; above whom there is no other God, and after whom there is no other God. And, since God is rational, therefore by [the] Word He created the things that were made; and God is Spirit, and by [the] Spirit He adorned all things: as also the prophet says: *By the word of the Lord were the heavens established, and by his spirit all their power.* Since then the Word establishes, that is to say, gives body and grants the reality of being, and the Spirit gives order and form to the diversity of the powers; rightly and fittingly is the Word called the Son, and the Spirit the Wisdom of God. Well also does Paul His apostle say: *One God, the Father, who is over all and through all and in us all.* For *over all* is the Father: and *through all* is the Son, for through Him all things were made by the Father; and *in us all* is the Spirit, who cries *Abba Father*, and fashions man into the likeness of God. Now the Spirit shows forth the Word, and therefore the prophets announced the Son of God; and the Word utters the Spirit, and therefore is Himself the announcer of the prophets, and leads and draws man to the Father.

6 This then is the order of the rule of our faith, and the foundation of the building, and the stability of our conversation: God, the Father, not made, not material, invisible; one God, the creator of all things: this is the first point of our faith. The second point is: The Word of God, Son of God, Christ Jesus our Lord, who was manifested to the prophets according to the form of their prophesying and according to the method of the dispensation of the Father: through whom all things were made; who also at the end of the times, to complete and gather up all things, was made man among men, visible and tangible, in order to abolish death and show forth life and produce a community of union between God and man. And the third point is: The Holy Spirit, through whom the prophets prophesied, and the fathers learned the things of God, and the righteous were led forth into the way of righteousness; and who in the end of the times was poured out in a new way upon mankind in all the earth, renewing man unto God.

7 And for this reason the baptism of our regeneration proceeds through these three points: God the Father bestowing on us regeneration through His Son by the Holy Spirit. For as many as carry [in them] the Spirit of God are led to the Word, that is to the Son; and the Son brings them to the Father; and the Father causes them to possess incorruption. Without the Spirit it is not possible to behold the Word of God, nor without the Son can any draw near to the Father: for the knowledge of the Father is the Son, and the knowledge of the Son of God is through the Holy Spirit; and, according to the good pleasure of the Father, the Son ministers and dispenses the Spirit to whomsoever the Father wills and as He wills.

8 And by the Spirit the Father is called Most High and Almighty and Lord of hosts; that we may learn concerning God that He it is who is creator of heaven and earth and all the world, and maker of angels and men, and Lord of all, through whom all things exist and by whom all things are sustained; merciful, compassionate and very tender, good, just, the God of all, both of Jews and of Gentiles, and of them that believe. To them that believe He is as Father, for in the end of the times He opened up the covenant of adoption; but to the Jews as Lord and Lawgiver, for in the intermediate times, when man forgat God and departed and revolted from Him, He brought them into subjection by the Law, that they might learn that they had for Lord the maker and creator, who also gives the breath of life, and whom we ought to worship day and night: and to the Gentiles as maker and creator and almighty: and to all alike sustainer and nourisher and king and judge; for none shall escape and be delivered from His judgment, neither Jew nor Gentile, nor believer that has sinned, nor angel: but they who now reject His goodness shall know His power in judgment, according to that which the blessed apostle says: *Not knowing that the goodness of God leadeth thee to repentance; but according to thy hardness and impenitent heart thou treasurest up for thyself wrath in the day of wrath and of the revelation of the righteous judgment of God, who shall render to every man according to his works.* This is He who is called in the Law the God of Abraham and the God of Isaac and the God of Jacob, the God of the living; although the sublimity and greatness of this God is unspeakable.

9 Now this world is encompassed by seven heavens, in which dwell powers and angels and archangels, doing service to God, the Almighty and Maker of all things: not as though He was in need, but that they may not be idle and unprofitable and ineffectual. Wherefore also the Spirit of God is manifold in [His] indwelling, and in

seven forms of service is He reckoned by the prophet Isaiah, as resting on the Son of God, that is the Word, in His coming as man. *The Spirit of God*, he says, *shall rest upon him, the Spirit of wisdom and of understanding, the Spirit of counsel and of might, [the Spirit of knowledge] and of godliness; the Spirit of the fear of God shall fill him.* Now the heaven which is first from above, and encompasses the rest, is [that of] wisdom; and the second from it, of understanding; and the third, of counsel; and the fourth, reckoned from above, [is that] of might; and the fifth, of knowledge; and the sixth, of godliness; and the seventh, this firmament of ours, is full of the fear of that Spirit which gives light to the heavens. For, as the pattern [of this], Moses received the seven-branched candlestick, that shined continually in the holy place; for as a pattern of the heavens he received this service, according to that which the Word spake unto him: *Thou shall make [it] according to all the pattern of the things which thou hast seen in the mount.*

10 Now this God is glorified by His Word who is His Son continually, and by the Holy Spirit who is the Wisdom of the Father of all: and the power(s) of these, [namely] of the Word and Wisdom, which are called Cherubim and Seraphim, with unceasing voices glorify God; and every created thing that is in the heavens offers glory to God the Father of all. He by His Word has created the whole world, and in the world are the angels; and to all the world He has given laws wherein each several thing should abide, and according to that which is determined by God should not pass their bounds, each fulfilling his appointed task.

11 But man He formed with His own hands, taking from the earth that which was purest and finest, and mingling in measure His own power with the earth. For He traced His own form on the formation, that that which should be seen should be of divine form: for [as] the image of God was man formed and set on the earth. And that he might becoming living, He breathed on his face the breath of life; that both for the breath and for the formation man should be like unto God. Moreover he was free and self-controlled, being made by God for this end, that he might rule all those things that were upon the earth. And this great created world, prepared by God before the formation of man, was given to man as his place, containing all things within itself. And there were in this place also with [their] tasks the servants of that God who formed all things; and the steward, who was set over all his fellow-servants received this place. Now the servants were angels, and the steward was the archangel.

12 Now, having made man lord of the earth and all things in it, He secretly appointed him lord also of those who were servants in it. They however were in their perfection; but the lord, that is, man, was [but] small; for he was a child; and it was necessary that he should grow, and so come to [his] perfection. And, that he might have his nourishment and growth with festive and dainty meats, He prepared him a place better than this world, excelling in air, beauty, light, food, plants, fruit, water, and all other necessaries of life: and its name is Paradise. And so fair and good was this Paradise, that the Word of God continually resorted thither, and walked and talked with the man, figuring beforehand the things that should be in the future, [namely] that He should dwell with him and talk with him, and should be with men, teaching them righteousness. But man was a child, not yet having his understanding perfected; wherefore also he was easily led astray by the deceiver.

13 And, whilst man dwelt in Paradise, God brought before him all living things and commanded him to give names to them all; *and whatsoever Adam called a living soul, that was its name.* And He determined also to make a helper for the man: for thus God said, *It is not good for the man to be alone: let us make for him a helper meet for him.* For among all the other living things there was not found a helper equal and comparable and like to Adam. But God Himself *cast a trance upon Adam and made him sleep*; and, that work might be accomplished from work, since there was no sleep in Paradise, this was brought upon Adam by the will of God; and God *took one of Adam's ribs and filled up the flesh in its place, and the rib which He took He builded into a woman; and so He brought her to Adam*; and he seeing [her] said: *This is now bone of my bone, flesh of my flesh: she shall be called woman, because she was taken from her husband.*

14 And Adam and Eve – for that is the name of the woman – *were naked, and were not ashamed*; for there was in them an innocent and childlike mind, and it was not possible for them to conceive and understand anything of that which by wickedness through lusts and shameful desires is born in the soul. For they were at that time entire, preserving their own nature; since they had the breath of life which was breathed on their creation: and, while this breath remains in its place and power, it has no comprehension and understanding of things that are base. And therefore they were not ashamed, kissing and embracing each other in purity after the manner of children.

15 But, lest man should conceive thoughts too high, and be exalted and uplifted, as though he had no lord, because of the authority and freedom granted to him, and so should transgress against his maker God, overpassing his measure, and entertain selfish imaginings of pride in opposition to God; a law was given to him by God, in order that he might perceive that he had as lord the Lord of all. And He set him certain limitations, so that, if he should keep the commandment of God, he should ever remain such as he was, that is to say, immortal; but, if he should not keep it, he should become mortal and be dissolved to earth from whence his formation had been taken. Now the commandment was this: *Of every tree that is in the Paradise thou shalt freely eat; but of that tree alone from which is the knowledge of good and evil, of it thou shalt not eat; for in the day thou eatest, thou shalt surely die.*

16 This commandment the man kept not, but was disobedient to God, being led astray by the angel who, for the great gifts of God which He had given to man, was envious and jealous of him, and both brought himself to nought and made man sinful, persuading him to disobey the commandment of God. So the angel, becoming by his falsehood the author and originator of sin, himself was struck down, having offended against God, and man he caused to be cast out from Paradise. And, because through the guidance of his disposition he apostatized and departed from God, he was called Satan, according to the Hebrew word; that is, Apostate: but he is also called Slanderer. Now God cursed the serpent which carried and conveyed the Slanderer; and this malediction came on the beast himself and on the angel hidden and concealed in him, even on Satan; and man he put away from His presence, removing him and making him to dwell on the way to Paradise at that time; because Paradise receiveth not the sinful.

17 And when they were put out of Paradise, Adam and his wife Eve fell into many troubles of anxious grief, going about with sorrow and toil and lamentation in

this world. For under the beams of this sun man tilled the earth, and it put forth thorns and thistles, the punishment of sin. Then was fulfilled that which was written: *Adam knew his wife, and she conceived and bare Cain*; and after him *she bare Abel*. Now the apostate angel, who led man into disobedience and made him sinful and caused his expulsion from Paradise, not content with the first evil, wrought a second on the brothers; for filling Cain with his spirit he made him a fratricide. And so Abel died, slain by his brother; signifying thenceforth that certain should be persecuted and oppressed and slain, the unrighteous slaying and persecuting the righteous. And upon this God was angered yet more, and cursed Cain; and it came to pass that everyone of that race in successive generations was made like to the begetter. And God *raised up* another son to Adam, *instead of Abel* who was slain.

18 And for a very long while wickedness extended and spread, and reached and laid hold upon the whole race of mankind, until a very small seed of righteousness remained among them: and illicit unions took place upon the earth, since angels were united with the daughters of the race of mankind; and they bore to them sons who for their exceeding greatness were called giants. And the angels brought as presents to their wives teachings of wickedness, in that they brought them the virtues of roots and herbs, dyeing in colours and cosmetics, the discovery of rare substances, love-potions, aversions, amours, concupiscence, constraints of love, spells of bewitchment, and all sorcery and idolatry hateful to God; by the entry of which things into the world evil extended and spread, while righteousness was diminished and enfeebled.

19 Until judgment came upon the world from God by means of a flood, in the tenth generation from the first-formed [man]; Noah alone being found righteous. And he for his righteousness was himself delivered, and his wife and his three sons, and the three wives of his sons, being shut up in the ark. And when destruction came upon all, both man and also animals, that were upon the earth, that which was preserved in the ark escaped. Now the three sons of Noah were Shem, Ham and Japheth, from whom again the race was multiplied: for these were the beginning of mankind after the flood.

20 Now of these one fell under a curse, and the two [others] inherited a blessing by reason of their works. For the younger of them, who was called Ham, having mocked his father, and having been condemned of the sin of impiety because of his outrage and unrighteousness against his father, received a curse; and all the posterity that came of him he involved in the curse; whence it came about that his whole race after him were accursed, and in sins they increased and multiplied. But Shem and Japheth, his brothers, because of their piety towards their father obtained a blessing. Now the curse of Ham, wherewith his father Noah cursed him, is this: *Cursed be Ham the child; a servant shall he be unto his brethren*. This having come upon his race, he begat many descendants upon the earth, [even] for fourteen generations, growing up in a wild condition; and then his race was cut off by God, being delivered up to judgment. For the Canaanites and Hittites and the Peresites and Hivites and Amorites and Jebusites and Gergasites and Sodomites, the Arabians also and the dwellers in Phoenicia, all the Egyptians and the Libyans, are of the posterity of Ham, who have fallen under the curse; for the curse is of long duration over the ungodly.

21 And even as the curse passed on, so also the blessing passed on to the race of him who was blessed, to each in his own order. For first of them was Shem blessed in these words: *Blessed be the Lord, the God of Shem; and Ham shall be his servant.* The power of the blessing lies in this, that the God and Lord of all should be to Shem a peculiar possession of worship. And the blessing extended and reached unto Abraham, who was reckoned as descended in the tenth generation from the race of Shem: and therefore the Father and God of all was pleased to be called the God of Abraham and the God of Isaac and the God of Jacob; because the blessing of Shem reached out and attached itself to Abraham. Now the blessing of Japheth is on this wise: *God shall enlarge unto Japheth, and he shall dwell in the house of Shem, and Ham shall be his servant.* That is to say: In the end of the ages he blossomed forth, at the appearing of the Lord, through the calling of the Gentiles, when God enlarged unto them the calling; and *their sound went out into all the earth, and their words to the end of the world.* The enlarging, then, is the calling from among the Gentiles, that is to say, the Church. *And he dwells in the house of Shem*; that is, in the inheritance of the fathers, receiving in Christ Jesus the right of the firstborn. So in the rank in which each was blessed, in that same order through his posterity he received the fruit of the blessing.

22 Now after the Flood God made a covenant with all the world, even with every living thing of animals and of men, that He would no more destroy with a flood all that grew upon the earth. And He set them a sign [saying]: *When the sky shall be covered with a cloud, the bow shall be seen in the cloud; and I will remember my covenant, and will no more destroy by water every moving thing upon the earth.* And He changed the food of men, giving them leave to eat flesh: for from Adam the first-formed until the Flood men ate only of seeds and the fruit of trees, and to eat flesh was not permitted to them. But since the three sons of Noah were the beginning of a race of men, God blessed them for multiplication and increase, saying: *Increase and multiply, and replenish the earth and rule it; and the fear and dread of you shall be upon every living thing of animals and upon all the fowls of the air; and they shall be to you for meat, even as the green herb: but the flesh with the blood of life ye shall not eat: for your blood also will I require at the hand of all beasts and at the hand of man. Whoso sheddeth a man's blood, in return for his blood shall it be shed.* For He made man the image of God; and the image of God is the Son, after whose image man was made: and for this cause He appeared in the end of the times that He might show the image [to be] like unto Himself. According to this covenant the race of man multiplied, springing up from the seed of the three. And *upon the earth was one lip*, that is to say one language.

23 And they arose and came from the land of the east; and, as they went through the land, they chanced upon the land of Shinar, which was exceeding broad; where they took in hand to build a tower. They sought means thereby to go up to heaven, and be able to leave their work as a memorial to those men who should come after them. And the building was made with burnt bricks and bitumen: and the boldness of their audacity went forward, as they were all of one mind and consent, and by means of one speech they served the purpose of their desires. But that the work should advance no further, God divided their tongues, that they should no longer be able to understand one another. And so they were scattered and planted out, and took possession of the world, and dwelt in groups and companies each according to

his language: whence came the diverse tribes and various languages upon the earth. So then, whereas three races of men took possession of the earth, and one of them was under the curse, and two under the blessing, the blessing first of all came to Shem, whose race dwelt in the east and held the land of the Chaldeans.

24 In process of time, that is to say, in the tenth generation after the Flood, Abraham appeared, seeking for the God who by the blessing of his ancestor was due and proper to him. And when, urged by the eagerness of his spirit, he went all about the world, searching where God is, and failed to find out; God took pity on him who alone was silently seeking Him; and He appeared unto Abraham, making Himself known by the Word, as by a beam of light. For He spake with him from heaven, and said unto him: *Get thee out of thy country, and from thy kindred, and from thy father's house; and come into the land that I will show thee*, and there dwell. And he believed the heavenly voice, being then of ripe age, even seventy years old, and having a wife; and together with her he went forth from Mesopotamia, taking with him Lot, the son of his brother who was dead. And when he came into the land which now is called Judaea, in which at that time dwelt seven tribes descended from Ham, God appeared unto him in a vision and said: *To thee will I give this land, and to thy seed after thee, for an everlasting possession*, and [He said] that his seed should be a stranger in a land not their own, and should be evil-entreated there, being afflicted and in bondage four hundred years; and in the fourth generation should return unto the place that was promised to Abraham; and that God would judge that race which had brought his seed into bondage. And, that Abraham might know as well the multitude as the glory of his seed, God brought him forth abroad by night, and said: *Look upon the heaven, and behold the stars of the heaven, if thou be able to number them: so shall thy seed be*. And when God saw the undoubting and unwavering certainty of his spirit, He bare witness unto him by the Holy Spirit, saying in the Scripture: *And Abraham believed, and it was counted unto him for righteousness*. And he was uncircumcised when this witness was borne; and, that the excellency of his faith should be made known by a sign, He gave him circumcision, *a seal of the righteousness of that faith which he had in uncircumcision*. And after this there was born to him a son, Isaac, from Sarah who was barren, according to the promise of God; and him he circumcised, according to that which God had covenanted with him. And of Isaac was Jacob born; and on this wise the original blessing of Shem reached to Abraham, and from Abraham to Isaac, and from Isaac to Jacob, the inheritance of the Spirit being imparted to them: for He was called the God of Abraham and the God of Isaac and the God of Jacob. And Jacob begat twelve sons, from whom the twelve tribes of Israel were named.

25 And when famine had come upon all the earth, it chanced that in Egypt alone there was food; and Jacob with all his seed removed and dwelt in Egypt: and the number of all that migrated was *threescore and fifteen souls*; and in four hundred years, as the oracle had declared beforehand, they became six hundred and sixty thousand. And, because they were grievously afflicted and oppressed through evil bondage, and sighed and groaned unto God, the God of their fathers, Abraham and Isaac and Jacob; He brought them out of Egypt by the hand of Moses and Aaron, smiting the Egyptians with ten plagues, and in the last plague sending a destroying angel and slaying their first-born, both of man and of beast: wherefrom He saved the children of Israel, revealing in a mystery the sufferings of Christ by the sacrifice

of a lamb without spot, and giving its blood to be smeared on the houses of the Hebrews as a sure precaution. And the name of this mystery is Passion, the source of deliverance. And dividing the Red Sea, He brought the children of Israel with all security to the wilderness; and as to the pursuing Egyptians, who followed them and entered into the sea, they were all overwhelmed; this judgment of God coming upon those who had iniquitously oppressed the seed of Abraham.

26 And in the wilderness Moses received the Law from God, *the Ten Words on tables of stone, written with the finger of God* (now the finger of God is that which is stretched forth from the Father in the Holy Spirit); and the commandments and ordinances which he delivered to the children of Israel to observe. And the tabernacle of witness he constructed by the command of God, the visible form on earth of those things which are spiritual and invisible in the heavens, and a figure of the form of the Church, and a prophecy of things to come: in which also were the vessels and the altars of sacrifice and the ark in which he placed the tables [of the Law]. And he appointed as priests Aaron and his sons, assigning the priesthood to all their tribe: and they were of the seed of Levi. Moreover this whole tribe he summoned by the word of God to accomplish the work of service in the temple of God, and gave them the Levitical law, [to shew] what and what manner of men they ought to be who are continually employed in performing the service of the temple of God.

27 And when they were near to the land, which God had promised to Abraham and his seed, Moses chose a man from every tribe, and sent them to search out the land and the cities therein and the dwellers in the cities. At that time God revealed to him the Name which alone is able to save them that believe thereon; and Moses changed the name of Oshea the son of Nun, one of them that were sent, and named him Jesus: and so he sent them forth with the power of the Name, believing that he should receive them back safe and sound through the guidance of the Name: which came to pass. Now when they had gone and searched and enquired, they returned bringing with them a bunch of grapes; and some of the twelve who were sent cast the whole multitude into fear and dismay, saying that the cities were exceeding great and walled, and the sons of the giants dwelt therein, so that it was [not] possible for them to take the land. And thereupon it fell out that all the multitude wept, failing to believe that it was God who should grant them power and subjugate all to them. And they spake evil also of the land, as not being good, and as though it were not worth while to undergo the danger for the sake of such a land. But two of the twelve, Jesus the son of Nun, and Caleb the son of Jephunneh, rent their clothes for the evil that was done, and besought the people not to be disheartened nor lose their courage; for God had given all into their hands, and the land was exceeding good. And when they believed not, but the people still continued in the same unbelief, God changed and altered their way, that they should wander desolate and sore smitten in the desert. And according to the days that they were in going and returning who had spied out the land – and these were forty in number – setting a year for a day, He kept them in the wilderness for the space of forty years; and none of those who were fullgrown and had understanding counted He worthy to enter into the land because of their unbelief, save only the two who had testified of the inheritance, Jesus the son of Nun and Caleb the son of Jephunneh, and those who were quite young and knew not the right hand and the left. So all the unbelieving

multitude perished and were consumed in the wilderness, receiving one by one the due reward of their want of faith: but the children, growing up in the course of forty years, filled up the number of the dead.

28 When the forty years were fulfilled, the people drew near to the Jordan, and were assembled and arrayed over against Jericho. Here Moses gathered the people together, and summed up all afresh, proclaiming the mighty works of God even unto that day, fashioning and preparing those that had grown up in the wilderness to fear God and keep His commandments, imposing on them as it were a new legislation, adding to that which was made before. And this was called Deuteronomy: and in it were written many prophecies concerning our Lord Jesus Christ and concerning the people, and also concerning the calling of the Gentiles and concerning the kingdom.

29 And, when Moses had finished his course, it was said to him by God: *Get thee up into the mountain, and die*: for thou shalt not bring in my people into the land. So he *died according to the word of the Lord*; and Jesus the son of Nun succeeded him. He divided the Jordan and made the people to pass over into the land; and, when he had overthrown and destroyed the seven races that dwelt therein, he assigned to the people the temporal Jerusalem, wherein David was king, and Solomon his son, who builded the temple to the name of God, according to the likeness of the tabernacle which had been made by Moses after the pattern of the heavenly and spiritual things.

30 Hither were the prophets sent by God through the Holy Spirit; and they instructed the people and turned them to the God of their fathers, the Almighty; and they became heralds of the revelation of our Lord Jesus Christ the Son of God, declaring that from the posterity of David His flesh should blossom forth; that after the flesh He might be the son of David, who was the son of Abraham by a long succession; but according to the spirit Son of God, pre-existing with the Father, begotten before all the creation of the world, and at the end of the times appearing to all the world as man, the Word of God *gathering up* in Himself *all things that are in heaven and that are on earth.*

31 So then He united man with God, and established a community of union between God and man; since we could not in any other way participate in incorruption, save by His coming among us. For so long as incorruption was invisible and unrevealed, it helped us not at all: therefore it became visible, that in all respects we might participate in the reception of incorruption. And, because in the original formation of Adam all of us were tied and bound up with death through his disobedience, it was right that through the obedience of Him who was made man for us we should be released from death; and because death reigned over the flesh, it was right that through the flesh it should lose its force and let man go free from its oppression. So *the Word was made flesh*, that, through that very flesh which sin had ruled and dominated, it should lose its force and be no longer in us. And therefore our Lord took that same original formation as [His] entry into flesh, so that He might draw near and contend on behalf of the fathers, and conquer by Adam that which by Adam had stricken us down.

32 Whence then is the substance of the first-formed [man]? From the Will and the Wisdom of God, and from the virgin earth. *For God had not sent rain*, the Scripture says, *upon the earth*, before man was made; *and there was no man to till the earth.* From this, then, whilst it was still virgin, God took dust of the earth and

formed the man, the beginning of mankind. So then the Lord, summing up afresh this man, took the same dispensation of entry into flesh, being born from the Virgin by the Will and the Wisdom of God; that He also should show forth the likeness of Adam's entry into flesh, and there should be that which was written in the beginning, *man after the image and likeness* of God.

33 And just as through a disobedient virgin man was stricken down and fell into death, so through the Virgin who was obedient to the Word of God man was reanimated and received life. For the Lord came to seek again the sheep that was lost; and man it was that was lost: and for this cause there was not made some other formation, but in that same which had its descent from Adam He preserved the likeness of the [first] formation. For it was necessary that Adam should be summed up in Christ, that mortality might be swallowed up and overwhelmed by immortality; and Eve summed up in Mary, that a virgin should be a virgin's intercessor, and by a virgin's obedience undo and put away the disobedience of a virgin.

34 And the trespass which came by the tree was undone by the tree of obedience, when, hearkening unto God, the Son of man was nailed to the tree; thereby putting away the knowledge of evil and bringing in and establishing the knowledge of good: now evil it is to disobey God, even as hearkening unto God is good. And for this cause the Word spake by Isaiah the prophet, announcing beforehand that which was to come – for therefore are they prophets, because they proclaim what is to come: by him then spake the Word thus: *I refuse not, nor gainsay: I gave my back to scourging, and my cheeks to smiting; and my face I turned not away from the shame of spitting.* So then by the obedience wherewith He obeyed *even unto death*, hanging on the tree, He put away the old disobedience which was wrought in the tree. Now seeing that He is the Word of God Almighty, who in unseen wise in our midst is universally extended in all the world, and encompasses its length and breadth and height and depth – for by the Word of God the whole universe is ordered and disposed – in it is crucified the Son of God, inscribed crosswise upon it all: for it is right that He being made visible, should set upon all things visible the sharing of His cross, that He might show His operation on visible things through a visible form. For He it is who illuminates the height, that is the heavens; and encompasses the deep which is beneath the earth; and stretches and spreads out the length from east to west; and steers across the breadth of north and south; summoning all that are scattered in every quarter to the knowledge of the Father.

35 Moreover He fulfilled the promise made to Abraham, which God had promised him, to make his seed as the stars of heaven. For this Christ did, who was born of the Virgin who was of Abraham's seed, and constituted those who have faith in Him *lights in the world*, and by the same faith with Abraham justified the Gentiles. For *Abraham believed God, and it was counted unto him for righteousness*. In like manner we also are justified by faith in God: for *the just shall live by faith*. Now *not by the law is the promise to Abraham, but by faith*: for Abraham was justified by faith: and *for a righteous man the law is not made*. In like manner we also are justified not by the law, but by faith, which is witnessed to in the law and in the prophets, whom the Word of God presents to us.

36 And He fulfilled the promise to David; for to him God had promised that *of the fruit of his body* He would raise up an eternal King, whose kingdom should

have no end. And this King is Christ, the Son of God, who became the Son of man; that is, who became the fruit of that Virgin who had her descent from David. And for this cause the promise was, *Of the fruit of thy body* – that He might declare the peculiar uniqueness of Him, who was the fruit of the virgin body that was of David, [even of Him] who was King over the house of David, [and] of whose kingdom there shall be no end.

37 Thus then He gloriously achieved our redemption, and fulfilled the promise of the fathers, and abolished the old disobedience. The Son of God became Son of David and Son of Abraham; perfecting and summing up this in Himself, that He might make us to possess life. The Word of God was made flesh by the dispensation of the Virgin, to abolish death and make man live. For we were imprisoned by sin, being born in sinfulness and living under death.

38 But God the Father was very merciful: He sent His creative Word, who in coming to deliver us came to the very place and spot in which we had lost life, and brake the bonds of our fetters. And His light appeared and made the darkness of the prison disappear, and hallowed our birth and destroyed death, loosing those same fetters in which we were enchained. And He manifested the resurrection, Himself becoming *the first-begotten of the dead*, and in Himself raising up man that was fallen, lifting him up far above the heaven to the right hand of the glory of the Father: even as God promised by the prophet, saying: *And I will raise up the tabernacle of David that is fallen*; that is, the flesh that was from David. And this our Lord Jesus Christ truly fulfilled, when He gloriously achieved our redemption, that He might truly raise us up, setting us free unto the Father. And if any man will not receive His birth from a virgin, how shall he receive His resurrection from the dead? For it is nothing wonderful and astonishing and extraordinary, if one who was not born rose from the dead: nay indeed we cannot speak of a resurrection of him who came unto being without birth. For one who is unborn and immortal, and has not undergone birth, will also not undergo death. For he who took not the beginning of man, how could he receive his end?

39 Now, if He was not born, neither did He die; and, if He died not, neither did He rise from the dead; and, if He rose not from the dead, neither did He vanquish death and bring its reign to nought; and if death be not vanquished, how can we ascend to life, who from the beginning have fallen under death? So then those who take away redemption from man, and believe not in God that He will raise them from the dead, these also despise the birth of our Lord, which He underwent on our behalf, that the Word of God should be made flesh in order that He might manifest the resurrection of the flesh, and might have pre-eminence over all things in the heavens, as the first-born and eldest offspring of the thought of the Father, the Word, fulfilling all things, and Himself guiding and ruling upon earth. For He was the Virgin's first-born, a just and holy man, godfearing, good, well-pleasing to God, perfect in all ways, and delivering from hell all who follow after Him: for He Himself was *the first-begotten of the dead*, the Prince and Author of life unto God.

40 Thus then the Word of God *in all things hath the pre-eminence*; for that He is true man and *Wonderful Counsellor and Mighty God*; calling men anew to fellowship with God, that by fellowship with Him we may partake of incorruption. So then He who was proclaimed by the law through Moses, and by the prophets of the Most High and Almighty God, as Son of the Father of all; He from whom all things are,

He who spake with Moses – He came into Judaea, generated from God by the Holy Spirit, and born of the Virgin Mary, even of her who was of the seed of David and of Abraham, Jesus the Anointed of God, showing Himself to be the One who was proclaimed beforehand by the prophets.

41 And His forerunner was John the Baptist, who prepared and made ready the people beforehand for the reception of the Word of life; declaring that He was the Christ, on whom the Spirit of God rested, mingling with His flesh. His disciples, the witnesses of all His good deeds, and of His teachings and His sufferings and death and resurrection, and of His ascension into heaven after His bodily resurrection – these were the apostles, who after [receiving] the power of the Holy Spirit were sent forth by Him into all the world, and wrought the calling of the Gentiles, showing to mankind the way of life, to turn them from idols and fornication and covetousness, cleansing their souls and bodies by the baptism of water and of the Holy Spirit; which Holy Spirit they had received of the Lord, and they distributed and imparted It to them that believed; and thus they ordered and established the Churches. By faith and love and hope they established that which was foretold by the prophets, the calling of the Gentiles, according to the mercy of God which was extended to them; bringing it to light through the ministration of their service, and admitting them to the promise of the fathers: to wit, that to those who thus believed in and loved the Lord, and continued in holiness and righteousness and patient endurance, the God of all had promised to grant eternal life by the resurrection of the dead; through Him who died and rose again, Jesus Christ, to whom He has delivered over the kingdom of all existing things, and the rule of quick and dead, and also the judgment. And they counselled them by the word of truth to keep their flesh undefiled unto the resurrection and their soul unstained.

42 For such is the state of those who have believed, since in them continually abides the Holy Spirit, who was given by Him in baptism, and is retained by the receiver, if he walks in truth and holiness and righteousness and patient endurance. For this soul has a resurrection in them that believe, the body receiving the soul again, and along with it, by the power of the Holy Spirit, being raised up and entering into the kingdom of God. This is the fruit of the blessing of Japheth, in the calling of the Gentiles, made manifest through the Church, standing in readiness to receive its dwelling in the house of Shem according to the promise of God. That all these things would so come to pass, the Spirit of God declared beforehand by the prophets; that in respect of them the faith of those who worship God in truth should be confirmed. For what was an impossibility to our nature, and therefore ready to cause incredibility to mankind, this God caused to be made known beforehand by the prophets; in order that, through its having been foretold in times long before, and then at last finding effect in this way, even as it was foretold, we might know that it was God who [thus] proclaimed to us beforehand our redemption.

43 So then we must believe God in all things, for in all things God is true. Now that there was a Son of God, and that He existed not only before He appeared in the world, but also before the world was made, Moses, who was the first that prophesied, says in Hebrew: *Baresith bara Elowin basan benuam samenthares*. And this, translated into our language, is: 'The Son in the beginning: God established then the heaven and the earth.' This Jeremiah the prophet also testified, saying thus: *Before the morning-star I begat thee: and before the sun [is] thy name*; and that is,

before the creation of the world; for together with the world the stars were made. And again the same says: *Blessed is he who was, before he became man*. Because, for God, the Son was [as] the beginning before the creation of the world; but for us [He was] then, when He appeared; and before that He was not for us, who knew Him not. Wherefore also His disciple John, in teaching us who is the Son of God, who was with the Father before the world was made, and that all the things that were made were made by Him, says thus: *In the beginning was the Word, and the Word was with God, and the Word was God. The same was in the beginning with God. All things were made by Him, and without Him was not anything made*: showing with certainty that the Word, who was in the beginning with the Father, and by whom all things were made, this is His Son.

44 And again Moses tells how the Son of God drew near to hold converse with Abraham: *And God appeared unto him by the oak of Mamre in the middle of the day. And looking up with his eyes he beheld, and, lo, three men stood over against him. And he bowed himself down to the earth, and said: Lord, if indeed I have found favour in thy sight*. And all that which follows he spake with the Lord, and the Lord spake with him. Now two of the three were angels; but one was the Son of God, with whom also Abraham spake, pleading on behalf of the men of Sodom, that they should not perish if at least ten righteous should be found there. And, whilst these were speaking, the two angels entered into Sodom, and Lot received them. And then the Scripture says: *And the Lord rained upon Sodom and Gomorrah brimstone and fire from the Lord out of heaven*: that is to say, the Son, who spake with Abraham, being *Lord*, received power to punish the men of Sodom *from the Lord out of heaven*, even from the Father who rules over all. So Abraham was a prophet and saw things to come, which were to take place in human form: even the Son of God, that He should speak with men and eat with them, and then should bring in the judgment from the Father, having received from Him who rules over all the power to punish the men of Sodom.

45 And Jacob, when he went into Mesopotamia, saw Him in a dream, *standing upon the ladder*, that is, the tree, which was set up from earth to heaven; for thereby they that believe on Him go up to the heavens. For His sufferings are our ascension on high. And all such visions point to the Son of God, speaking with men and being in their midst. For it was not the Father of all, who is not seen by the world, the Maker of all who said: *Heaven is my throne, and earth is my footstool; what house will ye build me, or what is the place of my rest?* and who *comprehendeth the earth with his hand, and with his span the heaven* – it was not He that came and stood in a very small space and spake with Abraham; but the Word of God, who was ever with mankind, and made known beforehand what should come to pass in the future, and taught men the things of God.

46 He it is who spake with Moses in the bush, and said: *Seeing have I seen the affliction of my people that is in Egypt; and I am come down to deliver them*. He it is who came forth and came down for the deliverance of the oppressed, bringing us out from the power of the Egyptians, that is, from all idolatry and impiety; and delivering us from the Red Sea, that is, delivering us from the deadly confusion of the Gentiles and the grievous vexation of their blasphemy. For in them the Word of God prepared and rehearsed beforehand the things concerning us. Then He set forth in types beforehand that which was to be; now in very truth He has brought us out

from the cruel service of the Gentiles, and a stream of water in the desert has He made to flow forth in abundance from a rock; and that rock is Himself; and has given twelve fountains, that is, the teaching of the twelve apostles. And the obstinate unbelievers He brought to an end and consumed in the wilderness; but those who believed on Him, and *in malice* were *children*, He made to enter into the inheritance of the fathers; whom not Moses, but Jesus puts in possession of the heritage: who also delivers us from Amalek by the expansion of His hands, and brings us to the kingdom of the Father.

47 So then the Father is Lord and the Son is Lord, and the Father is God and the Son is God; for that which is begotten of God is God. And so in the substance and power of His being there is shown forth one God; but there is also according to the economy of our redemption both Son and Father. Because to created things the Father of all is invisible and unapproachable, therefore those who are to draw near to God must have their access to the Father through the Son. And yet more plainly and evidently does David speak concerning the Father and the Son as follows: *Thy throne, O God, is for ever and ever: thou hast loved righteousness and hated unrighteousness: therefore God hath anointed thee with the oil of gladness above thy fellows.* For the Son, as being God, receives from the Father, that is, from God, the throne of the everlasting kingdom, and the oil of anointing above His fellows. The oil of anointing is the Spirit, wherewith He has been anointed; and His fellows are prophets and righteous men and apostles, and all who receive the fellowship of His kingdom, that is to say, His disciples.

48 And again David says: *The Lord said unto my Lord: Sit on my right hand, until I make thy enemies thy footstool. The rod of thy strength shall the Lord send forth from Sion; and rule thou in the midst of thy enemies. With thee in the beginning in the day of thy power, in the brightness of the holy ones: from the womb before the morning-star I begat thee. The Lord sware and will not repent: Thou art a priest for ever after the order of Melchisedec. And the Lord on thy right hand hath broken in pieces kings in the day of wrath: he shall judge among the Gentiles, he shall fill up the ruins, and shall break in pieces the heads of many on the earth. He shall drink of the brook in the way: therefore shall he lift up the head.* Now hereby he proclaimed that He came into being before all, and that He rules over the Gentiles and judges all mankind and the kings who now hate Him and persecute His name; for these are His enemies: and in calling Him God's priest for ever, he declared His immortality. And therefore he said: *He shall drink of the brook in the way; therefore shall he lift up the head*; proclaiming the exaltation with glory that followed on His humanity and humiliation and ingloriousness.

49 And again Isaiah the prophet says: *Thus saith the Lord God to my Anointed the Lord, whose right hand I have held, that the Gentiles should hearken before him.* And how the Christ is called Son of God and King of the Gentiles, that is, of all mankind; and that He not only is called but is Son of God and King of all, David declares thus: *The Lord said unto me: Thou art my Son, this day have I begotten thee. Ask of me and I will give thee the Gentiles for thy inheritance, and for a possession the utmost parts of the earth.* These things were not said of David; for neither over the Gentiles nor over the utmost parts did he rule, but only over the Jews. So then it is plain that the promise to the Anointed to reign over the utmost parts of the earth is to the Son of God, whom David himself acknowledges as his

Lord, saying thus: *The Lord said unto my Lord; Sit on my right hand*, and so forth, as we have said above. For he means that the Father speaks with the Son; as we showed a little before as to Isaiah, that he said thus: *God saith to my Anointed the Lord, that the Gentiles should hearken before him.* For the promise is the same by the two prophets, that He should be King: so that the speech of God is addressed to one and the same, I mean, to Christ the Son of God. Forasmuch as David says: *The Lord said unto me*, it is necessary to say that it is not David who speaks, nor any one of the prophets, in his own person: for it is not a man who speaks the prophecies; but the Spirit of God, assimilating and likening Himself to the persons represented, speaks in the prophets, and utters the words sometimes from Christ and sometimes from the Father.

50 So then right fitly Christ says through David that He converses with the Father; and right worthily does He say the other things concerning Himself through the prophets; as in other instances, so also after this manner by Isaiah: *And now thus saith the Lord, who formed me as his servant from the womb, to gather Jacob and to gather Israel unto him: and I shall be glorified before the Lord, and my God shall be a strength unto me. And he said: A great thing shall it be to thee to be called my servant, to stablish and confirm the tribe of Jacob, and to turn again the dispersion of Israel: and I have set thee for a light of the Gentiles, that thou shouldst be for salvation unto the end of the earth.*

51 Here, first of all, is seen that the Son of God pre-existed, from the fact that the Father spake with Him, and before He was born revealed Him to men: and, next, that He must needs be born a man among men; and that the same God *forms* Him *from the womb*, that is, that of the Spirit of God He should be born; and that He is Lord of all men, and Saviour of them that believe on Him, both Jews and others. For the people of the Jews is called Israel in the Hebrew language, from Jacob their father, who was the first to be called Israel: and Gentiles He calls the whole of mankind. And that the Son of the Father calls Himself *servant*, [this is] on account of His subjection to the Father: for among men also every son is the servant of his father.

52 That Christ, then, being Son of God before all the world, is with the Father; and being with the Father is also nigh and close and joined unto mankind; and is King of all, because the Father has subjected all things unto Him; and Saviour of them that believe on Him – such things do the Scriptures declare. For it is not feasible and possible to enumerate every scripture in order; and from these you may understand the others also which have been spoken in like manner, believing in Christ, and seeking understanding and comprehension from God, so as to understand what has been spoken by the prophets.

53 And that this Christ, who was with the Father, being the Word of the Father, was thereafter to be made flesh and become man and undergo the process of birth and be born of a virgin and dwell among men, the Father of all bringing about His incarnation – Isaiah says thus: *Therefore the Lord himself shall give you a sign: behold, the virgin shall conceive and shall bring forth a son, and ye shall call him Emmanuel: butter and honey shall he eat; before he knoweth or selecteth the evil, he chooseth the good: for, before the child knoweth good or evil, he rejecteth wickedness to choose the good.* So he proclaimed His birth from a virgin; and that He was truly man he declared beforehand by His *eating*; and also because he called

Him *the child*; and further by giving Him a name; for this is the custom also for one that is born. And His name is two-fold: in the Hebrew tongue Messiah Jesus, and in ours Christ Saviour. And the two names are names of works actually wrought. For He was named Christ, because through Him the Father anointed and adorned all things; and because on His coming as man He was anointed with the Spirit of God and His Father. As also by Isaiah He says of Himself: *The Spirit of the Lord is upon me: wherefore he hath anointed me to preach good tidings to the poor.* And [He was named] Saviour for this, that He became the cause of salvation to those who at that time were delivered by Him from all sicknesses and from death, and to those who afterwards believed on Him the author of salvation in the future and for evermore.

54 For this cause then is He Saviour. Now Emmanuel is, being interpreted, *With you God*; or as a yearning cry uttered by the prophet, such as this: *With us shall be God*; according to which it is the explanation and manifestation of the good tidings proclaimed. For *Behold*, He saith, *the virgin shall conceive and shall bring forth a son*; and He, being God, is to be with us. And, as if altogether astonished at these things, he proclaims in regard to these future events that *With us shall be God.* And yet again concerning His birth the same prophet says in another place: *Before she that travailed gave birth, and before the pains of travail came on, she escaped and was delivered of a man-child.* Thus he showed that His birth from the virgin was unforeseen and unexpected. And again the same prophet says: *Unto us a son is born, and unto us a child is given: and his name is called Wonderful Counsellor, Mighty God.*

55 He calls Him *Wonderful Counsellor*, meaning of the Father: whereby it is declared that the Father works all things together with Him; as is contained in the first book of Moses which is entitled Genesis: *And God said, let us make man after our image and likeness.* For there is seen in this place the Father speaking to the Son, the Wonderful Counsellor of the Father. Moreover He is also our Counsellor, giving advice; not compelling as God, even though He is *Mighty God*, [as] he says; but giving advice that we should forsake ignorance and acquire knowledge, and depart from error and come to the truth, and put away corruption and receive incorruption.

56 And again Isaiah says: *And they shall wish that they had been burned with fire: for unto us a child is born, and unto us a son is given; whose government is upon his shoulders, and his name is called Angel of great counsel. For I will bring peace upon the rulers, again peace and health unto him. Great is his rule, and of his peace there is no bound, upon the throne of David and upon his kingdom, to prosper and complete, to aid and undertake, in righteousness and judgment from this time forth and for evermore.* For hereby the Son of God is proclaimed both as being born and also as eternal King. But *they shall wish that they had been burned with fire* [is said] of those who believe not on Him, and who have done to Him all that they have done: for they shall say in the judgment, How much better that we had been burned with fire before the Son of God was born, than that, when He was born, we should not have believed on Him. Because for those who died before Christ appeared there is hope that in the judgment of the risen they may obtain salvation, even such as feared God and died in righteousness and had in them the Spirit of God, as the patriarchs and prophets and righteous men. But for those who

after Christ's appearing believed not on Him, there is a vengeance without pardon in the judgment. Now in this: *Whose government is upon his shoulder*, the cross is in a figure declared, on which He was nailed back. For that which was and is a reproach to Him, and for His sake to us, even the cross, this same is, says he,·His *government* being a sign of His kingdom. And, *Angel of great counsel*, he says; that is, of the Father whom He hath declared unto us.

57 That the Son of God should be born, and in what way He was to be born, and that He should be shown to be Christ – from what has been said it is plain how this was made known beforehand by the prophets. And in addition to this, in what land and among whom of mankind He was to be born and to appear, this also was proclaimed beforehand with words such as these. Moses in Genesis says thus: *There shall not fail a prince from Judah, nor a leader from his loins, until he shall come for whom it remaineth; and he shall be the expectation of the Gentiles: washing his robe in wine, and his garment in the blood of the grape.* Now Judah was the ancestor of the Jews, the son of Jacob; from whom also they obtained the name. And there failed not a prince among them and a leader, until the coming of Christ. But from the time of His coming the might of the quiver was captured, the land of the Jews was given over into subjection to the Romans, and they had no longer a prince or king of their own. For He was come, *for whom remaineth*, in heaven the kingdom; who also *washed his robe in wine, and his garment in the blood of the grape*. His robe as also His garment are those who believe on Him, whom also He cleansed, redeeming us by His blood. And His blood is said to be *blood of the grape*; for even as the blood of the grape no man maketh, but God produceth, and *maketh glad* them that drink thereof, so also His flesh and blood no man wrought, but God made. *The Lord Himself gave the sign* of the virgin, even that Emmanuel which was from the virgin; who also *maketh glad* them that drink of Him, that is to say, who receive His Spirit, [even] *everlasting gladness*. Wherefore also He is *the expectation of the Gentiles*, of those who *hope in Him*; because we expect of Him that He will establish again the kingdom.

58 And again Moses says: *There shall rise a star out of Jacob; and a leader shall be raised up out of Israel*; showing yet more plainly that the dispensation of His coming in flesh should be among the Jews. And from Jacob and from the tribe of Judah He who was born, coming down from heaven, took upon Him this economy of dispensation: for the *star* appeared in heaven. And by *leader* he means king, because He is the King of all the redeemed. And at His birth the star appeared to the Magi who dwelt in the east; and thereby they learned that Christ was born; and they came to Judaea, led by the star; until the star came to Bethlehem where Christ was born, and entered the house wherein was laid the child, wrapped in swaddling-clothes; and it stood over His head, declaring to the Magi the Son of God, the Christ.

59 Moreover Isaiah himself yet further says: *And there shall come forth a rod out of the roots of Jesse, and a flower from his root shall come forth. And the spirit of God shall rest upon him; the spirit of wisdom and of understanding, the spirit of counsel and of might, the spirit of knowledge and of godliness: the spirit of the fear of God shall fill him. Not according to opinion shall he judge, and not according to speech shall he reprove: but he shall judge judgment for the humble, and shew mercy to the humble of the earth. And he shall smite the earth with the word of his*

mouth, and with the breath of his lips shall he slay the impious man. And he shall be girt about his loins with righteousness, and with truth encompassed about his reins. And the wolf shall feed with the lamb, and the leopard with the kid, and the calf and the lion shall pasture together. And a sucking child shall put his hand on the hole of the asps, and on the lair of the offspring of the asps, and they shall not hurt him. And in that day there shall be a root of Jesse, and he that riseth up to rule the Gentiles: in him shall the Gentiles hope: and his rising up shall be honour. By these words he states that He was born from her who was of the race of David and of Abraham. For Jesse was the descendant of Abraham, and the father of David; (and David's) descendant the virgin was who conceived Christ. Now [as to] the *rod*: for this cause also Moses with a rod showed the mighty works to Pharaoh: and with other men also the rod is a sign of rule. And by *flower* he means His flesh; for from spirit it budded forth, as we have said before.

60 Now, *Not according to opinion shall he judge, and not according to speech shall he reprove: but he shall judge judgment for the humble, and shall show mercy to the humble on the earth* – [by this] he the more establishes and declares His godhead. For to judge without respect of persons and partiality, and not as favouring the illustrious, but affording to the humble worthy and like and equal treatment, accords with the height and summit of the righteousness of God: for God is influenced and moved by none, save only the righteous. And to show mercy is the peculiar attribute of God, who by mercy is able to save. And *He shall smite the earth with a word*, and *slay the impious* with a word only: this belongs to God who worketh all things with a word. And in saying: *He shall be girt about his loins with righteousness, and with truth encompassed about his reins*, he declares His human form and aspect, and His own surpassing righteousness.

61 Now as to the union and concord and peace of the animals of different kinds, which by nature are opposed and hostile to each other, the Elders say that so it will be in truth at the coming of Christ, when He is to reign over all. For already in a symbol he announces the gathering together in peace and concord, through the name of Christ, of men of unlike races and [yet] of like dispositions. For, when thus united, on the righteous, who are likened to calves and lambs and kids and sucking children, those inflict no hurt at all who in the former time were, through their rapacity, like wild beasts in manners and disposition, both men and women; so much so that some of them were like wolves and lions, ravaging the weaker and warring on their equals; while the women (were like) leopards or asps, who slew, it may be, even their loved ones with deadly poisons, or by reason of lustful desire. [But now] coming together in one name they have acquired righteous habits by the grace of God, changing their wild and untamed nature. And this has come to pass already. For those who were before exceeding wicked, so that they left no work of ungodliness undone, learning of Christ and believing on Him, have at once believed and been changed, so as to leave no excellency of righteousness undone; so great is the transformation which faith in Christ the Son of God effects for those who believe on Him. And he says: *Rising up to rule the Gentiles*, because He is to die and rise again, and be confessed and believed as the Son of God [and] King. On this account he says: *And His rising up shall be honour*: that is, glory; for then was He glorified as God, when He rose.

62 Wherefore again the prophet says: *In that day I will raise up the tabernacle of David that is fallen*: that body of Christ, which, as we have said before, is born of

David, he plainly declares as after death rising from the dead. For the body is called a tabernacle. For by these words he says that He who according to the flesh is of the race of David will be Christ the Son of God; and that He will die and rise again, and that He is in aspect a man, but in power God; and that He Himself will be as judge of all the world and as the only worker of righteousness and redeemer – all this the Scripture declared.

63 And again the prophet Micah speaks of the place where Christ should be born, that it should be in Bethlehem of Judaea, saying thus: *And thou, Bethlehem of Judaea, art thou the least among the princes of Judah? for out of thee shall come a prince who shall feed my people Israel.* But Bethlehem is the native place of David: so that not only in respect of the Virgin who bore Him is He of David's race, but also in respect of His birth in Bethlehem the native place of David.

64 And again David says that of his race Christ is to be born, [speaking] after this manner: *For David my servant's sake turn not away the face of thy Christ. The Lord sware truth unto David, and he will not disappoint him: Of the fruit of thy body will I set on thy throne: if thy children shall keep my covenant and my testimonies, which I covenanted with them, their sons for evermore [shall sit upon thy throne].* But none of the sons of David reigned for evermore, nor was their kingdom for evermore; for it was brought to nought. But the king that was born of David, He is Christ. All these testimonies declare in plain terms His descent according to the flesh, and the race and place where He was to be born; so that no man should seek among the Gentiles or elsewhere for the birth of the Son of God, but in Bethlehem of Judaea from Abraham and from David's race.

65 And the manner of His entry into Jerusalem, which was the capital of Judaea, where also was His royal seat and the temple of God, the prophet Isaiah declares: *Say ye to the daughter of Sion, Behold a king cometh unto thee, meek and sitting upon an ass, a colt the foal of an ass.* For, sitting on an ass's colt, so He entered into Jerusalem, the multitudes strewing and putting down for Him their garments. And by *the daughter of Sion* he means Jerusalem.

66 So then, that the Son of God should be born, and in what manner born, and where He was to be born, and that Christ is the one eternal King, the prophets thus declared. And again they told beforehand concerning Him how, sprung from mankind, He should heal those whom He healed, and raise the dead whom He raised, and be hated and despised and undergo sufferings and be put to death and crucified, even as He was hated and despised and put to death.

67 At this point let us speak of His healings. Isaiah says thus: *He took our infirmities and bare our sicknesses*: that is to say, He shall take, and shall bear. For there are passages in which the Spirit of God through the prophets recounts things that are to be as having taken place. For that which with God is essayed and conceived of as determined to take place, is reckoned as having already taken place: and the Spirit, regarding and seeing the time in which the issues of the prophecy are fulfilled, utters the words [accordingly]. And concerning the kind of healing, thus will He make mention, saying: *In that day shall the deaf hear the words of the book, and in darkness and in mist the eyes of the blind shall see.* And the same says again: *Be strong, ye weak hands and feeble and trembling knees: be comforted, ye that are of a fearful mind. Be strong, fear not. Behold, our God will recompense judgment: He will come and save us. Then shall the eyes of the blind be*

opened, and the ears of the deaf shall hear: then shall the lame man leap as an hart, and the tongue of the stammerers shall be plain. And concerning the dead, that they shall be raised, he says thus: *The dead shall be raised, and they that are in the tombs shall be raised.* And in bringing these things to pass He shall be believed to be the Son of God.

68 And that He shall be despised and tormented and in the end put to death, Isaiah says thus: *Behold, my son shall understand, and shall be exalted and glorified greatly. Even as many shall be astonished at thee, so without glory shall thy form be from men. And many races shall be astonished, and kings shall shut their mouths: for they to whom it was not declared concerning him shall see, and they who have not heard shall consider. Lord, who hath believed our report? and to whom hath the arm of the Lord been revealed? We declared before him as a child, as a root in a dry ground: and there is to him no form nor glory: and we saw him, and he had no form nor beauty: and his form was without honour, meaner than that of other men: a man in chastisement, and acquainted with the bearing of pain; for his face was turned away, he was dishonoured and made of no account. He beareth our sins, and for our sakes endureth pain: and we accounted him to be in pain and chastisement and affliction. But he was wounded for our iniquities, and was tormented for our sins. The discipline of our peace (was) upon him; by his stripes we were healed.* By these words it is declared that He was tormented; as also David says: *And I was tormented.* Now David was never tormented, but Christ [was], when the command was given that He should be crucified. And again by Isaiah His Word says: *I gave my back to scourging; and my cheeks to smiting: and my face I turned not away from the shame of spitting.* And Jeremiah the prophet says the same, thus: *He shall give his cheek to the smiter: he shall be filled with reproaches.* All these things Christ suffered.

69 Now what follows in Isaiah is this: *By his stripes we were healed. All we like sheep went astray: a man in his way went astray: and the Lord delivered him up to our sins.* It is manifest therefore that by the will of the Father these things occurred to Him for the sake of our salvation. Then he says: *And he by reason of his suffering opened not [his] mouth: as a sheep to the slaughter was he brought, as a lamb dumb before the shearer.* Behold how he declares His voluntary coming to death. And when the prophet says: *In the humiliation his judgment was taken away*, he signifies the appearance of His humiliation: according to the form of the abasement was the taking away of judgment. And the taking away of judgment is for some unto salvation, and to some unto the torments of perdition. For there is a taking away for a person, and also from a person. So also with the judgment – those for whom it is taken away have it unto the torments of their perdition: but those from whom it is taken away are saved by it. Now those took away to themselves the judgment who crucified Him, and when they had done this to Him believed not on Him: for through that judgment which was taken away by them they shall be destroyed with torments. And from them that believe on Him the judgment is taken away, and they are no longer under it. And the judgment is that which by fire will be the destruction of the unbelievers at the end of the world.

70 Then he says: *His generation who shall declare?* This was said to warn us, lest on account of His enemies and the outrage of His sufferings we should despise Him as a mean and contemptible man. For He who endured all this has an undeclarable generation; for by generation He means descent; [for] He who is His

Father is undeclarable and unspeakable. Know therefore that such descent was His who endured these sufferings: and despise Him not because of the sufferings which for thy sake He of purpose endured, but fear Him because of His descent.

71 And in another place Jeremiah says: *The Spirit of our face, the Lord Christ*; and how He *was taken in their snares, of whom we said, Under his shadow we shall live among the Gentiles*. That, being [the] Spirit of God, Christ was to become a suffering man the Scripture declares: and is, as it were, amazed and astonished at His sufferings, that in such manner He was to endure sufferings, *under whose shadow we said that we should live*. And by *shadow* he means His body. For just as a shadow is made by a body, so also Christ's body was made by His Spirit. But, further, the humiliation and contemptibility of His body he indicates by the shadow. For, as the shadow of bodies standing upright is upon the ground and is trodden upon, so also the body of Christ fell upon the ground by His sufferings and was trodden on indeed. And he named Christ's body a shadow, because the Spirit overshadowed it, as it were, with glory and covered it. Moreover oftentimes when the Lord passed by, they laid those who were held by divers diseases in the way, and on whomsoever His shadow fell, they were healed.

72 And again the same prophet [says] thus concerning the sufferings of Christ: *Behold how the righteous is destroyed, and no man layeth it to heart; and righteous men are taken away, and no man understandeth. For from the face of iniquity is the taking away of the righteous: peace shall be his burial, he hath been taken away from the midst*. And who else is perfectly righteous, but the Son of God, who makes righteous and perfects them that believe on Him, who like unto Him are persecuted and put to death? But in saying: *Peace shall be his burial*, he declares how on account of our redemption He died: for it is in the peace of redemption: and [also he declares] that by His death those who aforetime were enemies and opposed to one another, believing with one accord upon Him, should have peace with one another, becoming friends and beloved on account of their common faith in Him; as indeed they have become. But in saying: *he hath been taken away from the midst*, he signified His resurrection from the dead. Moreover because He appeared no more after His death and burial, the prophet declares that after dying and rising again He was to remain immortal, [saying] thus: *He asked life, and thou gavest [it] him, and length of days for ever and ever*. Now what is this that he says, *He asked life*, since He was about to die? He proclaims His resurrection from the dead, and that being raised from the dead He is immortal. For He received both *life*, that He should rise, and *length of days for ever and ever*, that He should be incorruptible.

73 And again David says thus concerning the death and resurrection of Christ: *I laid me down and slept: I awaked, for the Lord received me*. David said not this of himself, for he was not raised after death: but the Spirit of Christ, who [spake] also in other prophets concerning Him, says here by David: *I laid me down and slept: I awaked, for the Lord received me*. By sleep he means death; for He arose again.

74 And again David [says] thus concerning the sufferings of Christ: *Why did the Gentiles rage, and the people imagine vain things? Kings rose up on the earth, and princes were gathered together, against the Lord and his Anointed*. For Herod the king of the Jews and Pontius Pilate, the governor of Claudius Caesar, came together and condemned Him to be crucified. For Herod feared, as though He were to be an earthly king, lest he should be expelled by Him from the kingdom. But Pilate was

constrained by Herod and the Jews that were with him against his will to deliver Him to death: [for they threatened him] if he should not rather do this than act contrary to Caesar, by letting go a man who was called a king.

75 And further concerning the sufferings of Christ the same prophet says: *Thou hast repelled and despised us; and hast cast away thine Anointed. Thou hast broken the covenant of my servant; thou hast cast his holiness to the ground. Thou hast overthrown all his hedges; thou hast made his strongholds to tremble. They that pass on the way have ravaged him; he is become a reproach to his neighbours. Thou hast exalted the right hand of his oppressors; thou hast made his enemies to rejoice over him. Thou hast turned away the help of his sword, and gavest him not a hand in the battle. Thou hast removed and thrown him down from purification; thou hast overturned his throne upon the ground. Thou hast shortened the days of his time, and hast poured forth shame upon him.* That He should endure these things, and that too by the will of the Father, he manifestly declared: for by the will of the Father He was to endure sufferings.

76 And Zechariah says thus: *Sword, awake against my shepherd, and against the man [that is] my companion. Smite the shepherd, and the sheep of the flock shall be scattered.* And this came to pass when He was taken by the Jews: for all the disciples forsook Him, fearing lest they should die with Him. For not yet did they stedfastly believe on Him, until they had seen Him risen from the dead.

77 Again He says in the Twelve Prophets: *And they bound him and brought him as a present to the king.* For Pontius Pilate was governor of Judaea, and he had at that time resentful enmity against Herod the king of the Jews. But then, when Christ was brought to him bound, Pilate sent Him to Herod, giving command to enquire of him, that he might know of a certainty what he should desire concerning Him; making Christ a convenient occasion of reconciliation with the king.

78 And in Jeremiah He thus declares His death and descent into hell, saying: *And the Lord the Holy One of Israel, remembered his dead, which aforetime fell asleep in the dust of the earth: and he went down unto them, to bring the tidings of his salvation, to deliver them.* In this place He also renders the cause of His death: for His descent into hell was the salvation of them that had passed away.

79 And, again, concerning His cross Isaiah says thus: *I have stretched out my hands all the day long to a disobedient and gainsaying people.* For this is an indication of the cross. And yet more manifestly David says: *Hunting-dogs encompassed me: the assembly of evil-doers came about me. They pierced my hands and my feet.* And again he says: *My heart became even as wax melting in the midst of my body; and they put asunder my bones*, and again he says: *Spare my soul from the sword and nail my flesh: for the assembly of evil-doers hath risen up against me.* In these words with manifest clearness he signifies that He should be crucified. And Moses says this same thing to the people, thus: *And thy life shall be hanged up before thine eyes, and thou shalt fear by day and by night, and thou shalt not believe in thy life.*

80 And again David says: *They looked upon me, they parted my garments among them, and upon my vesture they cast lots.* For at His crucifixion the soldiers parted His garments as they were wont; and the garments they parted by tearing; but for the vesture, because it was woven from the top and was not sewn, they cast lots, that to whomsoever it should fall he should take it.

81 And again Jeremiah the prophet says: *And they took the thirty pieces of silver, the price of him that was sold, whom they bought from the children of Israel; and they gave them for the potter's field, as the Lord commanded me.* For Judas, being one of Christ's disciples, agreed with the Jews and covenanted with them, when he saw they desired to kill Him, because he had been reproved by Him: and he took the thirty *staters* of the province, and betrayed Christ unto them: and then, repenting of what he had done, he gave the silver back again to the rulers of the Jews, and hanged himself. But they, thinking it not right to cast it into their treasury, because it was the price of blood, bought with it the ground that was a certain potter's for the burial of strangers.

82 And at His crucifixion, when He asked a drink, they gave Him to drink vinegar mingled with gall. And this was declared through David: *They gave gall to my meat, and in my thirst they gave me vinegar to drink.*

83 And that, being raise from the dead, He was to ascend into heaven, David says thus: *The chariot of God [is] ten-thousandfold, thousands are the drivers: the Lord [is] among them in Sinai in [his] sanctuary. He ascended up on high, he led captivity captive: he received, he gave gifts to men.* And by *captivity* he means the destruction of the rule of the apostate angels. He declares also the place where He was to ascend into heaven from the earth. For *the Lord,* he says, *from Sion ascended up on high.* For over against Jerusalem, on the mount which is called [the Mount] of Olives, after He was risen from the dead, He assembled His disciples, and expounded to them the things concerning the kingdom of heaven; and they saw that He ascended, and they saw how the heavens were opened and received Him.

84 And the same says David again: *Lift up your gates, ye rulers; and be ye lift up, ye everlasting gates, and the King of glory shall come in.* For the everlasting gates are the heavens. But because the Word descended invisible to created things, He was not made known in His descent to them. Because the Word was made flesh, He was visible in His ascension; and, when the powers saw Him, the angels below cried out to those who were on the firmament: *Lift up your gates; and be ye lift up, ye everlasting gates, that the King of glory may come in.* And when they marvelled and said: *Who is this?* those who had already seen Him testified a second time: *The Lord strong and mighty, he is the King of glory.*

85 And being raised from the dead and exalted at the Father's right hand, He awaits the time appointed by the Father for the judgment, when all enemies shall be put under Him. Now the enemies are all those who were found in apostasy, angels and archangels and powers and thrones, who despised the truth. And the prophet David himself says thus: *The Lord said unto my Lord, Sit on my right hand, until I make thine enemies thy footstool.* And that He ascended thither, whence He had come down, David says: *From the end of heaven is his going forth, and his cessation even at the end of heaven.* Then he signifies his judgment: *And there is none that shall be hid from his heat.*

86 If then the prophets prophesied that the Son of God was to appear upon the earth, and prophesied also where on the earth and how and in what manner He should make known His appearance, and all these prophecies the Lord took upon Himself; our faith in Him was well-founded, and the tradition of the preaching [is] true; that is to say, the testimony of the apostles, who being sent forth by the Lord preached in all the world the Son of God, who came to suffer, and endured to the

destruction of death and the quickening of the flesh: that by the putting away of the enmity towards God, which is unrighteousness, we should obtain peace with Him, doing that which is pleasing to Him. And this was declared by the prophets in the words: *How beautiful are the feet of them that bring tidings of peace, and of them that bring tidings of good things.* And that these were to go forth from Judaea and from Jerusalem, to declare to us *the word* of God, which is *the law* for us, Isaiah says thus: *For from Sion shall come forth the law, and the word of the Lord from Jerusalem.* And that in all the earth they were to preach, David says: *Into all the earth went forth their speech, and their words to the ends of the world.*

87 And that not by the much-speaking of the law, but by the brevity of faith and love, men were to be saved, Isaiah says thus: *A word brief and short in righteousness: for a short word will God make in the whole world.* And therefore the apostle Paul says: *Love is the fulfilling of the law*: for he who loves God has fulfilled the law. Moreover the Lord, when He was asked which is the first commandment, said: *Thou shalt love the Lord thy God with all thy heart and with all thy strength. And the second is like unto it: Thou shalt love thy neighbour as thyself. On these two commandments,* He says, *all the law hangeth and the prophets.* So then by our faith in Him He has made our love to God and our neighbour to grow, making us godly and righteous and good. And therefore *a short word* has God made on the earth *in the world.*

88 And that after His ascension He was to be exalted above all, and that there shall be none to be compared and equalled unto Him, Isaiah says thus: *Who is he that entereth into judgment [with me]? Let him stand up against [me]. And who is he who is justified? Let him draw near to the Lord's Son. Woe unto you, for ye shall grow old as a garment, and the moth shall devour you. And all flesh shall be humbled and abased, and the Lord alone shall be exalted in the highest.* And that in the end by His name they should be saved who served God, Isaiah says: *And on those who serve me a new name shall be called, which shall be blessed upon the earth: and they shall bless the true God.* And that this blessing He Himself should bring about, and Himself should redeem us by His own blood, Isaiah declared, saying: *No mediator, no angel, but the Lord himself saved them; because he loved them and spared them: he himself redeemed them.*

89 That He would not send back the redeemed to the legislation of Moses – for the law was fulfilled in Christ – but would have them live in newness by the Word, through faith in the Son of God and love, Isaiah declared, saying: *Remember not the former things, nor bring to mind the things that were in the beginning. Behold I make new [things], which shall now spring up, and ye shall know [them]. And I will make in the wilderness a way, and in the waterless place streams, to give drink to my chosen race, and to my people whom I have purchased to declare my virtues.* Now a *wilderness* and a *waterless place* was at first the calling of the Gentiles: for the Word had not passed through them, nor given them the Holy Spirit to drink; who fashioned the new *way* of godliness and righteousness, and made copious *streams* to spring forth, disseminating over the earth the Holy Spirit; even as it had been promised through the prophets, that in the end of the days He should pour out the Spirit upon he face of the earth.

90 Therefore *by newness of the spirit* is our calling, and not *in the oldness of the letter*; even as Jeremiah prophesied: *Behold the days come, saith the Lord,*

that I will accomplish for the house of Israel and for the house of Judah the covenant of the testament which I covenanted with their fathers, in the day when I took them by the hand to lead them out of the land of Egypt: because they continued not in the covenant, and I regarded them not, saith the Lord. For this is the covenant of the testament that I will covenant with the house of Israel after those days, saith the Lord: I will put my laws into their minds, and write them in their hearts; and I will be to them a God, and they shall be to me a people: and they shall not teach any more every man his neighbour, and every man his brother, saying, Know the Lord: for all shall know me, from the least to the greatest of them. For I will pardon and be merciful unto the sins of their iniquities, and their sins will I remember no more.

91 And that these promises the calling from among the Gentiles should inherit, to whom also the new testament was opened up, Isaiah says thus: *These things saith the God of Israel: In that day a man shall trust in his Maker, and his eyes shall look to the Holy One of Israel: and they shall not trust in altars, nor in the work of their own hands, which their fingers have made.* For very plainly this was said of such as have forsaken idols and believed in God our Maker through the Holy One of Israel. And the Holy One of Israel is Christ: and He became visible to men, and to Him we look eagerly and behold Him; and we trust not in altars, nor in the works of our hands.

92 And that He should become visible amongst us – for the Son of God became Son of man – and be found of us who before had no knowledge [of Him], the Word Himself says thus in Isaiah: *I became manifest to them that sought me not; I was found of them that asked not for me. I said, Behold, here am I, to a race that called not on my name.*

93 And that this race was to become an holy people was declared in the Twelve Prophets by Hosea, thus: *I will call that which was not [my] people, my people; and her that was not beloved, beloved. It shall come to pass that in the place where it was called not my people, there shall they be called sons of the Living God.* This also is that which was said by John the Baptist: *That God is able of these stones to raise up sons to Abraham.* For our hearts being withdrawn and taken away from the stony worship by means of faith behold God, and become sons of Abraham, who was justified by faith. And therefore God says by Ezekiel the prophet: *And I will give them another heart, and a new spirit will I give them: and I will withdraw and take away the stony heart from their flesh, and I will give them another heart of flesh: so that they shall walk in my precepts, and shall keep my ordinances and do them. And they shall be to me for a people, and I will be to them for a God.*

94 So then by the new calling a change of hearts in the Gentiles came to pass through the Word of God, when *He was made flesh and tabernacled* with men; as also His disciple John says: *And his Word was made flesh and dwelt among us.* Wherefore the Church beareth much fruit of the redeemed: because no longer Moses [as] mediator nor Elijah [as] messenger, but the Lord Himself has redeemed us, granting many more children to the Church than to the first Synagogue; as Isaiah declared, saying: *Rejoice thou barren, that didst not bear.* The *barren* is the Church, which never at all in former times presented sons to God. *Cry out and call, thou that didst not travail: for the children of the desolate are more than of her which hath an husband.* Now the first Synagogue had as husband the Law.

95 Moreover Moses in Deuteronomy says that the Gentiles should be *the head*, and the unbelieving people *the tail*. And again he says: *Ye provoked me to jealousy with those that are no gods, and angered me with your idols: and I will provoke you to jealousy with that which is no nation, and with a foolish nation will I anger you.* Because they forsook the God who is, and worshipped and served the gods who are not; and they slew the prophets of God, and *prophesied for Baal*, who was the idol of the Canaanites. And the Son of God, who is, they despised and condemned, but they chose Barabbas the robber who had been taken for murder: and the eternal King they disavowed, and they acknowledged as their king the temporal Caesar. [So] it pleased God to grant their inheritance to the foolish Gentiles, even to those who were not of the polity of God and knew not what God is. Since, then, by this calling life has been given [us], and God has summed up again for Himself in us the faith of Abraham, we ought not to turn back any more – I mean, to the first legislation. For we have received the Lord of the Law, the Son of God; and by faith in Him we learn to love God with all our heart, and our neighbour as ourselves. Now the love of God is far from all sin, and love to the neighbour worketh no ill to the neighbour.

96 Wherefore also we need not the Law as a tutor. Behold, with the Father we speak, and in His presence we stand, being *children in malice*, and grown strong in all righteousness and soberness. For no longer shall the Law say, *Do not commit adultery*, to him who has no desire at all for another's wife; and *Thou shalt not kill*, to him who has put away from himself all anger and enmity; [and] *Thou shalt not covet thy neighbour's field or ox or ass*, to those who have no care at all for earthly things, but store up the heavenly fruits: nor *An eye for an eye, and a tooth for a tooth*, to him who counts no man his enemy, but all men his neighbours, and therefore cannot stretch out his hand at all for vengeance. It will not require tithes of him who consecrates all his possessions to God, leaving father and mother and all his kindred and following the Word of God. And there will be no command to remain idle for one day of rest, to him who perpetually keeps sabbath, that is to say, who in the temple of God, which is man's body, does service to God, and in every hour works righteousness. *For I desire mercy*, He saith, *and not sacrifice; and the knowledge of God more than burnt offerings. But the wicked that sacrificeth to me a calf is as if he should kill a dog; and that offereth fine flour, as though [he offered] swine's blood. But whosoever shall call on the name of the Lord shall be saved.* And there is *none other name* of the Lord *given under heaven whereby men are saved*, save that of God, which is Jesus Christ the Son of God, to which also the demons are subject and evil spirits and all apostate energies.

97 By the invocation of the name of Jesus Christ, crucified under Pontius Pilate, there is a separation and division among mankind; and wheresoever any of those who believe on Him shall invoke and call upon Him and do His will, He is near and present, fulfilling the requests of those who with pure hearts call upon Him. Whereby receiving salvation, we continually give thanks to God, who by His great, inscrutable and unsearchable wisdom delivered us, and proclaimed the salvation from heaven – to wit, the visible coming of our Lord, that is, His living as man – to which we by ourselves could not attain: for *the things which are impossible with men are possible with God.* Wherefore also Jeremiah saith concerning her [*i.e.* wisdom]: *Who hath gone up into heaven, and taken her, and brought her down from*

the clouds? Who hath gone over the sea, found her and will bring her for choice gold? There is none that hath found her way, nor any that comprehendeth her path. But he that knoweth all things knoweth her by his understanding: he that prepareth the earth for evermore, hath filled it with four-footed beasts: he that sendeth forth the light and it goeth; he called it, and it obeyed him with fear: and the stars shined in their watches, and were glad: he called them, and they said Here we be; they shined with gladness unto him that made them. This is our God: there shall none other be accounted of in comparison with him. He hath found out every way by knowledge, and hath given it unto Jacob his servant, and to Israel that is beloved of him. Afterward did he appear upon earth, and was conversant with men. This is the book of the commandments of God, and of the law which endureth for ever. All they that hold it fast [are appointed] to life: but such as leave it shall die. Now by *Jacob* and *Israel* he means the Son of God, who received power from the Father over our life, and after having received this brought it down to us who were far off from Him, when He *appeared on earth and was conversant with men*, mingling and mixing the Spirit of God the Father with the creature formed by God, that man might be *after the image and likeness* of God.

98 This, beloved, is the preaching of the truth, and this is the manner of our redemption, and this is the way of life, which the prophets proclaimed, and Christ established, and the apostles delivered, and the Church in all the world hands on to her children. This must we keep with all certainty, with a sound will and pleasing to God, with good works and right-willed disposition.

99 So that none should imagine God the Father to be other than our Creator, as the heretics imagine; [for] they despise the God who is, and make gods of that which is not; and they fashion a Father of their own above our Creator, and imagine that they have found out for themselves something greater than the truth. For all these are impious and blasphemers against their Creator and against the Father, as we have shown in the *Exposure and Overthrow of Knowledge falsely so-called.* And others again reject the coming of the Son of God and the dispensation of His incarnation, which the apostles delivered and the prophets declared beforehand, even such as should be the summing up of mankind, as we have shown you in brief: and such also are reckoned amongst those who are lacking in faith. And others receive not the gifts of the Holy Spirit, and cast away from themselves the prophetic grace, watered whereby man bears the fruit of life unto God: and these are they of whom Isaiah speaks: *For they shall be*, saith he, *as an oak that is stripped of leaves, and as a garden that hath no water.* And such are in no wise serviceable to God, seeing that they cannot bear any fruit.

100 So then in respect of the three points of our seal error has strayed widely from the truth. For either they reject the Father, or they accept not the Son and speak against the dispensation of His incarnation; or else they receive not the Spirit, that is, they reject prophecy. And of all such must we beware, and shun their ways, if in very truth we desire to be well-pleasing to God and to attain the redemption that is from Him.

Translation: J. Armitage Robinson

Introduction

There is little, if anything, in the Nicene formulae which is not present in embryonic or directional form in the works of Irenaeus. The cardinal place he holds in the way in which orthodox theology opens out to the full expression and significance of the Nicene faith has been underestimated generally in the lack of any systematic consideration of the relation between the influence he left and the achievement of the Nicene fathers, and particularly in the failure to accord his methodology in theology the foundational, directional and formative place it occupies. A comparison of what his work set out and clarified with the achievements of the Nicene fathers, for example, would suggest that the general thought established by Irenaeus is the *cardis*, on which they were able to move – the former was the hinge of the latters' door, both leading to that theological panorama set out by the Councils (and all the achievement of what lay behind them) of AD325, 381 and 451. Such themes are:

1 The internal and eternal relations of Father, Son and Holy Spirit, particularly the ground laid by Irenaeus of the ὁμοουσιος, the same substance, of the Son and the Father; the insistence that the Word is *semper co-existens*, ever co-exists with the Father; and hand in hand with this the oft repeated clear implication that the Spirit is likewise, his co-eternity being explicitly set out in *Adversus Haereses* IV:20:1,3, for example.
2 The external acts of God, showing that there is no disjunction between the Being and the activity of God by emphasizing clearly the mode of the Self-humbling of the eternal Son in the ὀικονομια, the ordering or dispensation of the Incarnation, thereby implying that what God is eternally in Himself, He is towards us in Jesus Christ.
3 The refusal to distinguish the Father from the Creator. There is one God who in the being of His Fatherhood is the Creator of all through His Son who is the Word, and the Holy Spirit.
4 The Royal Exchange and the Deification of Man by grace (that is, humanity's participation in the Divine life without ceasing to be human). The Son becomes what we are in order that we might become what he is. The parallel here with Athanasius's *De Incarnatione* LIV:3 is remarkable. There is also the emphasis here that Christ is God come as man, assuming the totality of what makes human existence. Therefore faith and godliness necessarily go hand in hand – the ground of Athanasius's dictum that we are to live a life in correspondence to God.
5 The growth of the child Jesus in wisdom and favour with God and man – the προεκοπτε, the cutting his way forward. Here is the foundation of Athanasius's comment on Christ ministering the things of God to man and the things of man

to God. It is also the hinterland of the observations by Basil and Gregory Nazianzen, in their respective ways, on the opening of the way for humanity to rise to knowledge of God. The emphasis on faith seeking understanding – that we believe in order to understand, rather than understand so that we may believe, set out definitively by Anselm of Canterbury so much later – is also found here as fundamental to Irenaeus's theology, in harness with the idea of God being beyond comparison, more than the comprehension of human thought, and elusive to description by human words.

6 The Holy Spirit, our knowledge of God and our godliness. Irenaeus is clear that the Spirit is not a creature. The Spirit is related inseparably to the Son, and, although the ὁμοουσιον of the Spirit is not drawn out, it is implied. The co-eternity of the Spirit with the Word and the Father is set out for example, in *Adversus Haereses* IV:20:1,3, as noted above. It is the Spirit who brings us into a community of union with God through Christ; we are raised by the Spirit to knowledge and communion with God and this can be an act of God alone. This communion is a sharing of the knowledge which God has of himself in his eternal Triadic relation.

These themes will be set out as they arise throughout the *Demonstration of the Apostolic Preaching*, which is a framework of Irenaeus's teaching.

Athanasius does not mention Irenaeus or acknowledge any dependence on his works. It is therefore impossible to claim without question that he was beholden directly to the works of Irenaeus. However, the insistence of the Nicene fathers on the received learning from earlier fathers, the tradition passed on to them, is a general enough consideration as to the recognition of Irenaeus's foundational and directional contribution in certain fields of theological endeavour. Moreover, there is a specific pointer to this. Socrates (*c.*AD380–450) comments that the fathers at the Council of Nicaea

> did not introduce any doctrine of their own devising into the church, but contented themselves with recording their sanction of these points which ecclesiastical tradition has insisted on from the beginning, and wise Christians have demonstratively taught. Such sentiments the ancient fathers have uniformly maintained in all their controversial writings. Irenaeus, Clemens, Appollinaris of Hierapolis, and Serapion who presided over the church at Antioch, assure us in their several works, that it was the generally received opinion that Christ in his incarnation was endowed with a soul.[1]

It is the mention by Socrates of the works of Irenaeus in the context of the Nicene fathers which is significant. That Eusebius of Caesarea also knowledgeably mentions the works of Irenaeus, suggests that the products of his theology were recognized widely at this time.[2] The references to Irenaeus and his works by Tertullian (*c.*AD160–225), Jerome[3] (*c.*AD342–420), Augustine of Hippo (*c.*AD354–430) and Theoderet[4] (*c.*AD 393–466) also bear out his lasting and wide influence and importance.

Equally, however, if full place has not been given to Irenaeus for his part in the whole progress of orthodoxy, the themes which are peculiarly Irenaean have not been explored in their fullness and set out in their richness of theological significance. Much has been written about his doctrine of recapitulation, for example, but generally this has been considered apart from (as with other of his doctrinal emphases) his theological method. Moreover, the doctrine of recapitulation is a secondary consequence of primary concerns in Irenaeus's case, of the nature of the incarnation and its relation to the act of creation – rather as in the same way Calvin's doctrine of predestination is a consequence of his more foremost concern of Christology.

It is methodology above and before all else which singles out Irenaeus and accords him a place of significance and establishes him indisputedly in it, in the development of theological thinking. All his doctrines are consequences of this method which not only has import for all areas of theological concern, but also provides him with both an immensity of direction of thought in his understanding of the nature of God in His Triadic existence, and the relation of the created realities in their dimension and nature to the Creator, and also an intensity within his pastoral insight concerning godliness and individuality.

There are particular reasons why the *Demonstration of the Apostolic Preaching* should be used as an entrance into Irenaean thought. It is an encheiridion, a pocket dogmatics. It is sent by Irenaeus as

> a more essential compendium of basic tenets, that by little you may attain to much, encompassing in a short word all the members of the body of truth and perceiving in brief the demonstration of the things of God.[5]

It was written after *Adversus Haereses.*[6] It is indeed a summary of that earlier, larger work, though without reference to the expositions of the various systems of the Gnostic heresy countered by Irenaeus there. It does mention such heresies, but only in passing, for it has a framework all of its own which is determined by the desire of Irenaeus to set out, on its own terms, the objective act and accomplished deed of God in reconciliation and revelation. The positive substance of the faith, appreciable on its own terms, is his business here. The *Demonstration of the Apostolic Preaching* is the very distillation of Irenaean thought. In its brevity lies its clarity – and this throws light on the involved argument of sections of the larger work.

This clear shortness reveals that Irenaeus established a methodology of theological thought and statement. He stresses the necessary relationship between faith and objective reality, and his use of words as precise and concise theological terms is determined and achieved by referring them to the nature of the object which confronts him and with which he is concerned, that is, the objective Truth of God Incarnate. Under the compulsion of that Self-giving and Self-witnessing of God in reconciliation and revelation, words and their deployment are bent by Irenaeus into appropriate use as fitting pointers to that unique mystery of the Word made flesh and the name of Jesus Christ. It is this appropriate usage, this paradigmatic propriety, which is the hallmark of Irenaeus's theological method.

Out of this come certain significant phrases as theological statements, and these lie behind much of the phraseology employed by later theologians as the terminology of scientific theology developed. For example, there is an affinity of inheritance between the language of Irenaeus and that used by Athanasius in terminology concerning Christ – He is the Word always existing with the Father, *semper co-existens*, or the beginning of ways, ἀρχη ὁδων, to give but two instances. The theological methodology is the same for both Irenaeus and Athanasius, and the choice and usage of words by the earlier is the key to an understanding of the implications of the language employed by the later.

But for both Irenaeus and Athanasius, theology was more than terminology. Faith and godliness were forged profoundly together, and the one theological virtue could not be true without the other. For both these fathers, theology was that which was cut, not only into the mind, but into the totality of human existence, body as well as soul. For it was this totality which the Word assumed and sanctified.

This methodology of theology and the resultant theological language employed, as formed out of that centre which is God's revelation and reconciliation, was refined as it was whetted against the heresies which both Irenaeus and Athanasius encountered. But the course which Irenaeus charted as he cut through the entanglements of the Gnostic heresy, was the same topography which Athanasius used as he moved with equal effect through Arian territory. Gnosticism lay behind Arianism, and the groundwork of Irenaeus is gone over by Athanasius as he moved on farther with his particular insights and contributions.

This sharpening of theological statement against the variety of Gnosticism opposed by Irenaeus in *Adversus Haereses* became the precision of orthodox formulae in the *Demonstration of the Apostolic Preaching*. The polarity of his theology is twofold. Both poles are considerations of the incarnation.

The first is the fact that although Irenaeus is concerned with the once-for-all given-ness of the faith, its totality and utter sufficiency in the incarnation, this does not mean that theology is regarded as a closed and complete system by which ultimate conclusions have, or can be, arrived at and stated. The demands of the mystery and the majesty and the autonomy of the objective reality of the Word made flesh that all human endeavour in speaking about this truth, because of the limitations and incapacity in which this exercise is undertaken by creatures confronted by their Creator, should be referred and tested against the integrity of this Self-giving truth again and again, prevents any theological inertia and petrifaction. These demands mean that the process of clearly perceiving and responsibly handing on this truth is a matter of theologia informata, theologia reformanda – rightly informed theology must always be theology constantly reforming. That is to say, theological method means that theological concepts and statements have to be referred back ever and again for scrutiny and refining against the prime, controlling and determinative Truth of the Word incarnate, and modified and clarified accordingly. Theology is debarred from thinking that it can encompass and contain, with rounded-off satisfaction, the truth of God within its own statements. Irenaeus is quite emphatic that there is a distinction between Truth and our statements about Truth, and that these statements, given this distinction, have to be viewed and understood and deployed in a particular way. It is this exercise which characterizes the science of theology.

Second, that the incarnation does not stand alone as an isolated truth, however fundamental it may be. Incarnation and creation are interlocked profoundly as two facets of the one act of the one God. It is in the light of the former that the latter is understood properly. Irenaeus's view of the relation between Creator and creation is Christocentric. It is his appreciation of the interlocking of the Being of God with the existence of His created handiwork in the incarnate Word, while yet preserving the integrities of the Divine nature and of the temporal/spatial reality in which we, as a significant part of that reality, live and move and have our being, which sets the theological pattern for subsequent ages. The union between the Divine and the human in the incarnation which does not compromise, change or dilute the integrities of God and man, and the subsequent bracketing together in a mutually respectful relation of Creator and creature, which Irenaeus states, sometimes explicitly, sometimes implicitly, anticipates the questions facing theology at a later time in his thought, but always fundamentally addresses itself to those perennial problems put to theology in one form or another, and which theology must endeavour not to avoid, but to meet, confront and debate, by reference to the Word made flesh, seeking no other expeditious road.

These themes are fundamental to the way in which the faith is unfolded in the *Demonstration of the Apostolic Preaching*. This short work by Irenaeus, 'who touched the Apostles' times', as Lancelot Andrewes[7] was later to say of him, was, and hopefully is, to use Armitage Robinson's phrase,[8] a '*Vade Mecum*' for an intelligent Christian. I would suggest that the influence of the directions it contains is greater than has been so far acknowledged, and that its re-establishment would be for present benefit and for profit in any age. Irenaeus himself so commends it:

> This, beloved, is the preaching of the truth, and this is the manner of our redemption, and this is the way of life, which the prophets proclaimed, and Christ established, and the Apostles traditioned, and the Church in all the world hands on to her children. This we must keep inviolate with a sound will and so be well-pleasing to God, with good works and properly centred mind.[9]

I have suggested, throughout the following comments on the sections of the *Demonstration*, that Irenaeus should be allowed to speak for himself as himself. By this I mean that all too often theologians and other historical persons are treated at the hands of their assessors as mere compendiums of earlier sources – amalgams of others' thoughts – and that if this is overdone, it cloaks the perception of them as individuals with original contributions made to the whole sweep of human endeavour. Obviously we are all beholden to others, but we are not thereby merely a mixture of others. I would suggest that in the field of academic studies too much time and effort is spent in dissecting the individual under scrutiny, so that the whole undertaking becomes as the work of atomists. I have only paid minimal attention, therefore, to sources behind Irenaeus, for I think that too much has been made of, for example, his being beholden, to such a great extent as some would have it, to Justin Martyr. By Irenaeus's own admissions, he would rather seem to stand as the passer on (and I am sure original developer of) that tradition about which we know little – the inheritance of Papias, Polycarp and those 'disciples of the apostles', and those who had kept company with John. In so doing, I do not mean to belittle critical scholarship. Far from it. But I wish to try to give Irenaeus the chance to be seen in the light of that side of him as the original, influential and therefore important, individual which I think he was.

I have also suggested that his mode of theological thought, while systematic, is intricate. I think it is to be seen as his production of circles of thought which emanate from the centre point of his theological thinking, the dispensation of the

Word made flesh, and from there go out in ever-widening circles, including many considerations, the various aspects and the totality of creation, as they expand, to the divine life and being of the triune God. Sometimes those circles widen out immediately to their final reach, but they all return, and in their returning mix and mingle with the outgoing ones, to the centre of their origin, the Person and acts of the Word made flesh who recapitulates all things in Himself and who is the very presence of God with us, accommodating Himself to our creaturely estate and endeavours.

I hope that this work will accomplish at least some increase in the appreciation of this theologian who has had such a varied reputation bestowed upon him by so many others.

Notes

1 Socrates: *Ecclesiastical History* III:7, cf. V:22.
2 Eusebius: *Ecclesiastical History* II:13:5; III:18:2; III:23:2–4; III:26:3; III:36:12; III:39:13; IV:7:4,9; IV:10; IV:11:1–5; IV:14:1–9; IV:18:9; IV:21; IV:25; IV:29:1–3; V:4:1–3; V:5:8; V:8:1–15; V:20:1–8; V:23:2; V:24:18; V:28:5; VI:13:9.
3 Jerome (and Gennadius): *Lives of Illustrious Men* IX, XVIII, XXIII, XXXV, CXXI.
4 Theoderet: *Dialogues* I–III; *Letters* CXLV, CLI.
5 Irenaeus: *Demonstration of the Apostolic Preaching* I.
6 *Ibid.* XCIX.
7 Lancelot Andrewes: *Sermon II of the Nativity.*
8 Irenaeus: *Demonstration of the Apostolic Preaching*, Introduction by J. Armitage Robinson, p. 2.
9 *Ibid.* XCVIII.

Chapter 1

Section 1: The Title – *Demonstration of the Apostolic Preaching*

The title itself is significant. Throughout the expression of the thought of Irenaeus there is no disjunction between word and act. There is no indulgence in 'bare words' of abstractions, philosophy for the sake of philosophy only, or of reducing the faith to a 'plausible system'[1]. Irenaeus condemns all such and regards the Christian faith as standing over against all such theorizing exercises. The faith is rather a matter of an active and demonstrable theology which speaks out to, and takes stock of, the realities of humanity and creation as seen in the light of the reality of the Creator. It speaks of the living and lively God who is as He acts and acts as He is. God demonstrates himself, and the Word is the demonstration of God. It is in this sense of 'active proof' that 'Demonstration' is used, as employed by Justin Martyr[2] citing to Trypho the prefigurement of the action and event of the resurrection and ascension of Christ in *Psalm XXIV*, and the antiphonal 'Who is this King of Glory? The Lord of Hosts, He is this King of Glory', as the question asked by the hosts of heaven not recognizing the 'uncomely and dishonoured'figure of Christ at the gates of heaven as they are commanded by the Father to open them to the King of Glory, and answered by the Holy Spirit. Επιδειξις – 'demonstration or proof' – as used here by Justin Martyr, is a word in which knowledge and being and action are involved. Irenaeus employs it likewise.

Theology is not concerned to ask 'Is there a God?' Irenaeus is not engaging in an apology for either the Gospel or its apostolic traditioning. He is setting out the one 'scope', that is (in the sense of σκοπος) the centre and horizon, the substance and the goal, of both scripture and tradition, for what it is in itself alone without any other consideration, and clearing the ground so that it can be perceived and allowed to speak for itself on its own terms. Irenaeus speaks of this in his larger work in terms of Christ being the 'treasure hid in the Scriptures'.[3] The primary question with which theology is concerned is 'Is there a Word of God?' For by His Word God demonstrates himself to be active and eternal Being who does not need to be discovered by the initiative of any philosophical system devised by human beings, but is himself his own proof. The Word made flesh means the Self-revelation of the invisible, immeasurable, incomprehensible and eternal God as the God who, in his grace, is involved with and committed to this observable, quantitative, physical and temporal creation. What God is eternally in Himself, He is towards us in Jesus Christ. This Jesus Christ is the 'scope' of the faith, for

> in no other way could we have learned the things of God, unless our Master, existing as the Word, had become man. For no other being had the power of revealing to us the things of the Father, except his own proper Word. For what other person 'knew the mind

> of the Lord' or who else 'has become His counsellor?' Again we could have learned in no other way than by seeing our Teacher and hearing His voice with our own ears, that, having become imitators of His works as well as doers of His words, we may have communion with Him . . . as the mighty Word and very man.[4]

This is the identity and nature of the Apostolic preaching or κερυγμα, for that 'kerugma' is the proclamation of that which has been demonstrated by God in Person by His incarnation, and which those who have heard and seen the Word of life have demonstrated correspondingly by their faith and godliness.

For Irenaeus there is a double demonstration – primarily of God's act involving His being in the incarnation of the Word, and secondarily of those who witness to this by their words and acts which point to Christ as the substance and circumference, the centre and the horizon, of their proclamation. The first is the σκοπος of the second. Faith, and the preaching of, and living out, the faith, if they be faith in truth, preaching in propriety, and that life which is in correspondence to God, are not detached from the Person of Christ. Any such disjunction would mean that they had become something else. 'Demonstration' as applied to the activity of the faithful, is the stamp, the impression, the likeness, of the Word made flesh upon them. By their words and action, the Word made flesh is perceived; through them He is made audible and visible and therefore demonstrated. This active faith is set out in sections 2 and 3 of the *Demonstration.*

Section 1: Faith and Godliness

The work is addressed in endearing terms to 'Marcianos'. Eusebius notes[5] that Irenaeus 'wrote a work dedicated to a brother Marcian'. The language used here in Section 1, the introduction, of the *Demonstration of the Apostolic Preaching*, would suggest that the name was indeed that of a friend and not a stylized device. In his youth, Irenaeus had seen, heard and been given a lasting impression of Polycarp (*c.*AD69–155), Bishop of Smyrna whom he eulogizes.[6] If not born in Smyrna, he at least had his early upbringing there and was of the Christian community in that place, hence his acquaintance with Polycarp. In the *Epistle of the Smyrnaens Concerning the Martyrdom of Polycarp*, mention is made of one Marcianos.[7] Euarestus, on behalf of the church at Smyrna, was the scribe who wrote of the circumstances of, and described, the recent martyrdom of Polycarp, producing this epistle which was then entrusted to Marcianos to carry it to Philomelium as the representative of the Christian community at Smyrna. This Marcianos must have been held in a position of regard by that church to be given this task. Whether or not this is the same Marcianos of Irenaeus's acquaintance must remain a conjecture, though the fact of the mutual link with Smyrna could point in this direction. Again, whether or not Marcianos is the 'dear friend' mentioned in the beginning of each of the books of *Adversus Haereses*, is also but surmise. However, if Marcianos were an individual known to Irenaeus, it would appear from the description in this first section of the present work as a 'compendium of basic tenets', or 'a manual of essentials'[8] and that it is so commended as a handier, succinct book as opposed to the lengthier, more detailed work (*Adversus Haereses*), that Marcianos was regarded as being familiar with that latter work, and could well have been the same person accorded the place of close acquaintance in both works. That the larger work referred to in this first section is indeed *Adversus Haereses*, is clear from the reference in section 99 – 'as we have shown in the Exposure and Overthrow of Knowledge falsely so-called' – the other title of that work.

Whatever the case, Irenaeus makes it appear that he was writing to someone domiciled at a distance from him – 'Would that it were possible for us to be always together . . . at the present time we are distant from one another in body . . . ' – presumably he being in Lyons and the recipient possibly in his well-known Smyrna. But once more surmise it must remain.

On the other hand, though the introduction would seem to be ruled out as a mere stylistic or literary device because of its specific address and detailed comments of a personal nature, the name Marcianos could have been employed as a personalized representation for the purpose of addressing the work to a particular body of persons – the Μαρκιανοι Marcianoi, the appellation used by Justin Martyr for the followers of the heretic Marcion. That the argument of this work could be directed towards persuading perhaps hesitant followers of Marcionism may be supported (though there is no direct attack on that heresy in the *Demonstration*) by several emphases of Irenaeus implying a criticism of that heretical scheme.

First, the place he gives to the prophets of the Old Testament in relation to the Father, Son and Holy Spirit, the God who is both Creator and Redeemer.[9] Second, the oft-repeated, emphatic linking of 'Father' with 'Creator' and the insistence that there is no disjunction between creation and Lordship, that is, there is not a Creator God and another God who is now Lord over that which is the work of the other.[10] Third, and following this as an extension (though it is equally applicable to various Gnostic tenets), the censure 'none should imagine God the Father to be other than our Creator, as the heretics imagine'[11] is significant as a principal statement in the summing up of the reasons for producing this work. This points back to Irenaeus's giving priority of place in the preceding argument to the title Father[12] and it is this which was to be paralleled so closely by Athanasius later in his assertion that God is known essentially through the Son as Father, that he has always been Father, and that he was not always Creator.[13] This will be discussed below in Chapter 13.

While there may be some grounds for supposing that Marcianus is the epitome of the disillusioned followers of Marcion against whose division of the Creator God of the Old Testament and the Good God of the New so much of the *Demonstration* is directed, the work contains no such phrase as the observation that the two covenants, the Old and the New, were

> unius et eisudem substantiae – of one and the same substance
>
> Utraque autem testamenta unus et idem paterfamilias produxit, Verbum Dei, Dominus noster Jesus Christus, qui et Abrahae et Moysi colluctus est – But one and the same householder produced both covenants, the Word of God, our Lord Jesus Christ, who spoke with both Abraham and Moses[14]

as might be expected in an anti-Marcion work. Irenaeus saw Marcion as the forerunner of much that led to the work of the gnostic Valentinus, and traces an evolution of gnosticism from him.[15] Irenaeus emphasizes the orthodox answer to that basically dualistic thought, from which sprang all the heresies he confronted, and which had their origin, in his view, beyond Marcion in the spawner of all heresies, the heresiarch Simon Magus, the Simon of Samaria mentioned in Acts VIII,[16] but at first are so clearly stated in the views of Marcion. Irenaeus has a unitary way of thinking, as opposed to a dualistic tendency in which Creator and creature, God and humanity, heaven and earth, spiritual and material, faith and works, are torn apart. His theological hallmark is to bracket all these profoundly together yet with their respective natures unimpaired. This unitary mode of thought is the result of his Christocentricity by which he constructs his theology out of a centre and on a foundation where God and humanity are united in the integrity of their natures in the Word made flesh.

The tone of the *Demonstration* is one of persuasion and the setting out positively of basic orthodox tenets. Dismissal of heresy is incidental, and for this reason, no obvious target is chosen. Whether or not the dedication to Marcianos is the literary device to so represent the unsure heretic sincerely searching for the truth, must yet again remain conjecture. Irenaeus notes the desire of 'Marcianos . . . to walk in godliness, which alone brings man to eternal life', is glad for him and exhorts him to 'keep the faith in its integrity that he may be well-pleasing to God who made you'.

The theme of faith and godliness as jointly the only possible expression of truth itself is introduced at the beginning and expanded in the following sections of the *Demonstration*. As a theme, it is the expression of his unitary way of thinking applied to the Christian existence. There can be no divorce of faith and works as the vocation of humanity, for it is to faith and works that humanity is called and from humanity the unity of faith and works is called by Truth, as our assent to, and acknowledgement of, that Truth as it confronts us in all the compelling authority of its Self-interpretation,[17] the majestic freedom of its Self-sufficiency[18] and the sufficient evidence of its Self-giving to us.[19] God is His own interpreter and He has set Himself before us in the Word made flesh who invokes faith, and faith expressed as godliness.

'Godliness', for Irenaeus, is not a quality which humanity achieves by its own volition and ability. It is not within human competence. It is primarily 'Godness', that is, what God essentially and eternally is in Himself and what He is towards us in Jesus Christ. Hence 'the mystery of godliness'[20] is not first or descriptively that state of piety which is the Christian stance; it is that God in all his Godness, without changing, compromising or diluting that Godness, takes the reality of our flesh and nature to himself at the incarnation. Godliness as applied as a description of the quality of human existence and action is a secondary matter, though necessarily following from the primary consideration. Here it refers certainly to the human but with respect to the priority of the Godliness of God, in that the reference is to participation in this Godliness, which is God's alone whereby He brings humanity into a 'community of union' (a favourite Irenaean phrase)[21] with himself in his assumption of human nature and flesh, raising it to newness through his cross, resurrection and ascension – 'the mystery of godliness' to which Paul refers. Godliness as applied to human quality, means the created counterpart of the uncreated God, humanity living a life by the sheer grace of God 'in correspondence with God', as Athanasius was to later say.[22] As life and light are inseparable and together are communion with God,[23] so faith and godliness are necessarily yoked one with the other and their union is the expression of love for God in communion with him.

This community of union is achieved by the grace of the Word and the Spirit. Irenaeus sets the concept out in terms of the royal exchange. This means that the Word of God

> did, through His transcendent love, become what we are, that He might bring us to be what He is Himself.[24]

> . . . the mighty Word and very man . . . thus has redeemed us through His own blood, giving His soul for our souls, and His flesh for our flesh, and has also poured out the Spirit of the Father for the union and communion of God and man, imparting indeed God to men by means of the Spirit, and, on the other hand, attaching man to God by means of His incarnation, and bestowing upon us at His coming immortality durably and truly, by means of communion with God.[25]

There is an interplay and an interdependence between 'faith and godliness', 'a community of union', 'light and life',[26] 'the image and likeness of God'[27] in Irenaeus's theology. They are all descriptive, complementary facets – indeed, interchangeable themes – of the one estate of humanity in God's creative vocation of humanity, an estate which is anchored beyond human competence and achievement in the sheer grace of the Word made flesh and his Spirit outpoured. They are all aspects of God's dispensation for us, our participation through the Spirit in the Word made flesh 'revealing God indeed to men, but presenting man to God'.[28] This Athanasius was to echo later in speaking of the Word becoming man that 'He might minister the things of God to us, and ours to God'.[29]

Faith and godliness born of 'pure and sound teaching is the way leading upwards for all who see it, lightened with heavenly light'. This enlightenment is not something which humanity may claim for itself through its own ability, mental achievement or natural disposition. It is not some 'inner light', the goal of self-discovery.

> For to follow the Saviour is to be a partaker of salvation, and to follow light is to receive light. But those who are in light do not themselves illumine the light, but are illumined and revealed by it. They certainly do not contribute anything to it, but, receiving the benefit, they are illumined by the light.[30]

This way is one, because it is a way of light, and light is simple and pure; it is in contrast to the alternative which is the fact that 'many and dark and contrary are the ways of them that see not'. The translation by J.P. Smith is preferable to that of Armitage Robinson here, in that it conveys with more emphasis the importance of the unifying and unitary nature of the truth, the way of truth and therefore of godliness and faith – 'a single upward path'.[31]

This is part of the unitary view of all things in relation to God which permeates Irenaeus's thought, whether it be the whole of creation as it exists as the one work of God, or the community of union of humanity with God, or the single-mindedness of the individual in godliness. It is important for a full appreciation of Irenaean theology to recognize and constantly hold in mind this unitary view of all existence, be it in its immensity or in its intensity, in relation to God, as a *cantus firmus* running through Irenaeus's works, determining and binding into one their contrapuntal variations.

This way of light as pure, simple and single, uniting man to God, is contrasted with the diverse, tortuous and labyrinthine ways of heresy separating man from God. There is implicit here the idea of contingency, which will be examined later in other aspects of Irenaeus's theology when these appear as we move through the text.

I wish to put forward a theological usage of the concept of contingency. The word, as I use it in the context of theological thought, conveys more than its common usage – dependent on, liable but not certain to happen, etc. I employ it with a double meaning: dependent on, certainly for the first aspect of it, but also established in its own integrity within that dependency, for the second. With regard to creation as contingent, this means that creation is utterly dependent on God for its beginning, the continuance of its existence and its fulfilment, the realization of its reason for being, yet it is not God or equal to Him, but has its own identity, nature, quality and existence. Analogous to this, but only as a parallel and not as an *analogia entis*, an analogy of being, is the later understanding of the mode of the existence of the human nature of Christ. That human nature has being, not of itself, but only within its union with the divine nature. Within that union it has its own identity and existence. The terms ἀνυποστασις, ἐνυποστασις, applied to the human nature of Christ in its relation to the divine, are again parallel here. The first means that outside its union with the divine existence, the humanity has no independent being, the second that within that union it does have its own being.

I suggest that here, an implicit idea of contingency impinges upon Irenaeus's understanding of human existence. Humanity is created to exist in a community of union with God. It is totally and utterly dependent upon God for its creation, its sustenance and its fulfilment through His Word and Spirit, His 'hands'.[32] Yet humanity is created with its own identity; it is not as the Creator –

> For you do not make God, but God made you. If you are God's workmanship, therefore, await the hand of your Maker which creates everything in due time . . . . But if you . . . show yourself ungrateful towards Him, because you were created [merely] man . . . you have at once lost both His workmanship and life. For to create is an attribute of the goodness of God; but to be created that of human nature.[33]

> And in this respect God differs from man, that God indeed makes, but man is made; and truly, He who makes is always the same; but that which is made must receive both beginning and middle, and addition and increase. And God does indeed create after a skilful manner, while, as for man, he is skilfully created.[34]

> For you, O man, are not an uncreated being, nor did you always co-exist with God as did His Word; but now, through His pre-eminent goodness, receiving the beginning of your creation, you gradually learn from the Word the dispensations of God who made you.[35]

Humanity exists only as the humanity God intended it to be in his creative purpose, that is, it exists only in its God-given natural integrity, in this contingent bond with God.

For life does not arise from us, nor from our own nature; but it is bestowed according to the grace of God . . . . Therefore he who shall preserve the life bestowed upon him, and give thanks to him who imparted it, shall receive also length of days for ever and ever. But he who shall reject it, and prove himself ungrateful, to his Maker, inasmuch as he has been created, and has not recognized him who bestowed, deprives himself of continuance for ever and ever.[36]

The recognition of the contingent bond is to 'give thanks'. And in that recognition of its true estate, humanity finds its liberty. The giving of thanks is not only a matter of verbal declaration by lips and tongue, but also of action by hand and foot, as it were – faith and godliness together. Thankfulness involves the totality of being so that it expresses the image of God by participation in and communion with the One who is himself the Image of God.[37]

For he [the Word] both showed forth the image truly, since he became himself what was his image; and he re-established the similitude after a sure manner, by assimilating man to the invisible Father through means of the visible word.[38]

It is by participation in the Word made flesh, and in this participation or communion with him realizing the image of God in the individual's totality, that each person finds the liberty of humanity.

Liberty is given to those who do him service with a willing mind and with all the heart.[39]

To be cut off from life is the lot of those who prefer their own zeal and are not subject to God.

But Irenaeus is insistent that the initiative, the continuance and the fulfilment of this contingent bond within which humanity has its own identity and freedom, is God's. Humanity's thankfulness does not create its community of union with God; it is merely its 'amen' to all that God has once and for all sufficiently done in bringing about the ground and the goal, the beginning and the end, and the sustaining of this bond, in the incarnation.

For, as much as God is in want of nothing, so much does man stand in need of communion with God. For this is the glory of man, to continue and remain permanently in God's service. Wherefore also did the Lord say to his disciples 'Ye have not chosen me, but I have chosen you', indicating that they did not glorify him when they followed him, but that, in following the Son of God, they were glorified by him . . . . We do participate in the glory of the Lord, who has both formed us, and prepared us for this, that, when we are with him, we may partake of his glory.[40]

. . . those . . . who despise the incarnation of the pure generation of the Word of God, defraud human nature of promotion into God, and prove themselves ungrateful to the Word of God who became flesh for them. For it was to this end that the Word of God was made man, and he who was the Son of God became the Son of man, that man, having been taken into the Word, and receiving the adoption, might become the son of God. For by no other means could we have attained to incorruptibility and immortality, unless we had been united to incorruptibility and immortality. But how could we be joined to incorruptibility and immortality, unless, first, incorruptibility and immortality had become that which we also are . . . ?[41]

It is in this 'single upward path' which Marcianos is exhorted to walk. He is counselled to 'make your course' in it. The language implies movement, progression and advancement. This, too, is one of Irenaeus's most constant themes; that the Christian life is a pilgrimage whereon the individual progresses more and more towards the ultimate vision of the glory of God in full communion with Him face to face. While this advancement is humanity's own, it nevertheless is not achieved by humanity moving on its own volition, perception and ability towards God. This movement and progress is made within the contingent relationship:

> God is also truly perfect in all things, himself equal and similar to himself, as he is all light, and all mind, and all substance, and the fount of all good; but man receives advancement and increase towards God. For as God is always the same, so also man, when found in God, shall always go on towards God. For neither does God at any time cease to confer benefits upon, or to enrich, man; nor does man ever cease from receiving the benefits, and being enriched by God.[42]

The simultaneity and juxtaposition of 'in God' and 'towards God' is itself a statement of contingency – we, and Marcianos, can only progress towards God as our own work of thankfulness as we are in God through union with his Word. This is a matter of God's sheer unmerited grace, in, by and through which we go towards God and are free for God. Our service of God is our perfect freedom.

The other way, that which leads to separating man from God, is the breaking of the bond of natural contingency and therefore is the work of the power of evil: 'the apostasy' –

> The apostasy tyrannized over us unjustly, and though we were by nature the property of the omnipotent God, alienated us contrary to nature, rendering us its own disciples.[43]

It will be noted that the dignity of humanity is expressed in its relation to God in, through and by the hands of God. We are made to progress in the image of God – that is, to advance towards God through, by and in the Word and Spirit. The 'image of God' as applied to humanity is a matter of moving towards the image of God – Christ himself – by the leading of the Spirit uttered by the Word. Perhaps Jerome's Latin rendering of the Hebrew of Genesis 1:26,27, in the Vulgate – *ad imaginem Dei*, rather than *in image Dei* – expresses this same dynamic interpretation. However, as we will see in the next section, the composition of human being is not regarded as a static, subjectivized image, but is a matter of body and soul in their totality related to God, which relation is regarded by Irenaeus as the 'spirit'. The *imago Dei* for Irenaeus is a dynamic, lively progress within the contingent bond of creature and Creator.

Notes

1 *suadela*: πιθανολογιας, cf. Irenaeus: *Adversus Haereses* I: preface 1–3.
2 Justin Martyr: *Dialogue with Trypho* XXXVI.
3 Irenaeus: *Adversus Haereses* IV:26:1.
4 Irenaeus: *Ibid.* V:1:1.

5 Eusebius: *Ecclesiastical History* V:26:1.
6 Irenaeus: *Adversus Haereses* III:3:4.
7 *Epistle of the Smyrnaens Concerning the Martyrdom of Polycarp* XX.
8 Justin Martyr: *Dialogue with Trypho* XXXV.
9 Irenaeus: e.g. *Demonstration of the Apostolic Preaching*, 5–6; cf. his appeal to the paradigmatic function of the prophets with regard to the incarnation, e.g. *Adversus Haereses* IV:34:1–2.
10 Irenaeus: e.g. *Demonstration of the Apostolic Preaching* 3–4; cf. *Adversus Haereses* IV:34:2–3, V:2:1.
11 Irenaeus: *Demonstration of the Apostolic Preaching* 98.
12 *Ibid.* 4–8.
13 Athanasius: e.g. *De Decretis* V:22; *Contra Arianos* 1:34.
14 Irenaeus: *Adversus Haereses* IV:9:1 (Paris edition, 1639 and Grabe edition, 1702, IV:21).
15 *Ibid.* I:27:2–I:28:1.
16 *Ibid.* I:23:1ff (cf. especially I:23:3 for the charge of dualism and embryonic Marcionism).
17 E.g. *ibid.* II:28:7; III:6:1–5; IV:6:3–7; IV:20:6,7; V:1:1; V:16:2.
18 E.g. *ibid.* I:22:1; II:preface 1; II:1:1–5; II:2:1–5; II:5:4; IV:14:1;IV:16:3–4; IV:17:1; IV:18:3,6; IV:20:1.
19 E.g. *ibid.* II:22:4; II:25:3; III:2:5; III:6:1–6; III:9:1; III:17:1; III:18:1,7;III:19-3; III:20:2; IV:24:2; V:1:1; V:2:1.
20 I Timothy III:16.
21 Irenaeus: e.g. *Demonstration* 6; *Adversus Haereses* (in the Armenian version) IV:34:4, V:1:1.
22 Athanasius: *De Incarnatione* V.
23 Irenaeus: *Adversus Haereses* V:27:2.
24 *Ibid.* V:preface.
25 *Ibid.* V:1:1.
26 *Ibid.* V:37:2.
27 *Ibid.* IV:20:1; IV:33:4; V:16:1–3.
28 *Ibid.* IV:20:6,7.
29 Athanasius: *Contra Arianos* IV:6.
30 Irenaeus: *Adversus Haereses* IV:14:1.
31 J.P. Smith: tr. *Proof of the Apostolic Preaching*, p. 47.
32 Cf., e.g. Irenaeus: *Adversus Haereses* IV: preface 3; IV:20:1; IV:39:3; V:1:3; V:5:1; V:6:1; V:28:4.
33 Irenaeus: *Adversus Haerese* IV:39:2.
34 *Ibid.* IV:11:2.
35 *Ibid.* II:25:3; cf. Fragment XXIV where the contrast is made between the constancy of God and the changeability of humanity.
36 Irenaeus: *Adveresus Haereses* II:34:3; cf. I:22:1; IV:11:2.
37 Irenaeus: cf. Section 2, *Demonstration of the Apostolic Preaching*.
38 Irenaeus: *Adversus Haereses* V:16:2.
39 *Ibid.* IV:11:4.
40 *Ibid.* IV:14:1; cf. III:20:2; IV:20:7.
41 *Ibid.* III:19:1.
42 *Ibid.* IV:11:2.
43 *Ibid.* V:1:1.

Chapter 2

Section 2: The Duty and Dignity of Humanity

The way of uniting man to God, and the ways whereby man is separated from God, concern the totality of what constitutes the human being. The former emphasizes the contingent bond between humanity and God in which bond alone humanity can be truly human – what it is in the creative purpose of God. Humanity exists in dependence to God, yet has its own nature, quality and identity within that relation, for it is other than the Creator; it is created. The latter underlines the breaking of the contingent bond by stressing the attempt of humanity to assert an independence and autonomy over against God, by which action it removes itself from the only ground of its essential being.

The image of God towards which humanity is made and which is the hallmark of its true quality is only found within the correct contingent relation to God. As we will see, Irenaeus insists that this relation is only achieved through the Persons and work of the Word and the Spirit and man's participation in such. Humanity's self-assertion, on the other hand, is summed up in Adam, the prime, patriarchal and recapitulative iconoclast, who breaks the image of God in so separating himself from God. He seeks the source and maintenance of life in his introversion and self-esteem which can neither give life nor sustain it, for only God, through his Word and Spirit, can do that.

> The rule of truth which we hold is that there is one God Almighty who made all things by his Word, and fashioned and formed, out of that which had no existence, all things which exist .... He who by his Word and Spirit makes and disposes and governs all things, and commands all things into existence – he who formed the world (for the world is of all) [that is, the totality of all created things] – he who fashioned man.[1]

The heretics have deviated from this rule of faith, and in so doing are

> thus proving themselves ungrateful to him who created them. Moreover they despise the workmanship of God, speaking against their own salvation, becoming their own bitterest accusers, and being false witnesses [against the dignity of humanity].[2]

That is why the heretics' 'doctrine is homocidal'.[3] Moreover, they deny the truth of the incarnation of the Word, by participation in which fact and event humanity is given the restoration and fulfilment of the image of God. In so doing, the heretics 'defraud human nature of promotion into God and prove themselves ungrateful to the Word of God who became flesh for them'.[4] They attack both the Creator, his love and grace, and the very root of the true being of humanity.

> Now man is a mixed organization of soul and flesh, who was formed after the likeness of God and moulded by his hands, that is, by the Son and Holy Spirit, to whom also he said, 'Let us make man'. This then is the aim of him who envies our life, to render men disbelievers in their own salvation and blasphemous against God the Creator.[5]

The way in which some heresy attacks any idea of the true relation of humanity to God in, by and through his Word and Spirit, is by elevating the 'spiritual' aspect of human being, to the disparagement of the 'physical'. Here, of course, is the rearing up of dualistic thought, wherein Creator and creature, heaven and earth, spiritual and corporal, soul and flesh, are sundered. To remove human existence in its totality, all that makes it human, from the Creator of it, will also involve a rending in that human existence itself. In this way they seek to 'spiritualize' the relation between Creator and creature by way of compensation for rejecting the full contingent relation between humanity and God. The 'spiritual' is related to God not by way of contingency, but by means of a mythological synthesis of same-quality being of Creator and creature. Such as advocate and hold to this view 'disallow the salvation of God's workmanship, which the flesh truly is'.[6] Here we must turn to examine in detail through this section in the *Demonstration of the Apostolic Preaching* how Irenaeus regards the totality of human being as the object of God's redeeming love in his Word and Spirit.

Faith and godliness concern the totality of what constitutes the human being. That totality is that 'man is a living being consisting of soul and body'. Irenaeus would appear, by this statement, to be advocating a bipartite view of human existence, that the human individual is a being compounded of a body and a soul. But in *Adversus Haereses*, he seems to sway between a bipartite and a tripartite interpretation of human existence.

> Now God shall be glorified in His handiwork, fitting it so as to be conformable to, and modelled after, His own Son. For by the hands of the Father, that is, by the Son and the Holy Spirit, man, and not a part of man, was made in the likeness of God. Now the soul and the spirit are certainly a part of the man, but certainly not the [entire] man; for the whole man consists in the commingling of the soul receiving the spirit of the Father, and the admixture of that fleshly nature which was moulded after the image of God.[7]

The heretics who disparage the physical existence of humanity.

> do not take this fact into consideration, that there are three things out of which, as I have shown, the complete man is composed – flesh, soul and spirit.[8]

Yet Irenaeus had written already

> Now man is a mixed organization of soul and flesh, who was formed after the likeness of God and moulded by His hands, that is, by the Son and the Holy Spirit, to whom also He said 'Let Us make man'.[9]

Clearly, what appears to be a contradiction requires resolution. The problem is further complicated in that in the Armenian of the *Demonstration of the Apostolic Preaching*, the word for 'spirit' is sometimes used instead of 'soul'. In speaking about 'godliness' in the *Demonstration*, Irenaeus remarks

> For godliness is obscured and dulled by the contamination and impurity of the flesh, and being broken and stained, loses its integrity if falsehood enter the soul [spirit] but it will be preserved in its beauty and integrity when truth is constant in the soul [spirit] and purity in the flesh.[10]

The argument in this Section 2 of the *Demonstration* is that faith is a matter of purity of soul and godliness likewise of the flesh. These two have to be conjoined; truth without godliness, faith without works, are a contradiction. The lack of one makes the other of no effect or profit. That is, godliness resides and is seen in the flesh, but it stems from, and exhibits the validity of, faith, which is concerned with the non-physical part of human being. So happily united, faith and works, truth and godliness 'bring man face to face with God'. I would suggest that the key to the resolution lies in both the context of where spirit, *spiritus*, πνευμα, as distinct from soul, *anima*, ψυχη, is used in *Adversus Haereses*, and in the instances where spirit is used as soul in the Armenian of the *Demonstration*.

'Spirit' in *Adversus Haereses* always occurs in the context of the creative act of God forming his handiwork, usually in conjunction with mention of his 'hands, his Word and Spirit'.[11] It is used in statements about the relation of humanity to God, first by the act of creation whereby humanity is made 'after the likeness of God' by His 'hands', second by the incarnation whereby man is 'attached' to God and the 'likeness' and 'image' renewed by the Word made flesh, third by the Word outpouring 'the Spirit of the Father'. And fourth in his treatment of the resurrection of the whole individual in terms of the resurrection of the incarnate Word. It will be noted that the Word stands central in all these discussions.

I would suggest that in each case, spirit as applied to the human being is not a constituent part of that creation – except where it is used as a synonym for soul in the Armenian of the *Demonstration of the Apostolic Preaching*, but rather the bond of the relation between God and humanity. It is the counterpart for the existence of the human being in the created dimension of the bond of eternal love which binds the Father and the Word, the Holy Spirit. In this, spirit is that which binds the creature to the Creator in contingent relation, and by it the creature is sustained in its own dimension and it is the principle of human life and existence as that created by God. The totality of body and soul inseparably united is borne, contained and vivified by what Irenaeus calls 'spirit'. In other words it is the ground of human being, which is the grounding of that being beyond itself in its necessary relation to its Creator. In this consists the image of God as applied to humanity.

The use of spirit as applied to the human is always within the context of, and therefore perceived by Irenaeus to be related especially to, the Holy Spirit. This is not to say that spirit is confined to the Holy Spirit, as though the Holy Spirit existed independently of, and could be in isolation from, the Word and the Father, any more than spirit is regarded as something which is autonomous and is not linked to both body and soul. Spirit as applied to the human is related to the Spirit as He exists in His relation to the Word and the Father, and as that creaturely correspondent, the spirit exists in relation to the body and the soul.

I would further suggest that spirit, in reference to the human being, can be seen as the participation in the Holy Spirit, or the communion of the Spirit (and therefore in, and of, the Spirit's relation to the Father and the Son) in Irenaeus's thought. This removes the seemingly contradictory meaning of respective statements about the composition of man as either bipartite or tripartite, the same opposing meanings as to whether man is given spirit or the Spirit, and the vexed question as to whether or not Irenaeus believes the soul to be immortal.

Here I would deem Irenaeus to have neither a bipartite nor a tripartite view of human being in the generally accepted ideas of such composition – namely that man is composed either of two or of three constituent parts. That he believes man to be created as soul and body is clear from several of Irenaeus's statements, but, as has been indicated, he also introduces the concept of 'spirit'. 'Spirit' – to extend the thesis of humanity's relation to God in terms of participation in the Holy Spirit or the communion of the Spirit – means for Irenaeus that necessary contingent bond to God which humanity, if it is humanity, must have. Man can only exist as soul of his body and body of his soul in their unity in the bond of spirit. To pursue the question of bipartite or tripartite existence is to follow a false trail. Irenaeus is not concerned, as Augustine later was, for example, to 'trinitize' man in order to reach an understanding of the Imago Dei. The image of God in which humanity is created is its relation to God. Man's is a relational existence, and as such spiritual and the image of God.

With regard to the first of these problems: if spirit is regarded as the fundamental essential of human existence in the sense of relation to God by which it has, and only can have, life, then the bipartite/tripartite dispute falls as an unnecessary question. The second would seem to be resolved by the fact that Irenaeus sometimes directly accredits man with the Holy Spirit's presence as sustaining him in life, and sometimes indirectly, as his context demands, via the spirit. This double usage seems to be held together in the following, which are but two examples among many:

> Now God shall be glorified in his handiwork, fitting it so as to be conformable to, and modelled after, his own Son. For by the hands of the Father, that is, by the Son and the Holy Spirit, man, and not a part of man, was made in the likeness of God. Now the soul and the spirit are certainly a part of the man, but not *the* man; for the perfect [that is, the 'whole' man, the totality of what he is] man consists in the commingling and the union of the soul receiving the spirit of the Father, and the admixture of that fleshly nature, which was moulded after the image of God . . . . For if one take away the substance of flesh, that is of the handiwork [of God], and understand that which is purely spiritual, such then would not be a spiritual man, but the spirit of man, or the Spirit of God. But when the spirit here blended with the soul is united to [God's] handiwork, the man is rendered spiritual and perfect because of the outpouring of the Spirit, and this is he who was made in the image and likeness of God. But if the Spirit be wanting to the soul, he who is such is indeed of an animal nature, and being left carnal shall be an imperfect being, possessing indeed the image [of God] in his formation, but not receiving the similitude through the Spirit; and thus is this being imperfect . . . . The commingling and union of all these [body, soul and spirit] constitutes the perfect man . . . . Those then are the perfect who have had the Spirit of God remaining in them, and have preserved their souls and bodies blameless, holding fast the faith of God, that is, that faith which is towards God . . . .[12]

Here the tripartite/bipartite descriptions are held together, but any contradiction as to an either/or between them are resolved if it is recognized that 'spirit' refers to that facet of existence which holds body and soul in a bond of contingent relation to

God. The perfection of the *imago Dei* which humanity is, is that relation of the embodied soul and the ensouled body to God in which they advance towards him in their inseparable unity as the entity of the human being. The image of God, for Irenaeus, is not a possession of the human being, but that for which it was created and towards which it moves – that which is mirrored in the whole human being as it advances in and towards the One who is Himself the Image of God.

These themes, scattered throughout his work, are found together in *Adversus Haereses* V:1ff: There they are attended by the underlying considerations, and couched in either explicit or implicit terms, of, faith and godliness, the 'Royal Exchange', and the community of union between God and humanity. In all these, the centrality of the Word is pivotal, for Irenaeus's anthropology is only worked out under his determinative and controlling Christology.

The theme of godliness, which has been touched upon previously in Section 1, follows Irenaeus's observation that 'man is a living being compounded of soul and flesh'. *Godliness*, as applied to man, is humanity's participation in the Godliness which is God's alone, that is, its 'community of union' with God in his Word assuming the totality of human being at the incarnation, and re-creating that humanity through his incarnate life, death, resurrection and ascension, and in the outpouring of the Holy Spirit binding us to him.

I would venture that in this passage there is an underlying concept of 'rightness' on which Irenaeus rests his view of the relation between humanity and God. And I would further hazard that this 'rightness' is expressed in the terminology of 'balance'. Straightaway, it must be said that this does not imply some philosophical tenet of 'rest' and 'immoveability' – rather, it is the active participation of humanity in the Godness of God, and the resultant endeavour of humanity through the Word as it progresses towards its fulfilment in God. This fulfilment is the complete 'rightness' where, face to face with God, humanity has its 'beauty and measure', its godliness balanced in the right relation to the Godness of God – God's creative order for humanity complete. 'Beauty and measure', both in what would have been the original Greek and in the Armenian extant text here, imply 'order, goodness, good being and integrity'. This beauty and measure is found in the humanity of the Word and humanity possesses it by virtue of the community of union it has with him. Thus, Irenaeus sums up the final state of the order and goodness of humanity in the Word made flesh:

> For there is the one Son who accomplished His Father's will; and one human race also in which the mysteries of God are wrought, 'which the angels desire to look into'; and they are not able to search out the wisdom of God, by means of which His handiwork, confirmed and incorporated with His Son, is brought to perfection; that His offspring, the First-begotten Word, should descend to the creature, that is, to what had been moulded, and that it should be contained by Him; and, on the other hand the creature should contain the Word, and ascend to Him, passing beyond the angels, and be made after the image and likeness of God.[13]

It may be, as Grabe suggests, that this end of Book V of *Adversus Haereses* is an insertion after a supposed loss of this part of the original text, but, even so, it sums up the essence of Irenaeus's thought. For Irenaeus, Adam was made as 'the figure of the One who was to come',[14] that is, Christ is, in the creative act of God, the exemplar of humanity. 'Beauty and measure' means the correspondence of humanity to its pattern in Christ.

This active rightness and balance comes through in such phrases as Irenaeus employs here. Concerning keeping the faith, that for him is a matter of purity of soul, holding 'faith towards God entire, neither adding thereto nor diminishing therefrom' – an observation which is underlined in the third section of the *Demonstration*, where he counsels the requirement to 'hold the rule of faith without deviation'. Purity of the flesh is the outward sign of this integrity of the faith which is held, by the abstinence from all evil works. Godliness will then be obvious in the quality of the totality of the faithful being, for it will, in the condition of that quality, 'keep itself in its beauty and measure'.

The constancy and unchangeableness of the faith is a principle of primary importance for Irenaeus. Here again, however, care has to be exercised in interpreting what he means by this. The faith means the expression of the knowledge of God; and that expression is a matter of truth in the soul and purity in the flesh. In other words, the human being is in a right relation with God, its faith corresponding to God's faithfulness in His Word, and the constancy and purity which it has as the expression of that faith are in correspondence to that Constancy in His Word which is the utterance of God's unchangeable love and to that Purity which is the articulation of God's refining holiness. Faith and right existence are one.

What is constant and unchangeable about the faith is its quality; the very nature of faith is its constancy and unchangeableness. Faith is the permission, freely offered, to share in the knowledge which God has of Himself as He exists as Father, Word and Spirit. It is not 'faith' in the existence of some distant divine object. Indeed such 'faith' is for Irenaeus, the hallmark of the heretic. Faith, if it be faith, is concourse and conversation with God, not speculation about him. Hence, purity of the flesh and the integrity of truth in the soul, the essential concomitants of faith, 'rejoice with one another, and are united and allied to bring man face to face with God'. And later in Section 12 of the *Demonstration*, Irenaeus construes Paradise, in which Adam was set, as the place of understanding, for

> so fair and good was this Paradise, that the Word of God continually resorted thither, and walked and talked with the man, figuring beforehand the things that should be in the future, (namely) that He should dwell with him and talk with him, and should be with men, teaching them righteousness.[15]

This faith is the necessary factor of human life, for that life can only be lived in communion with God and in the sharing of that knowledge God has of Himself. This Irenaus had drawn out in *Adversus Haereses*, and I quote here at some necessary length from parts of Book IV, and from two comments in Book V, for these best encapsulate in their measure the movement of his thought on the matter which is so condensed in the *Demonstration*.

> I have also largely demonstrated, that the Word, namely the Son, was always with the Father; and that Wisdom also, which is the Spirit, was present with Him, anterior to all creation . . .[16]

There is therefore one God, who by the Word and Wisdom created and arranged all things; but this is the Creator who has granted this world to the human race, and who, as regards His greatness, is indeed unknown to all who have been made by Him (for no man has searched out His height, either among the ancients who have gone to their rest, or any of those who are now alive); but as regards His love, He is always known through Him by whose means He ordained all things. Now this is His Word, our Lord Jesus Christ, who in the last times was made a man among men, that He might join the end to the beginning, that is, man to God. Wherefore the prophets, receiving the prophetic gift from the same Word, announced His advent according to the flesh, by which the blending and communion of God and man took place according to the good pleasure of the Father, the Word of God foretelling from the beginning that God should be seen by men, and hold converse with them upon earth, should confer with them, and should be present with His own creation, saving it, and becoming capable of being perceived by it, and freeing us from the hands of all that hate us, that is, from every spirit of wickedness; and causing us to serve Him in holiness and righteousness all our days, in order that man, having embraced the Spirit of God, might pass into the glory of the Father . . .[17]

For man does not see God by his own powers; but when He pleases He is seen by men, by whom He wills, and when He wills, and as He wills. For God is powerful in all things, having been seen at that time indeed, prophetically through the Spirit, and seen, too, adoptively through the Son; and He shall also be seen paternally in the kingdom of heaven, the Spirit truly preparing man in the Son of God, and the Son leading him to the Father, while the Father, too, confers incorruption for eternal life, which comes to every one from the fact of his seeing God. For as those who see the light are within the light, and partake of its brilliancy; even so, those who see God are in God, and receive of His splendour. But this splendour vivifies them . . . . And for this reason, He, beyond comprehension, and boundless and invisible, rendered Himself visible and comprehensible, and within the capacity of those who believe, that He might vivify those who receive and behold Him through faith. For as His greatness is past finding out, so also is His goodness beyond expression; by which having been seen, He bestows life on those who see Him. It is not possible to live apart from life, and the means of life is found in communion with God; but communion with God is to know God, and to enjoy His goodness.[18]

. . . For the glory of God is a living man; and the life of man consists in beholding God. For if the manifestation of God which is made by means of the creation, affords life to all living in the earth, much more does that revelation of the Father which comes through the Word, give life to those who see God.[19]

And through the Word Himself who had been made visible and perceptible, was the Father shown forth . . . for the Father is the invisible of the Son, but the Son the visible of the Father . . .[20]

But the Son, administering all things for the Father, works from the beginning even to the end, and without Him no man can attain the knowledge of God. For the Son is the knowledge of the Father, but the knowledge of the Son is in the Father, and has been revealed through the Son; and this was the reason why the Lord declared, 'No man knoweth the Son, but the Father, nor the Father, save the Son, and those to whomsoever the Son shall reveal.[21]

For in no other way could we have learned the things of God, unless our Master, existing as the Word, had become man. For no other being had the power of revealing to us the things of the Father, except His own proper Word. For no other person 'Knew the mind of the Lord', or who else 'has become His counsellor'?[22]

> . . . following the only true and steadfast Teacher, the Word of God, our Lord Jesus Christ, who did, through His transcendent love, become what we are, that He might bring us to be even what He is Himself.[23]

There is constancy and unchangeableness of faith because it is called forth by, and participates in, the invariable and unceasing love of God in which, by His Word and through His Spirit, He gives us to share his Self-knowledge. Faith in God, therefore, corresponding as it does to His faithfulness, is also a matter of love for God, analogous in its creaturely dimension, to the uncreated Love which He is as one God, Father, Word and Spirit. This is set out by Irenaeus in terms of St Paul's observation that 'Knowledge puffeth up, but love edifieth'.[24] He notes that this knowledge against which Paul inveighs is not the true knowledge of God, but that 'pretence of knowledge' by those who, falling away from love of God, imagine themselves perfect, rendering a God who is therefore imperfect, since God must be lesser than they in their estimation of themselves by their inflated egos. Rather than claiming to know the reason for one single thing in creation based on such supposed 'knowledge', it is better that one

> should believe in God, and continue in His love, than that puffed up through knowledge of this kind, he should fall away from that love which is the life of man; and that he should search after no other knowledge except Jesus Christ the Son of God who was crucified for us . . .[25]

Love calls, by the Word, from the depths of the mystery of God's incomprehensible and invisible Being to the depths of creaturely need and mortality. Deep calls to deep. This knowledge and love, the inseparable conjunction of which is true faith, is 'the life of man'. Faith, therefore, is not a matter of the supposed autonomy of the mind, for that regards the mind in isolation from the rest of being, but of the totality of being as a being of knowledge and love which acknowledges the whole human existence as the handiwork of God, created and redeemed by the Word. The constancy of faith is this necessarily attendant love, which itself is evoked by that which is constant in God, His love. The being of God is constant because it is a being of love as Father, Word and Spirit. It is not constant because it is, in any philosophical sense, a discovery by a projection of creaturely terms and their content into God, which thus postulates a divine existence unchanged and unchangeable, fixed and immovable, impervious to His creation, immune from its need. The love which God has within His eternal and divine relations, and the love which he bears towards His creation, is the constancy of God. So it is with the faith which is evoked by that love embodied in the Word made flesh. That faith, by the very necessity of its nature and quality, is love, and this love assures its constancy.

When Irenaeus writes of the faith of the church, the danger is to read his observations on the constancy and unchangeableness of that faith superficially, and tie them to an idea of fixed, rigid and static statements, neglecting to bear in mind insistence throughout his writings that love is a necessary concomitant of faith. He himself warns that truth and mere words must not be confused. We will look at this caution, and the accompanying theme of 'rightness' in detail in Section 3. But here, it may be noted, is a foreshadowing of this 'rightness' when, in writing of the disjunction between truth in the soul and evil works in the flesh, he qualifies this supposed truth claimed by any contradictory individual who asserts that he knows the truth yet persists in indulgent wrongdoing, by calling it a 'truth in words', as opposed to the constant truth allied to the purity of the flesh, the love and 'beauty and measure' of the godliness of an individual of which he writes in but the sentence before.

That truth is a matter of words might be the conclusion it is tempting to draw from Irenaeus's observations in *Adversus Haereses*. Such observations in the form of credal statements abound through this work.[26] He notes at the outset of his major work:

> The Church, though dispersed through the whole world, even to the ends of the earth, has received from the apostles and their disciples this faith . . .[27]

Then follows one of those credal statements. And towards the end of *Adversus Haereses*:

> I have pointed out the truth, and shown the preaching of the Church, which the prophets proclaimed . . . but which Christ brought to perfection, and the apostles have handed down, from whom the Church receiving [these truths], and throughout the world alone preserving them in their integrity, has transmitted them to her sons.[28]

Although he can write that the faith is 'well-compacted',[29] he does not claim, either by this or by these credal statements, that this faith is composed of hard and fast verbal formulae which encompass, enshrine and petrify the truth. Faith is a living and lively concern, for it is humanity's relation to the One who says 'I am that is'. In this section of the *Demonstration*, Irenaeus cites these words as being spoken to Moses by the Word. In *Adversus Haereses*,[30] where he also instances God's words to Moses, it is the Father who speaks them. In another section of that work, this time instancing the 'I am' passages in Isaiah, Irenaeus elaborates on the knowledge of the One who says 'I am that I am' in terms of the revelation by the Word.

> For neither in an ambiguous, nor arrogant, nor boastful manner does He say these things; but, since it was impossible without God, to come to a knowledge of God, He teaches men, through His Word, to know God.[31]

This particular passage of *Adversus Haereses* introduces a discussion on the knowledge of the Father of the Son and the Son of the Father; that what is proper to the Son is proper to the Father and what is proper to the Father is proper to the Son; that God cannot be known save by God:

> For the Son is the knowledge of the Father; but the knowledge of the Son is in the Father, and has been revealed through the Son.[32]

Faith, for Irenaeus, is not concerned with the question 'Is there a God?', but rather with the question 'Is there a Word of God?' That is to say, God is not a static proposition or possibility or non-possibility for philosophical discussion, but the demanding and acting and lively Creator and Redeemer of all things that are, in and by and through his co-eternal Word. God does not require us to provide proof of his existence. Only the God who reveals himself as his own Self-proof can command faith, which is the acceptance of that revelation and a life lived out in love towards, and thankfulness for, the fact that God acts as He is and is as He acts, and what He is and acts in Himself, He is and acts towards us in Jesus Christ, bringing us into a community of union with His very being in Him, the Word made flesh. Therein is the duty and dignity of humanity.

This is a duty and a dignity which rests on the rightness and balance of the double contingent relation of humanity *to* and *from* God who alone *is*. It is utterly dependent on God who through His Word has created, sustains and will fulfil all things that are, and who by that Word has made knowledge of Himself available to humanity in terms of its sharing in His Self-knowledge which He has as Father, Word and Spirit. Yet humanity is given by God its own created nature and identity. He is Creator; it is created.

> And in this respect God differs from man, that God indeed makes, but man is made; and truly, He who makes is always the same; but that which is made must receive both beginning, and middle, and addition, and increase. And God does indeed create after a skilful manner, while man, he is created skilfully . . . . For as God is always the same, so also man, when found in God, shall always go on towards God. For neither does God at any time cease to confer benefits upon or to enrich man; nor does man ever cease from receiving the benefits, and being enriched by God. For the receptacle of His goodness, and the instrument of his glorification, is the man who is grateful to Him who made him; and, again, the receptacle of His just judgment is the ungrateful man, who both despises His Maker and is not subject to His Word.[33]

The balance of double contingency is disturbed when humanity's status as humanity is stressed – the contingency *from* God – at the expense of the contingency *to* God, the recognition of God's creative care and loving-kindness in His Word on which humanity depends for its existence. Indeed, it can only exist in its own created nature and identity and quality – its contingency *from* God – in the holding of that dependence – its contingency *to* God. The refusal to see this is the essence of the heretics' mistaken and tragic teaching.[34] Thus it ought not to be that humanity should

> adopt an opinion contrary to God, supposing that the incorruptibility which belongs to him is his own naturally, and by thus not holding the truth, should boast with empty superciliousness, as if he were naturally like to God. For he (Satan) thus rendered him more ungrateful towards his Creator, obscured the love which God had towards man, and blinded his mind not to perceive what is worthy of God, comparing himself with, and judging himself equal to, God.[35]

There is a balance and a rightness in humanity's relation with God, and the perception of that balance and rightness is both the integrity of faith and purity of life, undertaken in thankfulness towards, and love for, God.

These themes of lively faith, the nature of truth, the revelation of God and the relation of creation and humanity to God are taken up in Section 3 of the *Demonstration*, and to this section we go.

Notes

1 Irenaeus: *Adversus Haereses* I:22:1.
2 *Ibid.*
3 *Ibid.* III:16:8.
4 *Ibid.* III:19:1.
5 *Ibid.* IV: Preface:4.
6 *Ibid.*
7 *Ibid.* V:6:1.
8 *Ibid.* V:9:1.
9 *Ibid.* IV:Preface:4.
10 Irenaeus: *Demonstration of the Apostolic Preaching* 2.
11 Irenaeus, e.g. *Adversus Haereses* V:6:1.
12 *Ibid.* V:6:1.
13 *Ibid.* V:36:3.
14 *Ibid.* III:22:3.
15 Irenaeus: *Demonstration of the Apostolic Preaching*. 12.
16 Irenaeus: *Adversus Haereses*. IV:20:3.
17 *Ibid.* IV:20:4.
18 *Ibid.* IV:20:5.
19 *Ibid.* IV:20:7.
20 *Ibid.* IV:6:6.
21 *Ibid.* IV:6:7; cf. IV:7:3.
22 *Ibid.* V:1:1.
23 *Ibid.* V:Preface.
24 I Corinthians VIII:1.
25 Irenaeus: *Adversus Haereses* II:26:1.
26 Irenaeus: cf., e.g., *Adversus Haereses* I:10:1; IV:24:1; V:Preface; *Fragments* LII–LIV.
27 Irenaeus: *Adversus Haereses* I:10:1.
28 *Ibid.* V:Preface.
29 *Ibid.* I:13:4.
30 *Ibid.* III:6:1.
31 *Ibid.* IV:5:1.
32 *Ibid.* IV:6:7.
33 *Ibid.* IV:11:2.
34 *Ibid.* II:10:1ff.
35 *Ibid.* III:20:1.

Chapter 3

Section 3: Truth and Faith

Belief, act and being are inextricably bracketed together in the opening of this section. The 'rule of faith' is to be held in its integrity, the commandments of God are to be obeyed, and belief in God means acknowledgement of Him in fear as Lord and in love as Father. It is to be noted that for Irenaeus God is never, barely, called 'Creator' as a title sufficient in itself. 'Creator' is juxtaposed always with 'Father'. It is a mark of heresy to separate the two nomenclatures. Thus, in writing of the heretics, Irenaeus notes that

> The apostles . . . according to these men's showing, are proved to be transgressors of the commandment, since they confess the Creator as God, and Lord, and Father, as I have shown – if He is not alone God and Father. Jesus, therefore, will be to them the author and teacher of such transgression, inasmuch as He commanded one Being should be called Father, thus imposing upon them the necessity of confessing the Creator as their Father, as has been pointed out.[1]

This emphasis on the knowledge of God as Father, in other words, Personally, through the Son, and only in that light as Creator, foreshadows Athanasius's insistence that

> It would be more godly and true to signify God from the Son and call him Father, than to name God from his works alone and call him Unoriginate.[2]

The knowledge of the Father by the Son and through the Spirit evokes the love of faith and the faith of love. To work from creation to a conjectural Creator is a bare mental proposition of intellectual arrogance and vaunted autonomy. It bypasses the basis of truth, the fullness of truth and therefore the integrity of that truth as it is in itself. The truth of God as He is in Himself is that truth concerned with Him as Personal Being and Being in Person. This gist of this third section of the *Demonstration* follows hard from the 'I am He that is' who sets out commandments in His relation to humanity, of the previous section.

The truth of God as He is in Himself produces faith. The way in which Irenaeus sets out the whole question of arriving at the knowledge of God involves many issues – the Word as the Self-revelation of God; the relation of that Self-revelation to scripture and tradition; the resultant nature of scripture and tradition and their relation; the relation between faith and understanding and truth dependent on scripture and tradition. These issues have a twofold, related theme underlying them. One part of this is his insistence on what was later called κατα φυσιν 'according to nature', thinking; the other is his emphasis on Christ as the σκοπος. 'the scope', of scripture and the proclamation of the church. This twofold theme, with its subsequent working out of those dependent issues, is one of the areas of mental achievement which calls for the weight, worth and import of Irenaeus's significance in theological endeavour to be recognized and due place assigned to him as a cardinal and decisive figure.

This mode of thought is set out clearly in a definitive statement as to the nature of truth in this third section, which statement also demonstrates Irenaeus's view of the relation between faith and understanding. 'The rule of faith' is to be observed and held without deviation, and 'the commandments of God' revered and obeyed in fear and love. This *doing* of the commandments is *produced by faith*. Irenaeus then immediately cites Isaiah VII:9: 'If ye believe not, neither shall ye understand.' That is, the rule of faith points to the God who is Lord and Father, the God *Who is,* and in His light knowledge is gained and the understanding of the relation between human being and divine Being expressed in observance of God's commandments.

The phrase 'the rule of faith' is paralleled in much of Irenaeus's works by the related phrase 'the rule of truth'. I would suggest that these are, in fundamental meaning, essentially and inseparably forged together, because for Irenaeus, as he explicitly writes in this section, *faith* rests on *truth*. They are both *rules* – that is, directive principles in the consistent process of our relation to the Truth of God in faith, the advancement of our being in a community of union with the Being of God in His Word and by His Spirit towards being brought face to face with the fullness of that Truth in the fulfilment of our existence.

'The rule of faith' does not imply here, or in any passages where the phrase, or its equivalent, 'the rule of truth', is mentioned in *Adversus Haereses*,[3] a document or set of fixed principles sufficiently and completely rounded off once and for all. Indeed in the larger work, Irenaeus is concerned to declare that truth cannot be encompassed by the human mind and its intellectual products.[4] There is a true and firm knowledge of God, but that does not mean that God has capitulated and all knowledge of things divine, heavenly or even earthly, can be our satisfied possession. There are some things which, set out in scripture, are plain, clear and unambiguous, 'which God has placed within the power of mankind'. Within the knowledge of such things, the mind, disciplined to studying them as they are set out, 'will make advancement in them'. It is here that 'the rule of faith' or 'the rule of truth', becomes the illuminating principle. This rule is the truth which our Lord openly declared to His disciples (and not by way of imparting secret knowledge to only a few of them skilled in 'arguments, enigmas and parables'), His words proclaiming

> that only one God, to the exclusion of all others, formed all things by His Word, whether visible or invisible, heavenly or earthly, in the water or under the earth, as I have demonstrated by the very words of Scripture; and since the very system of creation to which we belong testifies, by what falls under our notice, that one Being made and governs it.

This rule is also described elsewhere in *Adversus Haereses* as that which was established by St John combating the false knowledge of Cerinthus and the Nicolaitans:

> The disciple of the Lord therefore desiring to put an end to all such doctrines, and to establish the rule of truth in the Church, [says] that there is one Almighty God, who made all things by His Word, both visible and invisible, showing at the same time, that by the Word through whom God made the creation, He also bestowed salvation on the men included in the creation . . .[5]

The rule of truth covers the nature of God as He who alone is, and He who alone through His Word creates and redeems all things that are, visible and invisible, without exclusion. It is clear from the many instances where Irenaeus speaks of the rule of faith, or rule of truth, or the body of truth, or truth by itself (but a corpus is implied in such instances), or the tradition of the truth, that what is of import is not the exact words of this rule or body or tradition, but the substance of doctrine it conveys. The rule of truth or faith refers beyond itself to a centre in Truth itself, the Self-revelation of God, and it does so truthfully because it does it faithfully, pointing in a way that is in accordance with the nature of that Truth. Hence the rule is recounted by Irenaeus throughout *Adversus Haereses* in various forms, longer or shorter, with one emphasis or another, but all conveying essentially the same truth. Indeed, this truth, to retain its integrity, need not be conveyed by the written word at all. When Irenaeus remarks on this, he gives an expanded version of the rule. The tradition of truth is to be found clearly in, and therefore all uncertainty concerning it referred to,

> . . . the most ancient churches with which the apostles held constant intercourse, and learn from them what is certain and clear in regard to the present question . . . . For how should it be if the apostles themselves had not left us certain writings? Would it not be necessary to follow the course of the tradition which they handed down to those to whom they did commit the churches?
>
> To which course many nations of those barbarians who believe in Christ do assent, having salvation written in their hearts by the Spirit, without paper or ink, and carefully preserving the ancient tradition, believing in one God, the Creator of heaven and earth, and all things therein, by means of Christ Jesus, the Son of God; who, because of His surpassing love towards His creation, condescended to be born of the virgin, He Himself uniting man through Himself to God, and having suffered under Pontius Pilate, and rising again, and having been received up in splendour, shall come in glory, the Saviour of those who are saved, and the Judge of those who are judged, and sending into eternal fire those who transform the truth, despise His Father and His advent.[6]

Such passages are not composed of the recounting of creeds, though some of them may well reflect credal questions put to catechumens at their baptism. Rather they appear to be paraphrases and summaries of catechetical instruction, commentaries on the substance of the faith, and as such appear in a semi-credal form, again perhaps with baptismal credal phrases reflected or even repeated. But they are all designed and phrased to fit the particular use, or address the specific problem, with which Irenaeus was occupied in their respective contexts in his work.

In this section and in Sections 7 and 100 of the *Demonstration*, Irenaeus repeats the substance of the faith ('the faith . . . even as the Elders, the disciples of the Apostles, have handed down to us' – this Section; the 'three points' of faith through which baptism proceeds – Section 7; the 'three points of our seal' [that is, baptism] of truth – Section 100) in a trinitarian scheme, as he does in several instances in *Adversus Haereses*.[7] In all these, baptism is the context of their recounting.

What is significant in all the creed-like passages is that the truth itself is the rule. That is to say, the truth of God's Self-revelation in Christ to which the Spirit bears witness, determines the content of the rule – it is, in fact the content. Here we come to the factor of κατα φυσιν thinking, namely the direct relation of truth to statements about it. The truth is not created by statements concerning it; rather it bears witness to itself by determining what these statements shall be. They are formed by it under the compulsion and majesty and authority and sufficiency of its integrity. They do not validate the truth; they are validated by it in their alignment to its 'rightness'; it is in that aligning that their 'rightness' is formed, and in the exactitude of their verbal correspondence to its objective integrity that their 'rightness' consists. But they are still statements about truth; they are not the truth itself which alone resides in the integrity of the object as it is in itself. This is the other factor of κατα φυσιν thinking, that out of respect for the integrity of the object, statements about its truth are distinguished from that truth itself. They are not the truth and are not to be confused with it, for the truth itself and alone has autonomy, sufficiency, priority and advantage. Words, spoken or written, cannot measure up to it or contain it in its fullness. That is why Irenaeus inveighs against the heretics' 'truth in words'.

We may put it this way: the truth is the σκοπος, the 'scope', the content, substance, centre, goal and horizon, of these statements. They are paradigmatic, they point to the truth beyond themselves, and their 'rightness' in so pointing correctly to what the truth is in itself, is formed by the 'rightness', that is that integrity, which the truth of any object has as that object is in itself.

The σκοπος of scripture, Jesus Christ, is the principle of the harmony of all scripture (and, indeed, the harmony between scripture and tradition). Everything in the scriptures points to Him, and it is in the doctrine of Christ as the Self-revelation of God that we find the cohesion and the rationality of scripture. Christ is the σκοπος not only of scripture, but that which transmits the witness of scripture, the tradition of the church, stemming from Christ Himself through the apostles, and safeguarded by the succession of bishops. This is 'the only true and life-giving faith'.[8] This is why the scriptures are 'the ground and pillar of our faith'[9] for the tradition is the transmission of the truth to which the scriptures witness. The σκοπος binds tradition and succession in harmony to scripture in its primacy. This seems to be the underlying thought in *Adversus Haereses* III:Preface – 1:2. Moreover, Christ is that σκοπος of both the old and the new Testaments.

> For if anyone, therefore, reads the Scriptures with attention, he will find in them an account of Christ, and a foreshadowing of the new calling. For Christ is the treasure which was hid in the field, that is, in this world (for 'the field is the world'); but the treasure hid in the Scriptures is Christ, since He was pointed out by means of types and parables. Hence His human nature could not be understood, prior to the consummation of those things which had been predicted, that is, the Advent of Christ . . . . For every prophecy, before its fulfilment, is to men enigmas and ambiguities. But when the time has arrived, and the prediction has come to pass, then the prophecies have a clear and certain exposition. And for this reason, indeed, when at this present time the law is read to the Jews, it is like a fable; for they do not possess the explanation of all things pertaining to the advent of the Son of God, which took place in human nature; but when it is read by the Christians, it is a treasure, hid indeed in a field, but brought to light by the cross of Christ . . . .[10]

But even amongst the denizens of the Old Covenant, there were those who penetrated the mystery of the true content of that Covenant. Abraham

> knowing the Father through the Word, who made heaven and earth, confessed Him to be God; and having learned, by an announcement, that the Son of God would be a man among men, by whose advent his seed should be as the stars of heaven, he desired to see that day, so that he might himself embrace Christ; and, seeing it through the spirit of prophecy, he rejoiced.[11]

And as for the New Covenant:

> The only true and life-giving faith, which the Church has received from the apostles and imparted to her sons. For the Lord of all gave to His apostles the power of the Gospel, through whom also we have known the truth, that is, the doctrine of the Son of God; to whom also did the Lord declare: 'He that heareth you, heareth Me; and he that despiseth you, despiseth Me, and Him who sent Me'.[12]

There is but one and the same author of both Covenants:

> He [the Lord] did not teach that he who brought forth the old was one, and he who brought forth the new, another; but that they were one and the same . . . . But one and the same householder produced both covenants, the Word of God, our Lord Jesus Christ, who spoke with both Abraham and Moses, and who has restored us anew to liberty, and has multiplied that grace which is from Himself.[13]

In order to set out the necessity of perceiving the 'order and connection' of the scriptures,[14] Irenaeus uses the illustration of the image of a king constructed by a skilled craftsmen out of precious jewels. The heretics dismember the work of art, disconnecting the pieces, rearranging them, unartistically producing the figure of a dog or a fox, and claim that this is the likeness of the king. This is to suit the pattern of their own fables, which they substitute for the proper connection of scripture. That connection is Christ alone as the true content and horizon of the scriptures to which they point.

Christ unlocks the Old Testament, precisely because he is its horizon, goal, content and meaning, as he is of the New Testament to which the Old points. The paradigmatic nature of the scriptures, pointing beyond themselves to that content, is emphasized by Irenaeus in the above extracts. That content is the 'object' of theological study; it is He whom, as Irenaeus never tires of repeating throughout *Adversus Haereses*, the prophets announced and the apostles proclaimed and the church traditions.

Irenaeus's thought on the matter foreshadows the later, explicit use of σκοπος, for example by Athanasius who regards Christ Himself, as the Self-revelation of God, as the 'scope' of the scriptures and of the faith,[15] which point to him as their centre, content and horizon.

Christ as the Self-revelation of God is Himself the Truth. He is the One who *Is*. It is to Him that our thoughts are directed in faith that He is such, which faith comes from the evidence of scripture and the traditioning of the essence of scripture by the church. Out of that faith so directed comes knowledge and understanding. This faith is *produced by truth*, that is, the true witness of scripture and tradition pointing to Christ as the Truth. But neither scripture nor tradition are Christ. The truth of scripture and tradition rests on their paradigmatic role in accordance with the integrity of what He is in Himself. It is this witnessing in all propriety to the One who is Truth, which is the *rule of faith* or *rule of truth* directing us, and, because it is formed under the compulsive majesty of the autonomy and integrity of the Truth Himself, we have a sure faith in, a permissible knowledge of, and a legitimate way of speaking about, God, within our creaturely limitations.

All this means, as has been indicated already, that we have both a relation and a distinction between truth itself and our statements about truth. Truth is as it is; it has remained, does and will remain, so, in its integrity. Irenaeus distinguished the integrity of the truth of any thing from any other consideration, and emphasizes the sole creative role of that truth in bringing into being faith in it and in sustaining the knowledge of it through that faith. There is implicit in Irenaeus's thought an analysis and a development of κατα φυσιν thinking.

> Faith rests on things that truly are. For in things that are, as they are, we believe; and believing in things that are, as they ever are, we keep firm our confidence in them.[16]

The first consideration here is the integrity of the truth – 'things that are, as they are . . . as they ever are'. The truth of an object remains constant; it is what it was, what it is and what it will be, before, during and after our speaking about it, and whatever we may say about it. It is inviolate in its autonomy. The truth of God lies in the Gospel. There, and in the apostolic tradition, there is recorded

> the doctrine regarding God, pointing out that our Lord Jesus Christ is the truth, and that no lie is in Him . . . . The apostles, likewise, being disciples of the truth, are above all falsehood; for a lie has no fellowship with the truth . . . .[17]

This is greatly amplified in a later section of the same book in *Adversus Haereses*, where the centrality of Christ as the truth in scripture and tradition is exemplified: 'the doctrine of the apostles is open and steadfast, holding nothing in reserve'.[18] This is contrasted with the practice of the heretics, who first, by means of plausible words, imitate the phraseology of truth, and then initiate their converts in private into that which does not even have the appearance of truth.

> For error is plausible, and bears a resemblance to the truth, but requires to be disguised; while truth is without disguise, and therefore has been entrusted to children.[19]

That truth is 'without disguise', and has been 'entrusted to children', underlines Irenaeus's emphasis on the integrity of the truth, its authority, and our necessary growth in the compelling objectivity of the truth which we approach as children in wonder and reverence and without the presuppositions of the old and worldly wise. In other words, Irenaeus takes authority and certainty away from the vaunted autonomy of the mind, and places them firmly in the realm of the objective truth of any thing. The mind becomes the servant obedient to, the petitioner needful of, and the child requiring growth in, the integrity of that thing.

There can be no confusion, however, between our faith in, resultant knowledge of, and the statements by which we express and convey that faith and knowledge about God, and the Truth of God Himself. We have to distinguish between truth itself and our faith, knowledge and statements about it. Hence with regard to the whole process of faith, we have 'to bestow much pains on the maintenance thereof, in order that we may have a true comprehension of the things that are'. It is necessary to constantly reform our statements about truth against the measure which is truth itself.

The example of scripture itself warns us that there is a limit imposed upon us concerning our looking in to the 'how' of God – the mystery of the Being of God, his internal relations as Father, Son and Spirit, the depths of his decrees and the working of his acts.

> For we have learned from Scripture that God holds the supremacy over all things. But whence or in what way He produced it, neither has Scripture anywhere declared; nor does it become us to conjecture, so as, in accordance with our own opinions, to form endless conjectures concerning God, but we should leave such knowledge in the hands of God Himself . . . to God and His Word, to whom alone He said, 'Sit at my right hand, until I make Thine enemies Thy footstool! But as for us, we still dwell upon the earth, and have not yet sat down upon His throne. For though the Spirit of the Saviour that is in Him 'searcheth all things, even the deep things of God', yet to us 'there are diversities of gifts, differences of administrations, and diversities of operations'; and we, while upon the earth, as Paul also declares, 'know in part, and prophesy in part'. Since, therefore, we know but in part, we ought to leave all sorts of questions in the hands of Him who in some measure bestows grace on us . . . But when we reach points that are above us, and with respect to which we cannot reach satisfaction, [it is absurd] that we should display such an extreme of presumption as to lay open God, and things which are not yet discovered . . . .[20]

We must note that leaving all things in 'the hands of God', means that we surrender them to the Word and Spirit of God, in whose relation to each other and the Father the knowledge of the internal and eternal truth of God resides.

The second consideration is that there is process and a progress strongly implicit here – a constant reformation of our statements against the measure of the truth as it reveals itself to us. There is first faith in the integrity of the object, and then there is comprehension or understanding of that object: 'we must needs bestow much pains in the maintenance thereof, in order that we may have a true comprehension of the things that are'.

This is a process whereby we believe that we may understand, and in which faith and understanding gained move forwards together in mutual increase, with love for God. We make advancement in this progress until we are brought face to face with God in the fulfilment of all creation and the perfection of humanity. This advance in truth we will deal with in commenting on Section 12 of the *Demonstration*, but indicate it here by two characteristic quotations out of many such on this theme. After distinguishing between that knowledge which is God's alone, pertaining to his uncreated Existence and to his eternal Decrees, and that which can be ours legitimately in regard to our creaturely existence, Irenaeus remarks:

> is there complaint . . . that God should for ever teach, and man should for ever learn the things taught him by God? As the apostle has said on this point, that, when other things have been done away, then these three, 'faith, hope and charity, shall endure'. For faith, which has respect to our Master, endures unchangeably, assuring us that there is but one true God, and that we should truly love Him for ever, seeing that He alone is our Father; while we hope ever to be receiving more and more from God, and to learn from Him . . .[21]

And after distinguishing between the sufficiency and perfection of the Being of God as Creator and the existence of humanity as created and not self-sufficient, Irenaeus continues:

> . . . man receives advancement and increase towards God. For as God is always the same, so also man, when found in God, shall always go on towards God.[22]

The advancement towards God which Irenaeus perceives is always an advancement of the totality of human being. This perception is stated clearly whenever he mentions it throughout his works. Knowledge of God is possible only in the relation of the totality of created human being, body and soul, to the uncreated Existence of its Creator (see above on Section 2 on the Dignity and Duty of Humanity).

Irenaeus immediately yokes this knowledge of God with baptism. This he introduces here at the outset of a discussion on the content of the rule of faith, and reiterates towards the end of this discussion in Sections 7 and 8.

Baptism concerns the totality of the human being. It is 'the seal of eternal life, and is the new birth unto God, that we should no longer be the sons of mortal men, but of the eternal and perpetual God'. The ground of baptism is the 'Royal Exchange' whereby the Word becomes as we are that we might become as he is. The 'seal' of which Irenaeus writes is that which stamps a process as complete. The word 'seal' has a legal implication, in that it is the same as that affixed to a document to sign it as authoritative and functioning. Or, again, it is the superscription on a coin validating its worth. This 'seal' is the work of the Spirit in His relation to the Word and the Father:

> Wherefore we have need of the dew of God, that we be not consumed by fire, nor be rendered unfruitful, and that where we have an accuser there we may also have an Advocate, the Lord commending to the Holy Spirit His own man [that is, the human race], who had fallen among thieves, upon whom He Himself had compassion, and bound up his wounds, giving two royal denarii; so that we, receiving by the Spirit the image and superscription of the Father and the Son, might cause the denarii entrusted to us to be fruitful, counting out the increase to the Lord.[23]

Baptism is the establishment of the right relation of creation to the Creator, who has created all things by His Word, who is the Word made flesh, and who grants the Spirit in accordance with the will of the Father, to accomplish this 'rightness' of relation. It is a matter of note to perceive the implication of the first sentence of this following quotation as to the relation of incarnation to creation, namely that for God, being beyond created existence with its concomitants of time and space as expressions of its creaturely nature, incarnation and creation are simultaneous, and, as has been referred to previously (pp. 49, 50), creation is accomplished in the light of incarnation and Adam formed 'after as the figure of the One who was to come'. This is also abundantly clear from *Adversus Haereses* V:16:2 and from *Demonstration* 22, where the Adam, it is stated, is fashioned in accordance with the model of the body of Christ, and to this we will return in the consideration of that section. It is also to be noted in this quotation that the Father is stated explicitly to be 'Head of Christ'. This does not imply a blatant subordinationism regarding the Word, but is the relation of the Father to Christ, as the Word made flesh, who, assuming flesh and being born the Son of man, is come to do the will of the Father.

> For the Father bears the creation and His own Word simultaneously, and the Word borne by the Father grants the Spirit to all as the Father wills. To some He gives after the manner of creation what is made; but to others after the manner of adoption, that is, what is from God, namely generation. And thus one God the Father is declared, who is above all, and through all, and in all. The Father is indeed above all, and He is the Head of Christ; but the Word is through all things, and is Himself the Head of the Church; while the Spirit is in us all, and He is the living water, which the Lord grants to those who rightly believe in Him, and love Him, and know that 'there is one Father, who is above all, and through all, and in us all'.[24]

In this quotation, the Spirit is 'the water of life', in the previous, 'the dew of God'. The imagery of water and Spirit is extended by Irenaeus in the triple context of our Lord as the Bearer of the Spirit, of our Lord as the Son of God made the Son of man, and of the role of the Spirit in baptism, thus:

> And . . . giving to the disciples the power of regeneration into God, He said to them, 'Go and teach all nations, baptizing them in the name of the Father, and of the Son, and of the Holy Ghost'. For God promised, that in the last times He would pour Him [the Spirit] upon [His] servants and handmaids, that they might prophesy; wherefore He did also descend upon the Son of God, made the Son of man, becoming accustomed in fellowship with Him to dwell in the human race, to rest with human beings, and to dwell in the workmanship of God, working the will of the Father in them, and renewing them from their old habits into the newness of Christ.
>
> This Spirit . . . descended at the day of Pentecost upon the disciples after the Lord's ascension, having power to admit all nations to the entrance of life, and to the opening of the new covenant . . . . Wherefore also the Lord promised to send the Comforter, who should join us to God. For as a compacted lump of dough cannot be formed of dry wheat without fluid matter, nor can a loaf possess unity, so, in like manner, neither could we, being many, be made one in Christ Jesus without the water from Heaven. And as dry earth does not bring forth unless it receive moisture, in like manner we also, being originally a dry tree, could never have brought forth fruit unto life without the voluntary rain from above. For our bodies have received unity among themselves by means of the laver which leads to incorruption; but our souls, by means of the Spirit. Wherefore both are necessary, since both contribute towards the life of God, our Lord showing compassion upon that erring Samaritan woman . . . by pointing out, and promising to her living water, so that she should thirst no more . . . having in herself water springing up to eternal life. The Lord, receiving this [the Spirit] as a gift from His Father, does Himself confer it upon those who are partakers of Himself, sending the Holy Spirit upon all the earth.[25]

The Spirit here is the 'water from heaven',' the voluntary rain from above', 'water springing up to eternal life'. He is the true water of baptism, that which is signified by the sign of water in the administration of the rite. Sign and thing signified, while distinct are yet inseparable as they are brought together in the dispensation of God for the recreation of humanity. The use of the adjective voluntary means that it is by the will of God that the Spirit is so given. And the mode of giving, as outlined by Irenaeus here, suggests most strongly an implicit view that the Spirit proceeds *from* the Father *through* the Son, and that the Spirit is *sent* by the Father and *conveyed through* the Son – a view that became explicit in Athanasius's Trinitarian doctrine.[26]

While we will be dealing more directly with Irenaeus's Trinitarian thought when Section 8 and the first part of Section 9 of the *Demonstration* are considered, it is pertinent to note here that Irenaeus's doctrine of baptism in the name of Father, Son and Holy Spirit, is a matter first, of the Royal Exchange, whereby the Word in taking flesh becomes what we are in order that we might become what He is; second, that this becoming is the community of union of our life and the life of God as Father, Son and Holy Spirit; third, that the Spirit, given to us through the Word made flesh, gives us to God through the Word made flesh. There is, so to speak, a Christocentricity of the Spirit's presence and action both *to* us and *for* us. Third, baptism is in the *name* of Father, Son and Spirit. Name and existence are held together. God's name, as the principal statement in Section 2 states (and on which statement all which follows depends), is 'I am He that is'. To know God is to know His name, and to know His name is to know his Being, for it is that Being in which we are given a community of union being partakers of it in the Word through the Spirit.

Baptism is 'the new birth unto God' or, as Irenaeus calls it in Section 6 and in *Adversus Haereses*, 'our regeneration'. Such terminology is the language of new creation, new genesis, and coupled with the Holy Spirit, such indicates the creative role of the Spirit. It is the re-creation of humanity into its original status and dignity in its relation to the Creator. The relation between genesis and neo-genesis, creation and new creation, and the Spirit, will be examined in Section 5–7 of the *Demonstration*.

Notes

1 Irenaeus: *Adversus Haereses* IV:1:2.
2 Athanasius: *Contra Arianos* I:34; cf. De. Decr. 31.
3 Cf., e.g., Irenaeus: *Adversus Haereses* I:22:1; II:28:1ff; III:11:1,2.
4 For what follows cf. Irenaeus: *Adversus Haereses* II:28:1–9.
5 Irenaeus: *Adversus Haereses* III:11:1.
6 *Ibid.* III:4:1,2.
7 Cf., e.g., for closeness to Section 6 of The *Demonstration of the Apostolic Preaching*, Irenaeus: *Adversus Haereses* IV:33:7.
8 Irenaeus: *Adversus Haereses* III:Preface.
9 *Ibid.* III:1:1.
10 Cf. *ibid.* IV:24:2; IV:26:1; IV:33:15.
11 *Ibid.* IV:7:1; cf. section following.
12 *Ibid.* III:Preface.

13 *Ibid.* IV:9:1; cf. all that follows from 9:2 to 14:3.
14 *Ibid.* I:8:1.
15 Cf. Athanasius: *Contra Arianos* III:29.
16 Irenaeus: *Demonstration of the Apostolic Preaching* 3.
17 Irenaeus: *Adversus Haereses* III:5:1.
18 *Ibid.* III:15:1,2.
19 *Ibid.* III:15:2.
20 *Ibid.* II:28:7.
21 *Ibid.* II:28:3.
22 *Ibid.* IV:11:2.
23 *Ibid.* III:17:3.
24 *Ibid.* V:18:2.
25 *Ibid.* III:17:1,2.
26 Cf., e.g., Athanasius: *De sent. Dion.* 17; *De Syn.* 26; *Expositio Fidei* 4.

Chapter 4

Sections 3 (cont.)–4: the Deification of Man: God the Sole Lord of Creation

Baptism is to the end that 'we should no longer be the sons of mortal men, but of the eternal and perpetual God'. This is what 'faith occasions for us', and it has been handed down to us by 'the Elders, the disciples of the Apostles'. This latter phrase occurs again in *Adversus Haereses*[1] – in the Latin *presbyteri apostolorum discipuli*, and reflects Irenaeus's insistence on the continuity of the tradition with the original apostolic authority of those who companied with the Lord. It is also significant that it is used in the larger work in the same context of the 'gradation and arrangement of those who are saved, and that they advance through steps', which lies behind the assertion that by baptism 'we should no longer be the sons of mortal men, but of the eternal and perpetual God'.

Here the two disparate existences, of mortality and eternity, of man and God, are set out in terms of the significance of baptism through which the former finds its fulfilment and perfection in the latter. Irenaeus's observation, brief and concise here, does not imply that our humanity is dissolved and that we are changed out of our created nature and estate into something else. The first point to realize here is that, for Irenaeus, decay and death as the end of man are not God's creative intent for humanity. That is not to say that, in Irenaeus's belief, humanity is created perfect as the intent of God. We have to distinguish throughout his writings between that perfection which is God's and that perfection which belongs to humanity. God is perfect by the very fact of being God. Humanity's perfection is the fulfilment of its created estate. The perfection of God consists in the truth that

> He is a simple, uncompounded Being, without diverse members, and altogether like, and equal to Himself, since He is wholly understanding, and wholly spirit, and wholly thought, and wholly intelligence, and wholly reason, and wholly hearing, and wholly seeing, and wholly light, and the whole source of all that is good.[2]

And again:

> God is wholly perfect in all things, Himself equal and similar to Himself, as He is all light, and all mind, and all substance, and the fount of all good, but man receives advancement towards God . . . .[3]

Man's perfection is found in the fulfilment of that advance for which humanity is created. He is created with the potential and the means to so advance towards God. Humanity's perfection is the realization of the created estate; it is not as the perfection of God who is uncreated and constant to and within Himself. Hence God is 'perpetual . . . everlasting . . . continuing'. We have already noted the important distinction between God and humanity (p.54) held by Irenaeus; that 'God makes' but man 'is made'. We have to do with the emphasis in his theology that the difference between God and humanity, Creator and creation, is that of a qualitative nature. It is the characteristic of his heretical opponents that the difference between the divine and the human, the heavenly and the earthly which they postulate is, in the first instance, a quantitative matter – hence their speculation not only of a multiplicity of divine beings and creative agents, but also of the relation of the Word to the Father. Such are dealt with by them in terms of apparently qualitative difference but in fact quantitative, for their method of approach in such speculation is but the projection of creaturely limitations to a heightened degree. This leads to an entirely mistaken view of quality in that bigger and more powerful equals better, and is an eventual disparagement of creaturely nature. The only way in which the heretics can reach such heights is by their application of a dualism between body and soul, natural and spiritual, and this is why their observations on quality are artificial. That is also why their spiritual insistence is earth-bound, as is instanced by their observations on the relation of the Word to the Father:

> But ye pretend to set forth His generation from the Father, and ye transfer the production of the word of man, which takes place by means of a tongue, to the Word of God, and thus are righteously exposed by your own selves as knowing neither things human nor divine.[4]

The argument in *Adversus Haereses* IV:9:3 sets out the contrast between advancing in the truth of the one God and one salvation in His Word – 'the steps which lead man to God are not a few' – and the heretic's absurd movement towards greater and greater gods in an endless numerical progression – having found one and two then

> the progress of this man will consist in his also proceeding from a third to a fourth; and from this, again, to another and another: and thus he who thinks that he is always making progress of such a kind, will never rest in one God . . . but shall continually swim in an abyss without limits.[5]

What Irenaeus says in respect of the relation between the Old Covenant and the New in their similarity, is applicable to his distinction between Creator and creature:

> But greater and less are not applied to those things which have nothing in common between themselves, and are of an opposite nature, and mutually repugnant; but are used in the case of those of the same substance, and which possess properties in common, but merely differ in number and size . . . .[6]

'Greater' and 'less cannot be used of entities which are qualitatively different. They are certainly not applicable in a comparison of the divine and the human. Such statements lie behind the later development of this line of theological perception, which is critical of any attempt to blur the distinction between Creator and creature by the thoughtless application of temporal and spatial terms. Gregory Nazianzen's observations on the matter show the consistency of such an orthodox stance throughout the centures.[7] It is in such a theological emphasis as this in Irenaeus that we find the sharpening and clarification of theological language and modes of thought and the beginnings of systematic theology around the principles of κατα φυσιν thinking – the recognition of thinking in accordance to the nature of the object studied and the necessity of using terms appropriate to that nature. The awareness of the absurdity of the concept 'infinity', for example, as applied carelessly to any created dimension is behind Irenaeus's argument centring round the last quotation. God alone is Infinite by his uncreated Nature: all else is finite, being created.

This distinction between Creator and creature, and the resultant care required in thought and terminology concerning each and concerning their relation, runs as a constant theme through Books I and II of *Adversus Haereses*. That God is beyond comparison – later to be a distinctive Athanasian theme – is well laid out and repeated in one form or another as a ground in these first books, and taken up in the rest of the work. It is quite wrong to regard the first two books of *Adversus Haereses* as 'arid' and 'barren' of positive and constructive thought merely because they are taken up largely and negatively with the description of the heresies which Irenaeus is intent on refuting. In the midst of the detailed catalogue of heretical ideas and anti-heretical declamation, the very theological tools and terminology necessary to proclaim orthodox truth can be perceived in their shaping by Irenaeus as they are forged against the false reasoning of his opponents and shaped into a κατα φυσιν mode of theological endeavour in the light of God's Self-revelation. Thus:

> the account which we give of creation is one, harmonious with that regular order [of created things], for this scheme of ours is adapted to things which have been made.[8]

This is thinking in accordance with the nature of creation. Thinking in accordance with the nature of God in his Self-revelation is another matter. Irenaeus's advice, seeing that we cannot fathom out the truth of the whole of even creation, is:

> If, however, any one do not discover the cause of all those things which become objects of investigation, let him reflect that man is infinitely inferior to God . . . . For thou, O man, art not an uncreated being, nor didst thou always co-exist with God, as did His own Word; but now, through His pre-eminent goodness, receiving the beginning of thy creation, thou dost gradually learn from the Word the dispensations of the God who made thee. Preserve, therefore, the proper order of thy knowledge, and do not, as being ignorant of things really good, seek to rise above God Himself, for He cannot be surpassed . . . . For thy Former cannot be contained within limits; nor, although thou shouldst measure all this [universe], and pass through all His creation, and consider it in all its depth, and height, and length, wouldest thou be able to conceive of any other above the Father Himself.[9]

God is known only by God; He alone is His own interpreter, and is so towards creation by His Word and Spirit. It is utterly impossible to reach and understand God in His qualitative difference from us. Knowledge of God therefore is a matter of advancement in His Word as His Self-revelation. It is not an advancement in speculation concerning what is greater or more powerful than the last possible greatest or most powerful perceived by the ingenuity and conjecture of human philosophy; it is advancement in the Word as the Incomprehensible made comprehensible, the Invisible made visible, yet remaining as He is, consistent with His nature as Incomprehensible, Invisible. In revealing Himself to us, He does not capitulate to us and to the compounding dialectic of our limited minds. This advance in the Word is a progress in intellectual appreciation; it is an advance in love – that is, the love evoked by respect for what God is in himself, namely Love, and by the realization that what He is in Himself He is towards us in the Word and Spirit:

> As regards His greatness, therefore, it is not possible to know God, for it is impossible that the Father can be measured; but as regards His love (for this it is which leads us to God by His Word), when we obey Him, we do always learn that there is so great a God, and that it is He by Himself who has established, and selected, and adorned all things; and among the all things, both ourselves and this world . . . . It was not angels, therefore, who made us, nor who formed us, neither had angels power to make an image of God, nor anyone else, except the Word of the Lord, nor any power remotely distant from the Father of all things. For God did not stand in need of these, in order to the accomplishing of what He had determined with Himself beforehand should be done, as if He did not always possess His own hands. For with Him were always present the Word and Wisdom, the Son and the Spirit, by whom and in whom, freely and spontaneously, He made all things, to whom also He speaks, saying, 'Let Us make man after Our image and likeness'; He taking from Himself the substance of the creatures, and the pattern of things made, and the type of all the adornments in the world.[10]

We should note well how often, in writing of humanity's progress in the knowledge of God, Irenaeus always does so in the twofold context of life and love. The light of such knowledge of the divine is life itself and is undertaken in love. This light, life and love in their conjunction, are the necessary totality of creaturely correspondence to the Light, Life and Love which God is, and in relation to which the creature lives, moves and has its being.

> Those who see God are in God, and receive of His splendour. But [His] splendour vivifies them; those, therefore, who see God, do receive life. And for this reason, He, beyond comprehension, and boundless and invisible, rendered Himself visible, and comprehensible, and within the capacity of those who believe, that He might vivify those who receive and behold Him through faith . . . . He bestows life on those who see Him . . . and the means of life is found in fellowship with God; but fellowship with God is to know God, and to enjoy His goodness. Men therefore shall see God, that they may live, being made immortal by that sight, and attaining even unto God.[11]

And in warning against anyone who arrogantly claims knowledge for himself, and shuns the true knowledge of God given by God in His live, such a one will 'fall away from that love which is the life of men'.[12] This relation is expressed in terms of a 'community of union' with God in His Word and by His Spirit, and it is in this formulation of that relationship between God and humanity that the progress of humanity towards God – being made more like God – should be understood. It qualifies any idea of the 'deification' of humanity, which is never to be understood as the creature's status and nature as creature being denied and turned into the divine. Rather, it is the establishment of the creature as creature, in the fulfilment of its creaturely being in the perfection of its relation with God. That is why there is the constant Irenaean double phrase, or its emphatic equivalents meaning the same, a 'community of union'.[13] It is a 'union', but not a change or even a mixture. It is a 'community' because the natures of both parties to this union, the divine and the human, are safeguarded in their respective integrities and in their concourse and conversation one with another, in this relation.

That which disparages, demeans and destroys human being, death and all its foreshadowings in the manifestations of sin, is removed, and immortality and incorruptibility bestowed. But this does not mean that humanity as humanity alters, and that the human estate is transformed into the divine. Rather, it means the proper establishing of true humanity, which can only be done in humanity's right relation with God. So, of the perfection and fulfilment of all things, Irenaeus writes:

> For neither is the substance nor the essence of the creation annihilated (for faithful and true is He who established it), but 'the fashion of the world passeth away; that is, those things among which transgression has occurred, since man has grown old in them . . . and man has been renewed, and flourishes in an incorruptible state, so as to preclude the possibility of becoming old.[14]

The creature remains the created and the Creator is solely the uncreated; the priority of God stands even in the granting of that immortality and incorruptibility which is God's alone. Perfection and eternal life are not a matter of nature, but of grace. They are bestowed by God through the Royal Exchange of his Word becoming what we are that we might become what he is, and we are granted them as, led by the Spirit, we progress in the Word.

But this progress is essentially the Word's first and foremost. It is ours by participation in the progress of the Word made flesh as he moves through this human existence towards his cross, death, resurrection and ascension. This is his προεκοπτε, his 'cutting forward', his determination, his strong crying and tears, his face as a flint as he goes up to Gethsemane, Gabbatha and Golgotha. The Exchange is exact. The Word does not take any supposed 'ideal' flesh and nature, but Adamic flesh and nature:

> For it behoved Him who was to destroy sin, and redeem man under the power of death, that He should Himself be made the very same thing which he was, that is, man; who had been drawn by the sin into bondage, but was held by death, so that sin should be destroyed by man, and man should go forth from death. For as by the disobedience of the one man who was originally moulded from virgin soil, the many were made sinners, and forfeited life; so was it necessary that, by the obedience of one man, who was originally born from a virgin, many should be justified and receive salvation . . . God recapitulated in Himself the ancient formation of man, that He might kill sin, deprive death of its power, and vivify man.[15]

That is, he takes that flesh and nature which stands under the judgment and condemnation of the righteousness of God. He descends to the depths where we are that he might raise to the heights where he has gone. This we are permitted to do in community of union with Him through the flesh and nature He shares with us at the incarnation, in which community of union our flesh and nature become, in our progress, clothed in His Gospel and bestowed with life, light and immortality. We share His 'cutting forward' by participation in it.

> The Word says, mentioning His own gift of grace: 'I said, Ye are all the sons of the Highest, and gods; but ye shall die like men'. He speaks undoubtedly these words to those who have not received the gift of adoption, but who despise the incarnation of the pure generation of the Word of God, defraud human nature of promotion into God, and prove themselves ungrateful to the Word of God, who became flesh for them. For it was for this end that the Word of God was made man, and He who was the Son of God became the Son of Man, that man, having been taken into the Word, and receiving the adoption, might become the son of God. For by no other means could we have attained to incorruptibility and immortality, unless we had been united to incorruptibility and immortality. But how could we be joined to incorruptibility and immortality, unless, first, incorruptibility and immortality had become that which we also are, so that the corruptible might be swallowed up by incorruptibility, and the mortal by immortality, that we might receive the adoption of sons?[16]

> For as He became man in order to undergo temptation, so also was He the Word that He might be glorified; the Word remaining quiescent, that He might be capable of being tempted, dishonoured, crucified, and of suffering death, but the human nature being swallowed up in it, when it conquered, and endured, and performed acts of kindness, and rose again, and was received up. He therefore, the Son of God our Lord, being the Word of the Father, and the Son of man, since He had a generation as to His human nature from Mary – who was descended from mankind, and who was herself a human being – was made the Son of man. Wherefore also the Lord Himself gave us a sign, in the depth below, and in the height above, which man did not ask for, because he never expected that a virgin could conceive, or that it was possible that one remaining a virgin could bring forth a son, and that what was thus born should be 'God with us', and descend to those things which are of the earth beneath, seeking the sheep which had perished, which was indeed His own peculiar handiwork, and ascend to the height above, offering and commending to His Father that human nature which had been found, making in His own person the first fruits of the resurrection of man.[17]

This is strengthened by Irenaeus's insistence that the Word made flesh passes through all the ages of the human estate, from birth through youth and age to death.

> Wherefore also He passed through every stage of life, restoring to all communion with God.[18]

> For He came to save all through means of Himself – all, I say, who through Him are born again to God – infants, and children, and boys, and youths, and old men. He therefore passed through every age, becoming an infant for infants, thus sanctifying infants; a child for children, thus sanctifying those who are of this age, being at the same time made to them an example of piety, righteousness, and submission; a youth for youths, becoming an example to youths, and thus sanctifying them for the Lord. So likewise He was an old man for old men, that He might be a perfect Master for all, not merely as respects the setting forth of the truth, but also as regards age, sanctifying at the same time the aged also, and becoming an example to them likewise. Then, at last, He came on to death itself, that He might be 'the first-born from the dead, that in all things He might have the pre-eminence', the Prince of life, existing before all, and going before all.[19]

There is nothing of the creature's estate or circumstance which the Word has not recapitulated in Himself. This recapitulation is the necessary outcome of the incarnation, the Royal Exchange, and cannot be regarded but in that context. Its content is the presentation of God's handiwork with humanity at its heart and summed up in the humanity of Christ, back to him, in order that humanity 'might pass into the glory of the Father',[20] and that 'there shall be the new heaven and the new earth, in which the new man shall remain, always holding fresh converse with God'.[21] It is in this relation with God where humanity is affirmed in the propriety and integrity of its nature, as that which belongs to God alone and is created by him for this end, that the 'deification' of humanity is postulated by Irenaeus.

The phrase 'what is everlasting and continuing is made God' presents several difficulties. Armitage Robinson suggests[22] that the words 'made God' represent θεοποιεισθαι. He instances the use of this word by Hippolytus[23] and Athanasius[24], and notes that similar, though not exact, forms are used by Irenaeus in *Adversus Haereses*, but these instances are always qualified by the statement that man 'approximates' to the glory of God in his advance in faith, or that humanity may be called 'gods' but only by the grace of adoption. Again, in all instances where the progress of humanity towards God, and the fulfilment of that advance, the immortality of humanity is mentioned, Irenaeus makes an absolute distinction between God as Creator and all else, which is created and therefore qualitatively different from God. The state of blessedness which humanity will enjoy is certainly not that of being changed into God, but is that state where

> neither is the substance nor the essence of creation annihilated (for faithful and true is He who established it), but 'the fashion of the world passeth away'; that is, those things which transgression has occurred, since man has grown old in them . . . but when this fashion passes away, and man has been renewed, and flourishes in an incorruptible state, so as to preclude the possibility of becoming old, there shall be the new heaven and the new earth, in which the new man shall remain, always holding fresh converse with God.[25]

J.P. Smith's translation of what Armitage Robinson construes to represent θεοποιεισθαι, is more in keeping with the general tenor of Irenaeus's observations on the fulfilment of humanity. The exact equivalent of this phrase does not appear elsewhere in Irenaeus's works, as has been pointed out, and what might be deemed to be similar terms are hedged about with qualifications, safeguarding the respective uniqueness of God. Rather than rendering this, as Armitage Robinson does 'what is everlasting and continuing is made God', J.P. Smith translates it as 'the eternal and everlasting one is God',[26] thus making the phrase to refer to God as his unique nature and not to humanity as a commenting extension of what Irenaeus says of 'mortal men' becoming sons 'of the eternal and perpetual God'. 'Deification', in the sense of turning man into God, is not an option here in Irenaeus's thought.

Even in the perfection of its end humanity still retains its distinction as that which is *made*; God likewise is qualitatively unique as the *Maker*. But the fulfilment of humanity (and in this consists its 'deification') is that that which is made is brought into such a personal relation with its Maker through the One who became as we are in order to bring us to what He is, that the closest proximity, the most intimate converse, the direct seeing face to face, is the fullness of the community of union of humanity with God in which humanity's integrity as the handiwork of God is complete.

This making of man by God has a context. This is brought out in Section 4, and is elaborated in Sections 10–15. Here, however, the emphasis is on the assertion that whatever God has made, namely all things that are, is his sole possession. No other being, supposedly divine, or even quasi-divine, has right over what God has made.

This theme, of the sole right of God over creation, is a constantly repeated theme in the writings of Irenaeus. This repetition is mainly to underline opposition to Marcion's claim of a distinction between the God who created, the God of the old dispensation, and the God of the new. It also combats the plurality of creative emanations postulated by the various forms of gnosticism.

One point must be underlined throughout any discussion of Irenaeus's constant insistence on God as the sole Creator God and only Lord of all creation, and that is his assertion of the *transcendence* of God. For him, unlike the Valentinian heretics, and Marcion and his followers, for example, this is a *qualitative* issue, and not a *quantitative* matter. This is brought out in *Adversus Haereses* II:1:1ff. Here the argument centres round the concept of God as the 'pleroma', the fullness, of all things. There cannot be, writes Irenaeus, any Fullness above God, since God must contain all things and not Himself be contained.

The absurdity of the heretics' positions regarding the pleroma is then set out.[27] Either, the pleroma, with which is also understood the Creator, contains all things, including that which the heretics claim to be beyond it (and how can it do this?), or it must be wanting, since all is not contained, and therefore God is wanting. But if it is itself contained by what is claimed to be outside the pleroma, then there will be a pleroma within a pleroma. It is useless to speculate, as do the heretics that the pleroma and that which supposedly lies beyond it are separated by an infinite distance. For then there would be introduced a third category, greater than the other two, the pleroma and that which lies beyond it, which would contain them both. Each of them, so contained, would have sides bounding them which must have a beginning, a middle and an end. But again, the third existence would have bounds, because it meets the pleroma and that which lies beyond it, and this means that it too is bounded. For if it begins at the pleroma below, and ends at that which lies beyond the pleroma above, it must have definition of sides.

The same is true of the two Gods of Marcion, who will likewise be bounded by that which separates them, and contained by the immense interval which divides them one from the other. All this leads, according to Irenaeus, to endless absurdities of speculative infinities. God would not be the Fullness of all things. Instead we would 'of necessity wander forth after worlds without limits and gods that cannot be numbered'.[28] These gods will have beginnings, middles and ends, in relation one to the others. Moreover, they would all have their own territory and possession.

> These things then, being so, each deity will be contented with his own possessions, and will not be moved with any curiosity respecting the affairs of others; otherwise he would be unjust, and rapacious, and would cease to be what God is. Each creation, too, will glorify its own maker, and will be contented with him, not knowing any other; otherwise

> it would most justly be deemed an apostate by all the others, and would receive a richly-deserved punishment. For it must be either that there is one Being who contains all things, and formed in His own territory all those things which have been created, according to His own will; or, again, that there are numerous unlimited creators and gods, who begin from each other, and end in each other on every side; and it will then be necessary to allow that all the rest are contained from without by some one who is greater, and that they are each of them shut up within their own territory, and remain in it. No one of them all, therefore, is God. For there will be wanting to every one of them, possessing only a very small part when compared with the rest. The name of the Omnipotent will thus be brought to an end, and such an opinion will of necessity fall into impiety.[29]

In this way Irenaeus dismisses all mathematical concepts of God and the projection of spatial notions into him. He is quite adamant that we are faced with the choice of one God or none:

> For being driven away from Him who truly is, and being turned backwards, [such a person who does not rest content with the one Father] shall be for ever seeking, yet shall never find out God; but shall continually swim in an abyss without limits . . . .[30]

In the passage immediately preceding this, Irenaeus discusses the fact that the words 'greater' and 'less' can only be applied to existence which have the same generic natures, are of the same substance, and hold properties in common, merely differing in number and size. They cannot be addressed indiscriminately to existence of differing quality. So it is here. There are two concerns implicit here; first, that 'infinity', for Irenaeus, we may conclude, is God's alone. It is not applicable to created things which God contains as the pleroma of all things so brought into being. These have beginning, middle and end. God does not. Second, spatial concepts are therefore inapplicable to God; for, again, they pertain only to things which have beginning, middle and end. God is qualitatively different, and it is absurd to argue about him in quantitative terms, even if these are disguised in the dress of supposed infinities of created dimensions. In other words, God is beyond comparison.

This is a theme frequently found throughout Irenaeus's thought. There are attributes and qualities which

> may properly be said to hold good in men . . . [the heretics] ascribe those things which apply to men to the Father of all . . . they endow Him with human affections and passions. But if they had known the Scriptures, and been taught by the truth, they would have known, beyond doubt, that God is not as men are; and that His thoughts are not like the thoughts of men. He is . . . above these properties, and therefore indescribable. For He may well and properly be called an Understanding which comprehends all things, but He is not like the understanding of men; and He may most properly be termed Light, but He is nothing like that light with which we are acquainted.[31]

Again we come to the distinction between the Maker and the made to which reference has been made already. So too here

> But the things established are distinct from Him who has established them, and what have been made from Him who made them. For He Himself is uncreated, both without

> beginning and end, and lacking nothing . . . . The things which have been made by Him have received a beginning. But whatsoever things had a beginning, and are liable to dissolution, and are subject to, and stand in need of Him who made them, must necessarily in all respects have a different term applied.[32]

The very act of calling God 'God' or 'The Great King', means that 'The Being who can be so described admits neither of any other being compared with nor set above Him'.[33] This concept of God being beyond comparison was later emphasized greatly by Athanasius in his own struggle against Arianism.

Irenaeus dismisses any attempt to make a spatially quantitative difference between God and humanity, Creator and creation. The distinction is more profound. It is, he underlines, a qualitative distinction, and again emphasizes this, bearing in mind the relation between space and time, by showing that the same qualitative differentiation with regard to spatial measurement must be applicable to concepts regarding time as well. A consideration of what the act of creation implies must lead both to this awareness and to the conclusion that the one God, and no other, creates:

> Let them cease, therefore, to affirm that the world was made by any other; for as soon as God formed a conception in His mind, that was also done which He had thus mentally conceived.[34]

The impossibility of temporal divisions between God's thinking, expressing the thought and accomplishing the expressed thought in fulfilled deed is further expanded in terms both of the acts of God and the eternal generation of the Word. In other words, God is as He acts and acts as He is, His works *ad extra* corresponding to what He is *in se*. God's being and acts are not to be judged in terms of how humanity exists and moves:

> Now this blindness and foolish talking flow to you from the fact that you reserve nothing for God, but you wish to proclaim the nativity and production both of God Himself, of His Ennoea, of His Logos, and Life, and Christ; and you form the idea of these from no other than a mere human experience.[35]

Then follows a statement concerning the temporal sequence of the human process of thought, intention, word, and the expression of these successive factors in a series which takes time:

> But since God is all mind and reason, all active spirit, all light, and always exists one and the same, it is both beneficial for us to think of God, and as we learn regarding Him from the Scriptures, such feelings and divisions cannot be ascribed to Him. For our tongue, as being carnal, is not sufficient to minister to the rapidity of the human mind, inasmuch as that is of a spiritual nature, for which reason our word is restrained within us, and is not at once expressed as it has been conceived by the mind, but is uttered by successive efforts, just as the tongue is able to serve it.
>
> But you pretend to set forth His generation from the Father, and you transfer the production of the word of men which takes place by means of a tongue to the Word of God . . . .[36]

The projection of temporal sequence and spatial concerns into God was also roundly condemned by later fathers (to note but three examples, Basil in *Hexaemeron*[37] where the motif of the time lapse and the physical limitations of thought turned into speech by the tongue is taken up; Athanasius *Discourses against the Arians*,[38] where the theme of God being beyond comparison is stressed; and Gregory Nazianzen, *Orationes* XXVIII,[39] where the themes are parallel to Irenaeus's observations on the matter of God and space).

The dangers of creaturely modes of thought being projected into God and used to describe him are here surely grasped by Irenaeus who must be credited with setting out this problem in a systematic way so early and introducing it as a determinative factor and controlling consideration for theological methodology. The resultant necessity of distinguishing truth itself from our statements about truth (since limited human language is the only form with which we can operate) and the perception of theological statements as paradigmatic in nature, pointing to the truth which is greater than their compass, must also be accredited to him.

The removal of quantifying language as employed in speaking about God, which can only be on the same dimension and of the same nature as creation, and the realization that language which points to a qualitative difference between Creator and creature must be the concern of theology, lie behind Irenaeus's assertions that God is the sole God, that He alone is Lord of creation, that creation is His peculiar possession and territory. To use quantitative language can only lead to a myriad of absurdities concerning supposed infinites and infinities, and, in the last resort, to atheism, as quantifying can never achieve a solution without further contradiction from the concept of yet another quantity, which, in turn, when arrived at only stands vulnerable to fresh questioning.

Notes

1 Irenaeus: e.g. *Adversus Haereses* V:36:2; cf. IV:2:1; IV:32:1.
2 *Ibid.* II:13:3.
3 *Ibid.* IV:11:2.
4 *Ibid.* II:28:5:6.
5 *Ibid.* IV:9:3; cf., e.g. II:1:1ff.
6 *Ibid.* IV:9:2.
7 E.g. Gregory Nazianzen: *Orationes* XXVII:10:11.
8 Irenaeus: *Adversus Haereses* II:15:3.
9 *Ibid.* II:25:3,4.
10 *Ibid.* IV:20:1.
11 *Ibid.* IV:20:5,6.
12 *Ibid.* II:26:1.
13 Irenaeus: e.g. *ibid.* IV:20:4; V:1:1; *Demonstration of the Apostolic Preaching* 6.
14 Irenaeus: *Adversus Haereses* V:36:1.
15 *Ibid.* III:18:7.
16 *Ibid.* III:19:1.
17 *Ibid.* III:19:3.
18 *Ibid.* III:18:7.
19 *Ibid.* II:22:4.

20 *Ibid.* IV:20:4.
21 *Ibid.* V:36:1.
22 J. Armitage Robinson: *The Demonstration of the Apostolic Preaching*, note on p. 72.
23 E.g. Hippolytus: *Philos* X:34.
24 E.g. Athanasius: *De Incarnatione* 54.
25 Irenaeus: *Adversus Haereses* V:36:1.
26 St Irenaeus: *Proof of the Apostolic Preaching* 3, p. 49.
27 Irenaeus: *Adversus Haereses* II:1:2ff.
28 *Ibid* II:1:4.
29 *Ibid* II:1:5.
30 *Ibid* IV:9:3.
31 *Ibid* II:13:3,4.
32 *Ibid* III:8:3.
33 *Ibid* IV:2:5.
34 *Ibid* II:3:2.
35 *Ibid* II:28:4,5.
36 *Ibid.*
37 Basil: *Hexaemeron*, Homily II:7, Homily III:2.
38 e.g. Athanasius: *Contra Arianos* 1:3:57
39 Gregory Nazianzen: *Orationes* XXVIII:4–10.

Chapter 5

Sections 5–8: God as Spirit: the Relation of Humanity and Creation to the Triune God

The beginning of Section 5 emphasizes the claim that there is but one God. The nature of this one God is then elaborated upon in this and Section 6, and the corollary of this, its significance for humanity, is expounded by Irenaeus in Sections 7 and 8. This God has been demonstrated, 'shown forth', or 'shown to be'. The preceding argument of Sections 3 and 4 is then taken up and stated in terms of Trinitarian thought by way of sealing it or rounding it off. The argument now changes to a declaration of both what God is in Himself (*in se*) and what He does, as it were, outside Himself (*ad extra*). There is no disjunction between these, for God is as He acts and acts as He is. This is importantly implicit in this section. God is *rational* (λογιϰος) and therefore by his *Word* (λογος) he creates the things that are made. The play on these words is apparent in the Greek, and, as Armitage Robinson points out, in the Armenian of the extant text of the *Demonstration*. The rationality of God which He is in Himself is, in and by His Word, expressed in His creative act. There is a rationality of the created order, corresponding in its temporal/spatial dimension, to the uncreated Rationality of God.

In the same way, the nature of God is that he exists as *Spirit* so by the Spirit He adorns all things that are made. The peculiar office of the Spirit is thus set out, and it bears a relation to creation with regard to its form, its order and its beauty. When Irenaeus writes of the Spirit giving 'order and form to the diversity of powers' operative in the creation which are established bodily in the reality of existence by the Word, he may be combining the Greek conception of the universe as the *cosmos*, which term comes from ϰοσμειν 'to arrange' or 'to adorn', with the Hebrew understanding of the divine Wisdom as the source of beauty and dexterity as instanced in the verse from the Psalms (XXXIII:6) which he quotes. This juxtaposition of the particular works of the Word and the Spirit are found throughout *Adversus Haereses*. For example:

> . . . through His love and infinite kindness, He has come within reach of human knowledge (knowledge, however, not with regard to His greatness, or with regard to His essence – for that no man has measured or handled – but after this sort: that we should know that He who made, and formed, and breathed in them the breath of life, and nourishes us by means of the creation, established all things by His Word, and binding them together by His Wisdom – this is He who is the only true God).[1]

> . . . the same God who made all things by the Word and adorned them by Wisdom.[2]

> There is therefore one God, who by the Word and Wisdom created and arranged all things.[3]

It is to be noted that the Word and the Spirit are always juxtaposed, here in the creative act of God, but also in all other counsels, decisions and achievements of the divine will in the sustaining, redemption and fulfilling of creation. They are the direct, immediate and personal relation of God with his handiwork. He is the God who is, according to Section 8:

> creator of heaven and earth and all the world, and maker of angels and men, and Lord of all, through whom all things exist and by whom all things are sustained; merciful, compassionate, very tender, good, just, the God of all, both of Jews and of Gentiles, and of them that believe.[4]

In Section 5, when Irenaeus writes that 'God is Spirit' of the nature of God, we must be aware of the twofold use of 'Spirit' in Patristic writing in general, following, as it does, the biblical usage of the term as applied to God. God is described as 'Spirit' with regard to his transcendent, wholly-other, incorporeal, invisible, incomprehensible and uncreated Being. This application is comprehensive of all three Persons of the Trinity; it refers to Deity. It is in distinction from the corporeal nature of all created things – even the angels, where there is patristic reference to these, for though they are regarded as spirits and of a spiritual nature, there is still an infinite qualitative difference between their spiritual existence and the declaration that God is Spirit. 'Spirit' as applied to God, is without distinction of the Persons of the Trinity. This does not mean that the distinction between the Persons is blurred or even confused, for the term is employed of the ὀυσια, the one Being of the Godhead which the Persons have in common, the one and indivisible nature of the Trinity. Because God is 'Spirit', the direct and unthinking application of creaturely images to him is inappropriate and, indeed, impious and irreverent.

Moreover, the fact that the one qualitative term 'Spirit', is applied to God, Father, Word and Wisdom, rules out the multiplicity of Gods, divine and semi-divine agents of creation, postulated by the heretics in their various systems. 'Spirit' points to the oneness of God and his distinction from all else.

'Spirit' is used also and particularly of the third Person of the Trinity. The Holy Spirit coinheres with the Father and the Son, and as they are so too he is 'Spirit'. He utterly transcends, as they do in their eternal and ineffable Being, all created things, yet is universally present as God the Lord Holy and Almighty. It is to be noted that Irenaeus does not begin with an understanding of the Spirit gleaned from his presence with creation, but immediately appeals to the very existence of God himself – 'God is Spirit, and by the Spirit He adorns all things'.

I would regard the distinction which traditionally is made by some patristic scholars concerning the doctrine of the Trinity between the *economic* doctrine (that is, to deduce a doctrine of the Trinity through the external acts of God), and the doctrine of the Trinity as a statement of the internal and eternal relations of the Godhead, as artificial. It seems to me that, certainly in the case of Irenaeus, the awareness that God is as He acts and acts as He is, is always existent in his thought (even if not so explicitly stated) because of the juxtaposition of the being of God and His acts in so many of the statements of Irenaeus. Nor, would I suggest, is Irenaeus the only father in whom this perception is present.

It would, however, be anachronistic to credit Irenaeus with a full expression of the doctrine of the Spirit. Nevertheless, the implications of the later post-Nicene doctrine are present in his thought. The impression gained from Irenaeus's observations on the Holy Spirit is that the full divinity of the Spirit and his relation to the Father and the Son are taken for granted, and there is no particular cause for having to defend a doctrine of the Spirit as such. The struggle Irenaeus wages concerns the doctrine of the Word of God, the incarnation an the question 'Who is Jesus Christ?' On the working out and appreciation of this, for Irenaeus in his circumstances, a doctrine of the Spirit logically follows without question.

I would assert that the fullness of the later definition of the doctrine of the Holy Spirit is present in Irenaeus in, as it were, embryonic form, and therefore present in its potential. Indeed it could be said that the doctrine of the Spirit, as it is expressed by some of the later fathers, particularly post-Chalcedon, lacks the vibrancy of Irenaeus's statements concerning the Spirit and therefore his dynamic approach to the Spirit. It must be emphasized again that such an approach is not born out of what has been construed as 'economic' Trinitarianism, as, hopefully, we may see.

There are several most striking terms applied to both Spirit and Word, together and respectively by Irenaeus. These are here noted and then commented on. Both Word and Spirit are called the 'hands of God'.[5] Following this, the Spirit is described also, in the *Demonstration*, as 'the finger of God'.[6] God is 'glorified by His Word who is His Son continually, and by the Holy Spirit who is the Wisdom of the Father'.[7] The Word is *semper co-existens*, 'continually existent with, the Father',[8] and, in the context of such observations, Irenaeus not only takes it for granted that the Spirit is likewise *semper co-existens*, but indeed explicitly states this around the theme of the Self-sufficiency of God who does not stand in need of anything. That is to say, he is referring to the internal and ineffable relations of, and conversings within, the Godhead, primarily, and not resting his observations, in the first instance, on any work of God by which the Trinity can be *economically* deduced. Such work follows on as an act expressing what God is in Himself, for, again, there is the emphasis here that God is as He acts and acts as He is:

> For God did not stand in need . . . as if He did not possess His own hands. For with Him were always present the Word and Wisdom, the Son and the Spirit, by whom and in whom, freely and spontaneously, He made all things, to whom also He speaks, saying 'Let us make man after Our image and likeness'; He taking from Himself the substance of the creatures, and the pattern of things made, and the type of all the adornments in the world.[9]

(In the above passage, the rendering 'He taking from Himself', is as found in the 1884 Ante-Nicene Library translation. This is suspect, following the dubious Latin text of Grabe *ipse à semetipso substantiam creaturarum*, and is better construed as *He taking among Himself* (*apud*: following Harvey) as the context refers to the internal relations of the Trinity.) And again:

> I have also largely demonstrated, that the Word, namely the Son, was always with the Father; and that Wisdom also, which is the Spirit, was present with Him, anterior to all creation.[10]

The Spirit is never mentioned by Irenaeus in isolation from either or both the other two Persons of the Trinity. Irenaeus is the first theologian to bring into focus the work and Being of the Spirit in creation. Here in this section of the *Demonstration*, he links Word and Spirit in that making of all things, but with distinct roles in the accomplishing of that work.

The Word 'establishes, that is to say, gives body, and grants the reality of being'. The role of the Spirit is complementary: on the basis of what the Word does, the Spirit gives 'order and form to the diversity of powers'. It is the Father who creates, but does so through the Word and the Spirit, for he works in no other way than this in which is the consistency of the internal and eternal Triadic relation. Thus: 'establishing (*confirmans*) all things by His Word, and binding them together (*compingens*) by His Wisdom – this is He who is the only true God'.[11] As God is so He acts and as He acts so He is. He is Rationality itself and therefore He creates that which in its own dimension is rational. The Armenian and the Greek equivalents, as has been noted already, both play on the words that God is 'rational' (λογικος) and that by 'the word' (λογος) He created all things. God's Rationality consists in the fact that He is neither Wordless nor Spiritless. It is a dynamically Personal and sufficient Rationality of Order and Wisdom. Thus Irenaeus can describe the Word and the Wisdom, the Son and the Spirit, as 'the hands of God'. The 'hands of God' are not mere instrumental appendages, as it were, for it is with these hands that the Father converses.[12] They are divine and co-equal, inherent in the life of God. God's is a sufficient, active Existence. There is no question of any gnostic concept of a static deity requiring divine emanations and indebted of necessity to heavenly agents to fulfil its will.

This is possibly why Irenaeus does not dwell systematically on any explicit idea of the *procession* of the Son and Spirit in their relation to the Father and each other. We may say that the gnostics were the first theologians in that they were the first systematizers, for even if the content of their theology was capricious speculations, these at least were methodically arranged and set out. It would have been all too easy for such systems to subsume, consume and regurgitate any talk of procession regarding the Word and Spirit. So it may be deduced that although the necessity of opposing the prevailing systems of gnosticism sharpened the theology of Irenaeus and produced incisive insights to the deeper cutting in to the mysteries of the faith, it also tended to inhibit and blunt the explicit conclusions which might be constructed from the distinct implications which lie in his thought. For theological terminology in the matter had not yet been formulated in being whetted against trinitarian heresies as such, as a sufficiently sharpened safeguard for such conclusions. Hence a clear trinitarian doctrine may lie dormant, but is not roused to full voice in his statements.

The relation of Word and Spirit in Irenaeus's thought is, however, more complex than might be believed if the charge, sometimes levelled against him, of being somewhat primitive in Trinitarian doctrine, is accepted. The Spirit, in this relation, is construed in the context of the knowledge which God has of Himself. There are areas of knowing in which we are not competent, and never can be, because of our creaturely limitations. The scriptures are perfectly sufficient for us being 'spoken by the Word of God and His Spirit'.[13] But concerning the very Being of God 'We, inasmuch as we are inferior to, and later in existence than, the Word of God and His

Spirit, are to that degree, destitute of the knowledge of His mysteries'.[14] We are utterly dependent upon God for knowledge of him. God is not discovered by philosophical speculation on our part, or, indeed, by any other wit or ability or insight of humanity. Thus the definite, exclusive observation in Section 7 that

> Without the Spirit it is not possible to behold the Word of God, nor without the Son can any draw near to the Father: for the knowledge of the Father is the Son, and the knowledge of the Son of God is through the Holy Spirit; and, according to the good pleasure of the Father, the Son ministers and dispenses the Spirit to whomsoever the Father wills and as He wills.[15]

We may note the implied double οικονομια here. The Son 'ministers and dispenses' [literally 'ministerially dispenses' – that is, it is the Son's estate and office to do this] the Spirit according to the will of the Father. There is, therefore, an οικονομια of God as He is in Himself and an οικονομια of His acts which is the exact expression of His being. Moreover, because this observation about the knowledge of God is made within the context of baptism which is described as a movement from God to humanity and a corresponding movement whereby God brings humanity to him, there is a like οικονομια of our relation to God. (This, with regard to Irenaeus's doctrine of baptism will be expanded in later sections in the context of the incarnation of the Word and of the Virgin Mary. Suffice it to say here that the birth of Christ of the Virgin is regarded by Irenaeus as the accomplished event of God's redemption of humanity into which we are incorporated and become partakers. But this event stands not in isolation, but is the entrance to the whole 'cutting forward', the προεκοπτε, of Christ as He moves towards His passion, cross, resurrection and ascension. It is into that whole movement of the re-creation of our humanity (and all creation) in Him that we are incorporated in terms of His birth from the virgin in the power of the Holy Spirit. Baptism therefore involves a lifelong movement in faith and godliness fulfilled in resurrection.)

> The baptism of our regeneration proceeds through these three points: God the Father bestowing on us regeneration through His Son by the Holy Spirit. For as many as carry the Spirit of God are led to the Word, that is to the Son: and the Son brings them to the Father: and the Father causes them to possess incorruption.[16]

Again, we have to acknowledge here that there is the constant Irenaean emphasis on the fact that knowledge of God is never bare knowledge, in and for itself, but is inextricably woven with 'godliness'. Faith and godliness are inseparable, as has been noted in the comments on the substance of Section 1 of the *Demonstration*.

In all this, we are utterly dependent in the first instance upon God's gift of the Spirit of His Word amid the realities of our created existence, the 'Spirit of the Saviour that is in Him who' (in terms of I Corinthians II:10) 'searcheth all things, even the deep things of God'.[17] The Spirit is the conveyor of knowledge (and godliness) otherwise inaccessible to humanity, because He is the divine Personal knowledge which the Father has of the Son and the Son of the Father. The statement in *Adversus Haereses* IV:1:1 concerning the Spirit is that He announces the only God who rules over all, together with His Word. The Spirit does this in association with the Word. With regard to the internal relations of the Triune God, we find

Irenaeus saying of the Father that: 'His offspring and His similitude do minister to Him in every respect: that is, the Son and the Holy Spirit, the Word and Wisdom'.[18] This does not insinuate any subordination of the Son and Spirit to the Father; rather, it underlines the variety of function within the Godhead while yet maintaining the mutual and complementary roles of Word and Spirit. 'Ministering' does not imply 'servitude'; as an action it is the peculiar glory of the Word and the Spirit.

Irenaeus then juxtaposes Ephesians IV:16 and Galatians IV:6 – 'One God, the Father, who is over all and through all and in us all' – and the Pauline observation that the Spirit 'in us all' cries 'Abba Father', fashioning us into the likeness of God. The Being and acts of the Persons are set out in their relation to humanity. God the Father rules over all, brings all things into being through the Son, and makes us fitting subjects of the divine Lordship in the Spirit who being in us all evokes our acknowledgement of that dominion of God. This the Spirit does because it is His role to 'show forth the Word'.

But let us note that while the Spirit shows forth the Word, it is the Word 'who utters the Spirit'. The Spirit's role is determined by the fact that he is the Spirit of the Word, breathed through the Word by the Father. The cry of the Spirit, 'Abba Father', is the utterance of the Son in His eternal relation to the Father in the relations which the Godhead is. We therefore have at least an implicitly pointed trinitarian formula indicating the procession of the Spirit: that He comes 'through' the Son in such a way that the Son is personally present with us.

The relation of the triune God to his creation is not without its order. Nor is this order expressed only generally throughout all creation. It certainly is so expressed in its universality, for 'to complete and gather up all things' is the end of the will and action of God in the Word made flesh, who by that Word 'made all things'. But in its particularity, and, only insofar as it is this particularity, is it immense in its application. The relation between Creator and creation is such that God takes seriously the spatial/temporal structures and identities of His handiwork, and identifies Himself with them. At the heart of this particularity is the people of Israel, their unfolding narrative under the compulsion of the presence of the Word and Spirit, as the developing matrix out of which is taken the flesh and nature assumed by the Word. It is out of the womb of Israel in the person of Mary[19] that the Son of God is born a son of man and is this particular man Jesus for the bringing of all things into a community of union with God.

Hence the continual insistence that Mary is of 'Abraham's seed',[20] 'David's seed'[21] and

> . . . this King is Christ, the Son of God who became the Son of man; that is, who became the fruit of that virgin who had her descent from David. And for this cause the promise was, Of the fruit of thy body – that He might declare the peculiar uniqueness of Him, who was the fruit of the virgin body that was of David, (even of Him) who was King over the house of David, (and) of whose kingdom there shall be no end.[22]

Hand in hand with this insistence that there is a necessary place occupied by Israel in the dispensation of God for all creation, is the double emphasis that the two covenants, the old of Israel, the new of the Church, are in historical relation of continuity and fulfilment, and that the one God is the author of both.

> He [the Lord] did not teach that he who brought forth the old was one, and he who brought forth the new, another; but that they were one and the same . . . But one and the same householder produced both covenants, the Word of God, our Lord Jesus Christ, who spoke with both Abraham and Moses, and who has restored us anew to liberty, and has multiplied that grace which is from Himself.[23]

> For all the Apostles taught that there were indeed two testaments among the two peoples; but that it was one and the same God who appointed both for the advantage of those (for whose sakes the testaments were given) who were to believe in God, I have proved in the third book from the very teaching of the apostles; and that the first testament was not given without reason, or to no purpose, or in an accidental sort of manner; but that it subdued those to whom it was given to the service of God, for their benefit (for God needs no service from men), and exhibited a type of heavenly things, inasmuch as man was not yet able to see the things of God through means of immediate vision [the Latin has *per proprium visum*, indicating Irenaeus's emphasis on the propriety of Christ as the immediate self-revelation of God being himself the Son of the Father]; and foreshadowing the images of those things which exist in the Church, in order that our faith may be established firmly; and contained a prophecy of things to come, in order that man might learn that God has foreknowledge of all things.[24]

Because the one Householder is the Orderer of both covenants, both covenants are of one and the same substance, and that is the Word made flesh. He is the σκοπος of both, who spoke to Abraham, Moses and the prophets and appeared in the flesh, to which occurrence and to which new covenant the prophets and patriarchs looked: 'All things, therefore, are of one and the same substance, that is, from one and the same God'.[25] So emphatic is Irenaeus in this that he sees not only a continuity, in the sense of the new covenant following indubitably the old, but an actual transference unbound by temporal existence:

> Mary said, My soul doth magnify the Lord, and my spirit hath rejoiced in God my salvation – the rejoicing of Abraham descending upon those who sprang from him – those namely who were watching, and who beheld Christ and believed in Him; while on the other hand, there was a reciprocal rejoicing which passed backwards from the children to Abraham, who did also desire to see the day of Christ's coming. Rightly, then, did our Lord bear witness to him, saying, Your father Abraham rejoiced to see my day: and he saw it, and was glad.[26]

It is here in Sections 5 and 6 that Irenaeus begins to make mention and draw out the importance of the 'prophets', that is, the old covenant. He introduces the theme which is elaborated in later sections and summed up in steps in Sections 30 and 40, until its full implications are drawn out in Sections 43ff. Indeed, the sections from 16ff which recount the fall, the flood, the giving of the law and the subsequent history of Israel, are paralleled precisely by the account of the fulfilment of all these events and the significance of the people within them in the establishing of the new covenant in the Word made flesh.

The general insistence by Irenaeus on the covenants being of one and the same substance, and therefore on the indispensability of the Old Testament, is a counterblast against Marcionism. As has been noted in the comments on Section 1, there is no direct attack on Marcionism in the *Demonstration*. Nevertheless, the positive teaching here guards his readers against any temptation of tendency towards that particular heresy. The continuity of the two covenants, and the fact that the same God is author of both, is accentuated in Sections 5 and 6 by Irenaeus's observations on the Holy Spirit.

The prophets themselves, by the Spirit, announced the Son of God, and, by that Spirit, the Son is Himself the 'announcer of the prophets'. That is to say, He is His own message in the prophets and was personally with them in the exercise of their office. He is the substance of their message. In the prophets the Son is operative in the Spirit, and 'leads and draws man to the Father'. The advent of the Son in the flesh is no happenchance occurrence: it has a hinterland of deliberate and necessary preparation. Irenaeus clearly understands this background of the old covenant, the dispensation of the epic of Israel, to be an indispensable part of the drawing and leading of humanity to God. It is the integral prelude to the fulfilment of God's whole ὀιχονομια whereby He gathers all things into a community of union with the ὀιχονομια of his eternal existence.

It is the same Spirit who, in his relation to the Word, operates both covenants:

> For the one and the same Spirit of God, who proclaimed by the prophets what and of what sort the advent of the Lord should be, did by these elders give a just interpretation of what had been truly prophesied; and He did Himself by the apostles announce that the fullness of the times of the adoption had arrived, that the kingdom of heaven had drawn nigh, and that He was dwelling within those that believe on Him who was born Emmanuel of the virgin.[27]

God is personally active towards and in His creation by the Word and the Spirit, an action, as has been noted at once immense in its sweep of all creation and intense in its personal expression first in the old covenant and then in the fact and event of the Word made flesh. As Irenaeus notes, the Son, according to the witness of the Spirit, pre-exists with the Father.

> at the end of the times appearing to all the world as man, the Word of God, gathering up in Himself all things that are in heaven and that are on earth.
> So then He united man with God, and established a community of union between God and man.[28]

The gathering up of all things has as its focus and ground the incarnation establishing this community of union between God and humanity. The 'hands of God', the Word and the Spirit, are in the dispensation of God, both inclusively cosmic and scrupulously detailed in their activity and presence.

What is of import here is the activity of God and the involvement of the being of God towards and in humanity and creation is immediately personal. Irenaeus is abundantly clear that the relation of creation and humanity to God is not a relation of mechanical, impersonal dependence on an impersonal Creator, detached, unmoved and unaffected by his creative decree. This is the attitude of the gnostics who, as compensation for this belief, have to construct a mythological synthesis of graded emanations to compensate for and to give meaning to this perceived relation and bridge the resultant dualism between Creator and creature, heaven and earth, spiritual and material, splitting asunder creation and redemption and distorting the true meaning of the purpose, order and fulfilment of creation and the place and significance of humanity within it. In total contradiction to this, Irenaeus constantly underlines the fact that God is first and foremost 'Father', and only as Father is Creator, tender, compassionate and committed in love to His handiwork. Word and Spirit lead us to the Father. The three Persons are Persons-in-relation. In their relations consist their Personhood, and this is so not only in their intrinsic being, but in their acts. Within that person-related knowledge which is our participation in the knowledge which God has of Himself as He exists as Father, Word and Spirit, we, at the heart of creation, recognize Him as Creator and Redeemer of all things. In Sections 5 and 6, creation and redemption are inseparably bracketed together, and all dualisms, diving, cosmological and anthropological are swept aside by implication. Here in the insistence that the Father/Creator is one, and that God is only Creator on the basis of His Fatherhood, is the foundation of that dictum of Athanasius (in his case against the Arians with their gnostic background) that it is 'more godly and true to signify God from the Son and call him Father, than to name God from his works alone and call him Unoriginate'.[29]

It is the loving, sustaining and fulfilling personal interaction of God with His handiwork, through and by His Word and Spirit, which typifies Irenaeus's view of the relation between creation, humanity and God. It is a unitary view, whereby the totality of creation with humanity at its centre, is viewed only in its relation to the Father/Creator through and in the Word and Spirit. It is a Trinitarianly Christocentric interpretation, which is, in terms of the credal construction of Section 6, 'the order of the rule of our faith, and the foundation of the building, and the stability of our conversation'.[30]

Notes

1 Irenaeus: *Adversus Haereses* III:24:2.
2 *Ibid.* IV:20:2.
3 *Ibid.* IV:20:4; cf. IV:20:1.
4 Irenaeus: *Demonstration of the Apostolic Preaching* 8.
5 Irenaeus: *Adversus Haereses* IV:Preface:4; IV:20:1; V:1:3; V:6:1; V:28:4.
6 Irenaeus: *Demonstration of the Apostolic Preaching* 26.
7 *Ibid.* 10.
8 Irenaeus: *Adversus Haereses* II:25:3; II:30:9; cf.III:18:1.
9 *Ibid.* IV:20:1.
10 *Ibid.* IV:20:3.
11 *Ibid.* III:24:2, cf., e.g., IV:20:2,4.
12 *Ibid.* II:28:2.
13 *Ibid.*
14 *Ibid.*
15 Irenaeus: *Demonstration of the Apostolic Preaching* 7.
16 *Ibid.*
17 Irenaeus: *Adversus Haereses* II:28:7.
18 *Ibid.* IV:7:4.
19 *Ibid.* III:16:2ff.
20 Irenaeus: *Demonstration of the Apostolic Preaching* 35, 40.
21 *Ibid.* 40.
22 *Ibid.* 36; cf., e.g., Irenaeus *Adversus Haereses* III:9:2.

23 Irenaeus: *Adversus Haereses* IV:9:1.
24 *Ibid.* IV;32:2, cf. IV:32:1; cf.V:17:3, etc.
25 *Ibid.* IV:9:1.
26 *Ibid.* IV:7:1.
27 *Ibid.* III:21:4.
28 Irenaeus: *Demonstration of the Apostolic Preaching* 30, 31.
29 Athanasius: *Contra Arianos* 1:34; cf. De Decr. 31.
30 Irenaeus: *Demonstration of the Apostolic Preaching* 6.

Chapter 6

Sections 9–10: The Heavens in the Service of God: the Background to the Making of Man

Irenaeus now turns to the making of humanity in the context of the service of God by all creation according to the dispensation of its various orders. He makes it abundantly clear from the outset, in terms of one of his constant refrains, that God does not require such service because of any divine necessity. The reason for the employment in the service of God by the different orders of created being is 'that they may not be idle and unprofitable and ineffectual' – that they should exist in the integrity of their own identity which they hold from Him and find, in the thankful acknowledgement of that relation of their particular identities to the Creator, the Fullness of that integrity. All created entities are *made*; God alone is the *Maker*. Between the two estates of *made* and *Maker*, there is a qualitative distinction. We have noted this already in terms of the doubly contingent relation which the creature has towards and from the Creator in Section 1 (see pp. 40ff). The purpose of creation is to show gratitude to God for its being. He does not require such thanks, but the unfeigned articulation of it by the created entity, with humanity at its centre, expresses the rightness of the mode of its existence, the integrity of its identity as that which is created, which integrity it has only in its contingent relation to the Creator, the recognition of which evokes its gratitude. Thus:

> But all things which proceed from Him, whatsoever have been made, and are made, do indeed receive their own beginning of generation, and on this account are inferior to Him who formed them, inasmuch as they are not unbegotten. Nevertheless they endure, and extend their existence into a long series of ages in accordance with the will of God their Creator; so that He grants them that they should be thus formed at the beginning, and that they should so exist afterwards.
>
> For as the heaven which is above us, the firmament, the sun, the moon, the rest of the stars, and all their grandeur, although they had no previous existence, were called into being, and continue throughout a long course of time according to the will of God, so anyone who thinks thus respecting souls and spirits, and, in fact, respecting all created things, will not by any means go astray, inasmuch as all things that have been made had a beginning when they were formed, but endure as long as God wills that they should have an existence and continuance .... For life does not arise from us, nor from our own nature; but it is bestowed according to the grace of God. And therefore he who shall preserve the life bestowed upon him, and give thanks to Him who imparted it, shall receive also length of days for ever and ever. But he who shall reject it, and prove himself ungrateful to his Maker, inasmuch as he has been created, and has not recognized Him who bestowed (this), deprives himself of (this) continuance for ever and ever ...

> For the will of God ought to govern and rule in all things, while all other things give way to Him, are in subjection, and devoted to His service.[1]

In examining these sections of the *Demonstration*, the main emphases in Irenaeus's doctrine of creation should be kept in mind. The first of these is that God creates all things out of nothing. There is no pre-existent material, co-equal with God in his eternity, out of which he moulds and shapes the created entities. 'Before' creation there is, solely, God. Because we, as creatures, require to have material out of which to form and make things, we cannot transfer this necessity of the qualitative dimension of our existence to God, and think that he too requires something on which to work in order to bring creation into being.

> For to attribute the substance of created things to the power and will of Him who is God of all, is worthy both of credit and acceptance. It is also agreeable, and there may be well said regarding such a belief, that the things which are impossible with men are possible with God. While men indeed cannot make anything out of nothing, but only out of matter already existing, yet God is in this point pre-eminently superior to men, that He Himself called into being the substance of His creation, when previously it had no existence.[2]

The second emphasis is that, just as there is, in the beginning, solely God, so this God is the sole Creator, and therefore all things created are his – the whole creation is his possession and *territory*. This is set out in some detailed discussion at the beginning of *Adversus Haereses*, Book II. This in the context of the absurdity of the two gods of Marcion, which gods, of necessity, will be circumscribed and limited by the distance which separates them in their distinctive and contrary natures (an apparently qualitative distinction between good and evil which degenerates into a quantitative one because of the error Marcion shares with the gnostics – though he would have shunned their blatantly mythological bases and allegorical treatment of scripture – of projecting concepts with a creaturely content into the nature of his deities). This is also in the context of the many creators of the gnostic heretics (who operate with a highly evident quantitative limitation with regard to them). None of the creators of the gnostic theories, each one having a greater than he above him, could be the *pleroma, the fullness*, of all things, but would himself be contained by that which is greater than He. The postulation of there being several creators would mean that each had his own territory and therefore be bounded by the others and their respective spheres of creation. They would be limited creators with beginning, middle and end.

This is set out by Irenaeus in the other context of the equal absurdity of projecting measurement into considerations of deity. He abhors and forbids the transference of perceptions fitted only for the creaturely dimension into God:

> These (gods) . . . and others which are above and below, will have their beginnings at certain points, and so on ad infinitum; so that their thoughts will never rest in one God, but, in consequence of seeking after more than exists, would wander away to that which has no existence, and depart from the true God . . . .
>
> . . . thus our opinions will have no fixed conclusion or certainty, but will of necessity wander forth after worlds without limits, and gods that cannot be numbered.[3]

The third emphasis is that God creates directly by Himself alone; there is neither an agent of creation called into being, nor does anything that is called into being go on to create outside the will and purpose of God that which is in addition to itself. God, as Father, Word and Wisdom, exists and creates. Creation, and the ordering of it all, are His by His will and action alone. Creation is not other than that which is by the decree and fiat of God alone. Otherwise, the claim that angels brought creation into being would mean either, that they were more powerful than God since they had successfully opposed His will, or, that God was careless and inferior in that He took no notice to such things taking place. As it is, all things, without exclusion, are created directly as the will of the Father by the Word of God, and are created in and as the order which is willed for them individually and in relation to each other.[4] God stands in no need of agents to accomplish His creative will and *fiat*. To suppose otherwise is, again, a matter of the result of projecting human limitations into God.

> This manner of speech may perhaps be plausible or persuasive to those who know not God, and who liken Him to needy human beings, and to those who cannot immediately and without assistance form anything, but require many instrumentalities to produce what they intend. But it will not be regarded as at all probable by those who know that God stands in need of nothing, and that He created and made all things by His Word, while He neither required angels to assist Him in the production of those things which are made, nor of any power greatly inferior to Himself, and ignorant of the Father, nor of any defect or ignorance, so that man might be formed who should know Him [this follows Massuet's suggestion as to the meaning of this last clause]. But He Himself in Himself, after a fashion which we can neither describe nor conceive, predestinating all things, formed them as He pleased, bestowing harmony on all things, and assigning them their own place, and the beginning of their creation. In this way He conferred on spiritual things a spiritual and invisible nature, on super-celestial a celestial, and on angels an angelical, on animals an animal, on beings that swim a nature suited to the water, and on those that live on the land one fitted for the land – on all, in short, a nature suitable to the character of the life assigned them – while He formed all things that were made by His Word that never wearies.
>
> For this is a peculiarity of the pre-eminence of God, not to stand in need of other instruments for the creation of those things which are summoned into existence. His own Word is both suitable and sufficient for the formation of all things, even as John, the disciple of the Lord, declares regarding Him: All things were made by Him, and without Him was nothing made.[5]

Implicit here is that which is elsewhere openly stated, and this is the fourth emphasis in Irenaeus's doctrine of creation: that all things are created to be the context of humanity in its acquiring of, and advance in, the knowledge of God, the fulfilment and end of which is immortality in its community of union with God. Thus, in section 11:

> . . . (man) was free and self-controlled, being made by God for this end, that he might rule all those things that were upon the earth. And this great created world, prepared by God before the formation of man, was given to man as his place, containing all things within itself.[6]

This theme is stated emphatically in *Adversus Haereses*:

> . . . I have set forth the causes for which God permitted these things to be made, and have demonstrated that all such have been created for the benefit of that human nature which is saved, ripening for immortality . . . .[7]

The fifth emphasis, arching over these others, is that creation is an act of the love of God. It is the overflowing love of God bringing into being an entity other than Himself which may, in the relation of the respective integrities of that which is *made* and of Him who is the *Maker*, share His eternal life in a 'community of union' with Him. It is this love of God which means that creation and redemption are so closely bound for Irenaeus. Creation and incarnation are but the two sides of the one act of the love of God towards what He makes. The incarnation and the whole sweep of the earthly existence of the Word made flesh is the recapitulation of His own handiwork. For example:

> There is therefore one God, who by the Word of Wisdom created and arranged all things; but this is the Creator who has granted this world to the human race, and who, as regards His greatness, is indeed unknown to all who have been made by Him (for no man has searched out His height, either among the ancients who have gone to their rest, or any of those who are now alive); but as regards His love, He is always known through Him by whose means He ordained all things. Now this is His Word, our Lord Jesus Christ, who in the last times was made a man among men, that He might join the end to the beginning, that is, man to God.[8]

> With God there are simultaneously exhibited power, wisdom and goodness. His power and goodness in this: that of His own will He called into being and fashioned things having no previous existence; His wisdom in His having created things parts of one harmonious and consistent whole; and those things which, through His super-eminent kindness, receive growth and a long period of existence, do reflect the glory of the uncreated One, of that God who bestows what is good ungrudgingly.[9]

It is because God creates in love that – in opposition to the two gods of Marcion – His justice and His mercy are one in creation and that His justice is to be seen as an expression of His love towards creation in that it should keep to that course in which only it can be as it should be and preserve its identity and integrity. This is set out in *Adversus Haereses* III:25:1ff, where Irenaeus notes that Plato was more godly than Marcion, combining the justice and goodness of God in *Timaeus* VI.

The love of God is the precondition for all the other emphases in Irenaeus's doctrine of creation: that God alone creates all things out of nothing, and that out of no necessity within or without His existence, and that this creation, with humanity at its centre, is begun, sustained and fulfilled in what he calls in *Adversus Haereses* III:Preface, the 'rich and ungrudging' love of God.

The best precise statement of Irenaeus's doctrine of creation, in which all these emphases are present in one form or another, is:

> He made all things freely, and by His own power, and arranged and finished them, and His will is the substance of all things . . . the one only God who created all things, who alone is Omnipotent, and who is the only Father founding and forming all things visible

> and invisible, such as may be perceived by our senses and such as cannot, heavenly and earthly, 'by the Word of His power'; and He has fitted and arranged all things by His Wisdom, while He contains all things, but He Himself can be contained by no one: He is the Former, He the Builder, He the Discoverer, He the Creator, He the Lord of all; and there is no one besides Him or above Him . . . . There is only one God, the Creator – He who is above every Principality and Power and Dominion and Virtue: He is Father, He is God, He the Founder, He the Maker, He the Creator who made those things by Himself, that is through His Word and His Wisdom – heaven and earth, and the seas, and all things that are in them. He is just: He is good . . . He is the Father of our Lord Jesus Christ.[10]

There is an *Adversus Haereses* a passage on which these sections of the *Demonstration* form an extended comment on the same theme:

> For the Son, who is the Word of God, arranged these things [that is, the dispensation of the knowledge of God through himself the Word], beforehand from the beginning, the Father being in no want of angels, in order that He might call the creation into being, and form man, for whom also the creation was made; nor, again, standing in need of any instrumentality for the framing of created things, or for the ordering of those things which had reference to man; while (even though) He has a vast and unspeakable number of servants. For His offspring and His similitude do minister to Him in every respect; that is, the Son and the Holy Spirit, the Word and Wisdom; whom all the angels serve, and to whom they are subject.[11]

It will be noted that in this statement of the doctrine of creation, Irenaeus centres the whole relation of all the orders of creation on the Father through the Word and Spirit. It is an account which has as its context his observation that the Father is known only through the Son, for the Son knows the Father, is sent by the Father and reveals the Father. This knowledge is our sharing in the knowledge which the Father has of the Son and the Son of the Father:

> For no one can know the Father, unless through the Word of God, that is, unless by the Son revealing; neither can he have knowledge of the Son, unless through the good pleasure of the Father. But the Son performs the good pleasure of the Father; for the Father sends, and the Son is sent, and comes . . . .[12]
>
> For the Lord taught us that no man is capable of knowing God, unless he be taught of God; that is, God cannot be known without God: but that this is the express will of the Father, that God should be known. For they, to whomsoever the Son has revealed Him, shall know Him.[13]
>
> And for this purpose did the Father reveal the Son, that through His instrumentality He might be manifested to all, and might receive those righteous ones who believe in Him into incorruption and everlasting enjoyment (now to believe in Him is to do His will) . . . . The Father has revealed Himself to all by making His Word visible to all: and, conversely, the Word has declared to all the Father and the Son, since He has become visible to all.[14]
>
> For by means of the creation itself, the Word reveals God the Creator; and by means of the world, the Lord the Maker of the world; and by means of the formation (of man), the Artificer who formed him . . . . By the law and the prophets did the Word preach both Himself and the Father . . . . And through the Word Himself who had been made visible and discernible, was the Father shown forth . . . for the Father is the invisible of the Son, but the Son the visible of the Father.[15]

> He therefore who was known, was not a different being from Him who declared, No man knoweth the Father, but one and the same, the Father making all things subject to Him; while He received testimony from all that He was very man, and that He was very God, from the Father, from the Spirit, from angels, from the creation itself, from men, from apostate spirits and demons, from the enemy, and, last of all from death itself. But the Son, administering all things for the Father, works from the beginning even to the end, and without Him no man can attain the knowledge of God. For the Son is the knowledge of the Father; but the knowledge of the Son is in the Father, and has been revealed through the Son; and this was the reason why the Lord declared: No man knoweth the Son but the Father; nor the Father, save the Son, and those to whomsoever the Son shall reveal (Him). For 'shall reveal' was said not with reference to the future alone, as if (only) then the Word had begun to manifest the Father when He was born of Mary, but it implies impartially throughout all time. For the Son, being present with His own handiwork from the beginning, reveals the Father to all; to whom He wills, and when He wills, and as the Father wills. Wherefore, then, in all things and through all things, there is one God the Father, and one Word, and one Son, and one Spirit, and one salvation to all who believe in Him.[16]

What lies behind the course of the argument here is that the creation is the possession of the Father who has created it by His Word and that this creation is peculiarly related to the Word: it is the sphere of His revealing presence. There is no natural theology here whereby, behind the back of the Word, as it were, a knowledge of God is possible by direct observation and subsequent conceptualization of the created dimension to reach the divine. That, indeed, is the very heresy of the gnostics. Irenaeus is subjecting the whole of the temporal/spatial dimension to the being and activity of the revealing Word, who uses it as His sphere of revelation to humanity, first in His speaking to Israel through the patriarchs and prophets, and then in His incarnation. The patriarchs and prophets and the whole people of Israel who believe in the Father through this action and presence of the Word within the created order, are the witnesses to the One who is Lord over the created order, as are those who believe through the fulfilment of all to which Israel pointed, the very Person of the Word made visible in the Flesh, and in His visibleness making the invisible Father known. It is here in the Word made flesh that all the orders of creation are seen in the light of the integrity of the purpose of their creation – to be the sphere of the revelation of God that all may be brought to that knowledge of God which is immortality. For this reason, the whole of the created order, in all its diversity, is the theatre of the praise and service of God, for it is the trysting place of the Word of God with humanity, which presence and particular activity all entities within creation serve.

It is this which I believe to be the meaning behind these sections in the *Demonstration*, their content, structure and order. I would suggest that there is a deliberate transference of emphasis away from cosmology and to the nature of the God who has created the cosmos. Section 9, following the burden of the content of Section 8 that 'the sublimity and greatness of this God is unspeakable', this God being 'to all alike sustainer and nourisher and king and judge . . . none shall escape and be delivered from his judgment, neither Jew nor Gentile, nor believer that has sinned, nor angel', begins with the statement 'Now this world is encompassed by seven heavens, in which dwell powers and angels and archangels'. There is no speculation by Irenaeus with regard to hierarchies of angelic orders. There is merely an order of 'service of God', for he notes that it is in this that these are all occupied. Indeed, in *Adversus Haereses*, he scrupulously avoids any such speculation with regard to angelic orders. Such conjecture would have been close to the very systems of emanations of creative agents from the divine to which the gnostic heresies in their various forms adhered and which they promulgated. Irenaeus is decisively against all such speculation:

> If, however, they labour to maintain that, while all material things, such as the heaven and the whole world which exists below it, were indeed formed by the Demiurge, yet all things of a more spiritual nature than these – those namely which are above the heavens, such as Principalities, Powers, Angels, Archangels, Dominions, Virtues – were produced by a spiritual process of birth . . . then, in the first place, we prove from the authoritative scriptures that all things which have been mentioned, visible and invisible, have been made by one God . . . . (These men) indeed utter nothing of a sensible nature, but rave about untenable opinions . . . . Let them inform us what is the nature of things invisible, recount the number of the Angels and the ranks of Archangels, reveal the mysteries of the Thrones, and teach us the difference between the Dominions, Principalities, Powers and Virtues. But they can say nothing respecting them . . . .[17]

Irenaeus goes on to point out that the scriptures do speak clearly of spiritual creatures in the heavens, and that St Paul, caught up into the third heaven and 'again carried away into paradise', testifies that there are spiritual things, but these are not possible for any one to articulate.[18] These heretics are hardly superior to St Paul in their supposed knowledge and utterances concerning such.

What Irenaeus does here is to remove the significance of the heavens from the heavens as they are in themselves (the belief in seven heavens was soon to be discredited and discarded largely under advance in cosmological thinking), and place it in the 'manifold indwelling of God', that is, the Holy Spirit. The seven forms of service, represented by the seven heavens, are primarily and fundamentally the ways of the ministering relation of the Spirit to the incarnate Word. Irenaeus appeals to the quotation from Isaiah XI:2ff which he treats as a prophecy of the Spirit resting upon the incarnate Word – the Spirit of wisdom, understanding, counsel, might, knowledge (which is omitted in this section by oversight as it is included in the lists in Section 59 and in *Adversus Haereses* III:9:3 and III:17:3), godliness and fear. There is no cosmological speculation. Indeed, Irenaeus is adamant that there is no succession of heavens as an ascending series in themselves by their own nature: 'nor are there a series of heavens . . . madly dreamt of . . .'.[19] Here the significance of the heavens as seven in number is not found in themselves but in the substance to which they point, namely the virtues of the activity of the Spirit. Neither here is there any rumination in questions of angelic hierarchy. There is only the emphasis on creation and the heavens of it as the theatre of God's revelation in His Word and by His Spirit. All things, earthly and heavenly, are made to serve this. Irenaeus subjugates any supposed order of the heavens to the order given by Isaiah regarding the virtues of the Spirit, beginning with the heaven typified by wisdom as the highest, down to the lowest, 'this firmament of ours', as that characterized by the 'fear of that Spirit which gives light to the heavens'. In this Irenaeus is following the biblical dictum that 'the fear of the Lord is the beginning of wisdom'.

The Spirit 'gives light to the heavens'. Angels and Archangels and all the heavenly host themselves require the illumination of the knowledge of God. According to Irenaeus, it is the Son or Word who reveals God to them, but this does not, in Irenaeus's doctrine of the relation of Word and Spirit, contradict the Spirit as giving light to the heavens and their denizens:

> ... the Son, eternally co-existing with the Father, from of old, even from the beginning, constantly reveals the Father to Angels, Archangels, Powers, Virtues, and to all whom He wills that God should be revealed.[20]

As a pattern of these heavens so illuminated, Irenaeus remarks that Moses, having seen such things as he talked with God on the mount, was commanded to put the seven-branched candlestick perpetually shining in the holy place. This is a type of the church, for 'the church preaches the truth everywhere, and she is the seven-branched candlestick which bears the light of Christ'.[21]

In Irenaeus's comments here and in *Adversus Haereses*, there is an interplay, and a progression of thought concerning, the seven-branched candlestick of the old covenant pointing Israel to the light of Christ proclaimed to all the world by the church. The light of the old covenant points in the first instance to the order and service of the heavens which, in turn, witness in their content and service to the virtues of the Spirit resting on the incarnate Word. It is through the humanity of the Word, by which we are joined in a community of union with God, that we rise from the fear of God through godliness and knowledge to the understanding of God and true wisdom.

It is thus, in this whole work of creation and fulfilment, with its ordering and serving beings, that 'God is glorified by His Word who is His Son continually, and by the Holy Spirit who is the wisdom of the Father of all'. By that Word and Wisdom all things have been created, sustained and fulfilled and humanity brought and presented to God.

Irenaeus calls the *powers* of the Word and Wisdom 'Cherubim and Seraphim'. Origen (*Commentary on Romans* III:8) identifies the Word and the Spirit with the two cherubim over the mercy seat, while in *De Principiis* (I:3:4 and IV:3:26) he identifies them with two seraphim, which, according to his interpretation of Isaiah VI:3 on which he is commenting, alone cover the face and feet of God with their wings, thus making them distinct from other angelic or heavenly orders who require revelation from these two as Son and Spirit who cry 'Holy, Holy, Holy, is the Lord God of Sabaoth: the whole earth is full of Thy glory', thereby indicating that they alone know God and the extent of his creation. Origen also appeals to Habbakuk (III:2) for the statement which he applies to the two seraphim and therefore to the Son and the Spirit, 'In the midst of the two living things, or the two lives, Thou wilt be known'. Here Origen is referring to the knowledge possessed, and the revelation given, by Word and Spirit. Origen notes that his Hebrew teacher indicated that the two seraphim in Isaiah were to be so equated with the Word and the Spirit. It is more than likely that Irenaeus here is taking the same viewpoint, namely, not that there are personified powers of the Word and Spirit which are called 'Cherubim' and 'Seraphim', but that the Old Testament, in the vision of Isaiah, points forward in the appearance in the prophetic vision of these heavenly beings to the fullness of the Word and Spirit who alone know and reveal God. His mention of cherubim and seraphim come immediately after his comments at the end of Section 9 on 'pattern of the heavens' which Moses received in the shape of the seven-branched candlestick. The sense of this passage in Section 10 would then, in this same sense, be understood as 'the Word and Wisdom, which are called Cherubim and Seraphim' (by the prophet Isaiah as a pattern and prophetic prefiguration of Word and Wisdom).

The statement concerning the Word – 'who is His Son continually' – is noted by Armitage Robinson to be unclear. It is not certain whether 'continually' should be annexed to 'Son' or to 'glorified'. However, if it qualifies 'Son', it is only another example of Irenaeus's important reference to the Son as *semper co-existens* with the Father.[22] Irenaeus is the first father to state clearly the co-eternity of the Son and the Spirit with the Father.

Section 10 ends with a declaration of the creation and dispensation of 'the whole world'. This is qualified by the statement 'and in the world are the angels', and followed by bounds of being and service which God has established throughout creation. The term 'angel' for Irenaeus seems to indicate 'quality' of service, the power behind every particular 'appointed task' within creation. There is, as has been noted, no speculation as to the natures and hierarchies of angelic beings throughout the writings of Irenaeus. Rather, what takes note in his thought is that angels tend to be self-effacing, and point beyond themselves to the God who is glorified in whatever sphere of creation which they occupy. If there are angels 'in the world', this reminds Irenaeus's readers that just as the heavens glorify God and serve him, so too the realities of this earth, and, amongst these and above them all, that particular handiwork of God to which Irenaeus now turns in sections 11 and 12, the making of humanity.

Notes

1 Irenaeus: *Adversus Haereses* II:34:2–4.
2 *Ibid.* II:10:4.
3 *Ibid.* II;1:3,4; see II:1:1–5.
4 *Ibid.* II:2:1–3.
5 *Ibid.* II:2:4,5.
6 Irenaeus: *Demonstration of the Apostolic Preaching* 11.
7 Irenaeus: *Adversus Haereses* V:29:1.
8 *Ibid.* IV:20:4.
9 *Ibid.* IV:38:3.
10 *Ibid.* II:30:9.
11 *Ibid.* IV:7:4.
12 *Ibid.* IV:6:3.
13 *Ibid.* IV:6:4.
14 *Ibid*: IV:6:5.
15 *Ibid.* IV:6:6.
16 *Ibid.* IV:6:7.
17 *Ibid.* II:30:6.
18 *Ibid.* II:30:7,8.

19 *Ibid.* II:30:9.
20 *Ibid.* II:30:9.
21 *Ibid.* V:20:1.
22 E.g. *Ibid.* II:30:9; IV:20:1 and IV:20:3 (with the Spirit).

Chapter 7

Sections 11–12: The Substance and Production of Humanity: the Image of God

Irenaeus's statements on the composition and duty of human being have been noted already under Section 2 (see pp. 45ff.). Here in these sections of the *Demonstration*, Irenaeus puts the making of man in the context of its background in the preceding sections concerning all creation, particularly the heavenly, and the glory it gives to God. The opening phrase of this Section 11 is forceful in setting out that which is peculiar to man by way of contrast with all that has gone before as background.

The creation of humanity is singled out as that which is accomplished, in contradistinction to all the other creative activity of God, in a particular way by 'the hands of God'. This last phrase is a favourite expression of Irenaeus for the Word and the Spirit.[1] From its formation onwards, humanity never escapes these hands of God.[2] An example of the constant care of the hands of God for humanity is set out by Irenaeus in a passage which links the translation of Enoch and Elijah in their bodies, to the placing of man in paradise:

> For by means of the very same hands through which they were moulded at the beginning, did they receive this translation and assumption. For in Adam the hands of God had become accustomed to set in order, to rule, and to sustain His own workmanship, and to bring it and place it where they pleased.[3]

By using the phrase 'the hands of God', Irenaeus seeks to indicate that there is an intimate, immediate, continuing and unique interrelation of the Triune Being of the Creator as Father, Word and Spirit, and the created being of man, between the Uncreated and this particular creature, between the Maker and the made.

The man is made by God from that which is 'purest and finest' from the earth. Two points may be noted here. The first is that 'purest and finest' indicates the essential goodness of man so made: this is opposed to the dualism of the heretics in which all that is material or corporeal is regarded as evil and the product of evil. The second is the linking of 'purest and finest' and 'virgin' soil. Irenaeus dwells constantly elsewhere on the quality of the dust so used by God. This is usually done in a parallelism with the incarnation. For example:

> For as by the disobedience of the one man who was originally moulded from virgin soil, the many were made sinners and forfeited life; so it was necessary that by the obedience of one man, who was originally born from a virgin, many should be justified and receive salvation.[4]

It may be remarked here that all that is implied in this juxtaposition of virgin soil with virgin birth is an instance of that unitary approach to creation in its relation to the Father/Creator through the Word and Spirit in both creation and redemption which are profoundly bracketed together in Irenaeus's thought. Indeed, this conjunction of creation and redemption forms the axis round which that unitary way of thinking employed by Irenaeus revolves, as opposed to the direction of the dualistic approach to Creator and creation which characterizes the thought of his gnostic and Marcionite antagonists. This correlating of the making of man from virgin soil and the incarnation of the Word from the virgin, is part of a wider parallelism which will be noted as comment is made on the relevant sections of the *Demonstration*.

The same theme of the creation of man from the virgin earth (virgin because it had not yet been rained upon, tilled and sown with seed) is taken up in Section 32 of the *Demonstration* with words and phrases paralleled exactly in *Adversus Haereses*. This section from the larger work reads:

> And as the protoplast himself, Adam, had his substance from untilled and as yet virgin soil ('for God had not yet sent rain, and man had not tilled the ground') and was formed by the hand of God, that is by the Word of God . . . .[5]

Section 32 in the *Demonstration* mentions that which it is necessary to examine here if the usage of the phrases in this present section of the *Demonstration* – 'mingling in measure His own power with the earth. He traced His own form on the formation . . . as the image of God was man formed and set on the earth' – are to be understood. Irenaeus begins Section 32 with the question and answer: 'Whence then is the substance of the first-formed (man)? From the Will and Wisdom of God, and from the virgin earth.'[6] Here we have a parallel with the birth from the virgin being a matter of the will and power of God: the making of man is a matter of the grace of God alone. The 'substance' of Adam is not only from the virgin earth, but from 'the Will and Wisdom of God'. His birth from the virgin is, according to Section 32, used by our Lord in his recapitulation of Adam, His own handiwork, made from the virgin soil, as

> the same dispensation of entry into the flesh, being born from the Virgin by the Will and Wisdom of God: that He also should show forth the likeness of Adam's entry into flesh, and there should be that which was written in the beginning, man after the image and likeness of God.[7]

It is to be noted that Irenaeus is insistent on the fact that the incarnation is a matter of the will and power of God, and not a human endeavour and production. Thus it is that he underlines:

> He promised that the King should be 'of the fruit of his (David's) belly', which was appropriate to a virgin conceiving, and not 'of the fruit of his loins' nor 'the fruit of his reins', which expression is appropriate to a generating man and a woman conceiving by a man. In this promise (to David) therefore, the scripture excluded all virile influence, although it certainly is not mentioned that He who was born was not from the will of man.[8]

Joseph 'the virile influence', being the sign of human will and power, is excluded. The incarnation of the Word is solely a matter of the will and power of God, and therefore the grace of God. The birth from the virgin is the sign of this: the creation of man from the virgin soil, which is 'purest and finest' not having been rained upon, or touched in any way, likewise. All but the direct Will and Wisdom of the one God is excluded from this act. Man is the product of no other author. Any beginning of humanity as postulated by the gnostics is ruled out by this intimate and immediate relation between Maker and the substance by which humanity is humanity.

Section 32 states that the 'substance of the first-formed man' is 'from the Will and the Wisdom of God, and from the virgin earth'. Does this mean that humanity is composed of the substance of earth and the substance of God, that it enjoys an existence which is an amalgam of God and dust? The wording of this Section 11 might also seem to add weight to such an interpretation – God 'mingling in measure His own power with the earth'. However, this has to be seen in the context of Section 5 where it is stated that

> the Word establishes, that is, gives body and grants the reality of being, and the Spirit gives order and uniformity to the diversity of powers; rightly and fittingly is the Word called the Son, and the Spirit the Wisdom of God.[9]

The 'taking from the earth that which is purest and finest', is the 'giving body and granting reality of being'. The 'mingling in measure His own power' is the 'giving of order', the placing of this creature with a particularly significant status with the 'uniformity of the diversity of powers'. The man's substance is that he is made of earth by the Hands of God, God's Word and Wisdom, and that his status is, as Section 11 goes on to remark, that 'as the image of God was man formed and set on the earth'.

Any idea that Irenaeus is advocating a mythological synthesis between the substance of the dust of the earth and the substance of the Creator as that which man is, would entirely contradict his insistence of man being in a community of union with God. That community of union for Irenaeus, as we have noted previously (see comment on Section 1, pp. 38ff), is that man is created and exists in a relation of double contingency with God – he holds his beginning and existence in utter dependence upon God, yet God grants him a beginning and existence which is his own in his integrity as a creature. We may again appeal to the three passages in *Adversus Haereses* which we noted previously:

> For you do not make God, but God made you . . . to create is an attribute of the goodness of God, but to be created that of human nature.[10]

> God differs from man, that God indeed makes, but man is made; and truly, He who makes is always the same; but that which is made must receive both beginning and middle, and increase and addition. And God does indeed create after a skilful manner, while, as for man, he is skilfully created.[11]

> For you. O man, are not an uncreated being, nor did you always co-exist with God as did His Word; but now, through His pre-eminent goodness, receiving the beginning of your creation, you gradually learn from the Word the dispensations of the God who made you.[12]

This other constant emphasis of Irenaeus is he insists that humanity is led by Word and Spirit and progresses to God: 'man receives advancement and increase towards God. For as God is always the same, so also man, when found in God, shall always go on towards God'.[13] The 'in God' and 'towards God' in their juxtaposition, as we have noted already in the comments on Section 1 (p. 42), is a statement of that double contingency – *we* progress, it is our movement, but it is only so insofar as we are *in God* through union with His Word and led by His Spirit. An important emphatic view of Irenaeus as an aspect to this is found in Section 12 – namely that man is created as a child and has to grow to come to his perfection.

These two emphases of Irenaeus, found constantly throughout *Adversus Haereses* and in one form or another in the *Demonstration*, rule out any interpretation of man as a creature/divine synthesis.

Reference may be made again to that section in *Adversus Haereses*, which at first sight in the Ante-Nicene Library translation both rules out and yet supports this interpretation:

> For with Him were always present the Word and Wisdom, the Son and the Spirit, by whom and in whom, freely and spontaneously, He made all things, to whom also He speaks, saying, Let us make man after our image and likeness; He taking from Himself the substance of the creatures, and the pattern of things made, and the type of all the adornments of the world.[14]

We have looked partly at this topic already (see p. 102). Here we may say that 'He taking from Himself' should be construed as 'He taking among Himself'. In this case there is no idea put forward that God takes of his own 'substance' in the making of man. This quotation from *Adversus Haereses* is dealing with the conversing of the Persons regarding creation, that is to say, God takes counsel among Himself, as Father, Word and Spirit to involve Himself in creation.

We can only interpret 'mingling with his own power', therefore, in terms of God's 'working', as we can only with Section 32, which paraphrased would then read: 'Whence then is the substance of the first-formed man? From the virgin earth by the power of the working of the Will and Wisdom of God.' The distinction between Creator and creature is paramount in Irenaeus's thought. The modes of expression he employs in Sections 11 and 32 are surely to be regarded as underlining the unique relationship which this particular creature, man, enjoys with God as is clear from the especial counsel which the Father has with His Word and Wisdom concerning the nature and status of this creature made for this relation, and the careful workmanship He employs in the bringing into being of this creature by His Hands, His Word and Spirit.

That workmanship results in the creature being made 'after the image and likeness of God'. Here we must look at this phrase in terms of Irenaeus's twofold usage of it, namely that man is made after the image and likeness of God, yet will be made so. The phrase has both present and future implications. The 'image of God' as applied to humanity is not, in Irenaeus's thought, a once and for all and complete endowment. Humanity will only come to its full realization as this particular workmanship of God, the estate to which He has appointed it, the purpose for which He has destined it and the relation to Himself with which He has endowed it, when in full community of union with God through the incarnate Word we see God face to face which is immortality. The progress, the leading, the development, the advance, the furthering from an infantile state to the adult, the gradual movement towards God of humanity in and through and by the Word and Spirit, are themes which are scattered throughout *Adversus Haereses*.

These instances of this theme are too numerous to mention, but are perhaps best summed up in the passage from that larger work which is in the context of the observation that God did not create man perfect at the beginning and setting out the reasons for this.[15] This is an important passage, setting out God's respect for the fragility of the creature, its incapability of being able to bear the full weight of His glory, and His dispensation of the incarnate Word, who passes through all the ages of human existence in order to enable the total estate of humanity to bear Him. God could have created man perfect, for everything is possible for him. But that which is created, God recognizes, is not as He is, who is Perfect, but by very virtue of the fact that it is created and not, as He, uncreated, it falls short of the perfect. Humanity, if it is to be humanity in the created integrity of its identity, could not receive perfection at the beginning, being yet an infant. As infants we all require to grow, advance and be exercised in 'perfect discipline'. We have not the capacity to receive God, or even, if receiving such perfection, containing it, and even, again, if containing it, retaining it. For humanity had (and has)

> the sentient faculties of the soul still feeble and undisciplined in the practice of things pertaining to God . . . . It was for this reason that the Son of God, though He was perfect, passed through the state of infancy in common with the rest of mankind, partaking of it thus not for His own benefit, but for that of the infantile stage of man's existence, in order that men might be able to receive Him. There was nothing, therefore, impossible to and deficient in God [merely because] man was not an uncreated being; but this merely applied to him, man, who was lately created.[16]

The Word came as an infant, recapitulating all the stages of human growth, that that growth might be towards God and fulfilled in 'beholding Him'. Just as a mother nourishes her child with that which is suitable to the child's development, so

> He did this, when He appeared as man, that we, being nourished, as it were, from the breast of His flesh, and having, by such a course of milk nourishment, become accustomed to eat and drink the Word of God, may be able also to contain in ourselves the Bread of immortality, which is the Spirit of the Father.[17]

Here the 'Royal Exchange' is implied – God fitting Himself in His Word to our estate, that our estate may become the bearer of the Holy Spirit. The advance in this process is argued by Irenaeus in this passage – and here it is clear that God's Will and power are indeed His working in creation, and not a bestowal of his 'substance'.

> With God there are simultaneously exhibited power, wisdom and goodness. His power and goodness in this – that of His own will he called into being, and fashioned, things having no previous existence; His Wisdom – in having made created entities parts of one harmonious and consistent whole; and those things, which through His super-eminent kindness receive growth, and a long period of existence, do reflect the glory of the

> uncreated One, of that God who bestows what is good ungrudgingly. For from the very fact of these things having been created, they are not (of the status) of uncreated; but by their continuing in being throughout a long course of ages, they shall receive a faculty of the Uncreated through the gratuitous bestowal of eternal existence upon them by God. And thus in all things God has the pre-eminence, who alone is the uncreated, the first of all things, and the primary cause of the existence of all, while all other things remain under God's subjection. But being in subjection to God is continuance in immortality, and immortality is the glory of the uncreated One. By this arrangement, therefore, and these harmonies, and a sequence of this nature, man, a created and worked being, is rendered after the image and likeness of the uncreated God – the Father planning everything well and giving His commands, the Son carrying these into execution and performing the work of creation, and the Spirit nourishing and increasing – but man making progress day by day and ascending towards the perfect, that is, approximating to the uncreated One. For the uncreated is perfect, that is, God. Now it was necessary that man should in the first instance be created; and having been created, should receive growth; and having received growth, should be strengthened; and having been strengthened, should abound; and having abounded, should recover (his lost estate); and having recovered, should be glorified; and being glorified, should see his Lord. For God is He who is yet to be seen, and the beholding of God is productive of immortality, but immortality renders one nigh to God.[18]

Humanity is not, Irenaeus continues, to be impatient, confusing that which is human with that which is divine, either by ascribing the limitations and infirmities of human nature to God, or by wishing

> themselves to be even now like God their Creator . . . . For (dumb animals) bring no charge against God for not having made them men; but each one, just as it has been created, gives thanks that it has been (so) created. But we cast blame on Him, because we have not been made gods from the beginning, but at first merely men, then at length gods; although God has adopted this course out of His pure loving-kindness . . . . He declares, Ye are gods, and ye are all sons of the Highest. But since we could not sustain the power of divinity, He adds, But ye shall die like men, setting forth both truths . . . by His foreknowledge He knew the infirmity of human beings, and the consequences which would flow from it, but through (His) love and (His) power, He shall overcome the substance of our human nature. For it was necessary at first that this nature should be demonstrated; then, after that which was mortal should be conquered and swallowed up by immortality, and the corruptible by incorruptibility, and that man should be made after the image and likeness of God . . .[19]

This is the context for appreciating Irenaeus's understanding of the meaning and significance of humanity being created 'after the image and likeness of God'. It is a Christocentric understanding, for, for Irenaeus, Christ alone is *the* Image of God. He is 'the visible of the Father', the Father being 'the invisible of the Son'.[20] The Word is invisible until He assumes human flesh and nature. At the incarnation the Image of God is demonstrated clearly in a Christocentric manner, for there is seen the restoration and establishment of the 'similitude', or 'likeness' to this Image of God, after which man is made. For humanity, in the union of human flesh and nature with the Word, is in Jesus Christ , in perfect relation with God as it advances and is led in a community of union with God through him. Thus the image of God is not a quantitative, formal or physical consideration by itself and for itself and in the first instance: it is found primarily in the qualitative, relational existence which stamps human estate and dignity as being just that only in its relation with God through his Word after whose image man is made.

> This Word was manifested when the Word of God was made man, assimilating Himself to man, and man to Himself, so that by means of resemblance to the Son, man might become precious to the Father. For in times long past it was said that man was created after the image of God, but it was not shown [here a distinction is made between *said* and *shown*]; for the Word was as yet invisible, after whose image man was created. Wherefore also he lost the similitude easily. When, however, the Word of God became flesh, He confirmed both these: for He both showed forth the image truly, since He became what was His image; and He re-established the similitude after a sure manner, by assimilating man to the invisible Father by means of the visible Word.[21]

In Section 11, 'He traced His own form on the formation', refers not to any shape of God as He exists in his eternal and triune Being. This God is beyond comparison: words applied to this God fail: descriptions are expressly forbidden for the sublimity of God is far beyond our comprehension. Bearing in mind the Christocentricity of Irenaeus in the whole question of the relation of humanity to God in what is essentially the complementarity of creation and incarnation, the two sides of the one act of God, 'His form' refers to the form of the incarnate Word. That is, we are faced with that which pulls us up short in the thought of Irenaeus – that humanity is created according to the pattern of the humanity which the Word assumes. In other words, the sequence is not that humanity has a form which the Word at His incarnation has to take, but that the Word made flesh, in the dispensation of God who, beyond time and space orders the temporal/spatial character of creation, is the pattern which is traced on humanity, and appears as such. So, in Section 22, Irenaeus states:

> For He made man the image of God; and the image of God is the Son, after whose image man was made; and for this cause He appeared at the end of the times that He might show the image (to be) like unto Himself.[22]

It is unfortunate that our present western mode of thought cannot accommodate the nuances of ancient Hebrew ways of thinking. Irenaeus knew Hebrew, and would have been aware of the nuances and varied meanings of the preposition *B*^{e} – generally translated in its application to 'the image of God' in Genesis Chapter 1, as *in*, so that this is the commonly accepted meaning, that man is created in the image of God. Jerome, later, likewise knowing Hebrew, translates the Hebrew preposition in his Vulgate bible as *ad*. This preposition has a range of applications – 'in', 'by', 'for', 'to', 'towards' and so on. It is the latter two which Jerome chose, and it is to be noted that Irenaeus's usage is more commonly 'after the image of God'. 'Towards' or 'after' both indicate a dynamic interpretation rather than the static and formalized 'in'. Indeed 'after' and 'towards' together would sum up Irenaeus's insistence that man, made so, still has this image to achieve as the Word and Spirit lead him to the Father when humanity's existence, after and towards the image of God, will be fulfilled.

Irenaeus is certainly flexible in his application of the phrase 'the image of God'. Yet – and although this is not the opinion of some scholars (for example Denis

Minns O.P. in his *Irenaeus* in the *Outstanding Christian Thinkers Series*, published by Chapman, 1994) – I think that a synthesis of his scattered and sometimes apparently contradictory statements can be achieved if we take his usage to mean (and a careful marshalling and comparison of the texts, I believe, permits this) that man is created 'after the likeness of the image of God'. It is the 'likeness', the 'similitude', which establishes and restores the 'image' in the incarnation of the Word. If we refer back to and read again the quotation from *Adversus Haereses* instanced above, then this would seem indeed to set out the relation between the 'likeness' and the 'image' in Irenaeus's thought. It is as the 'likeness is re-established' by the incarnate Word, we having been made after the likeness of the image of God, that the image is shown clearly and we advance in a community of union with God in the incarnate Word towards our ultimate perfection in that image. In our making, advance and fulfilment, the 'image of God' is construed as a dynamic relation with our Creator.

One aspect of Irenaeus's usage of the making of humanity in terms of *image* and *likeness*, is that of the 'freedom' and 'rationality' of the human being. However, I would suggest that wherever this occurs in *Adversus Haereses* that we ought to exercise caution and not transfer modern notions of the freedom and autonomy of the individual to second-century patristic thought. 'Freedom' and 'rationality' for Irenaeus is qualified in these instances by either a direct or an oblique reference to 'obedience'. Section 11's mention of man created 'free and self-controlled' does not necessarily mean what is now commonly accepted and understood by these terms. The whole saga of the creation of humanity and its placing in paradise and its role *vis- à-vis* creation there, culminates in the stricture in section 15:

> But, lest man should conceive thoughts too high, and be exalted and uplifted, as though he had no lord, because of the authority and freedom granted to him, and so should transgress against his maker God, overpassing his measure, and entertain selfish imaginings of pride in opposition to God; a law was given to him by God, in order that he might perceive that he had as lord the Lord of all. And He set him certain limitations, so that, if he should keep the commandment of God, he should ever remain such as he was, that is to say, immortal; but, if he should not keep it, he should become mortal and be dissolved to earth from whence his formation had been taken.[23]

The commandment given to man was that he should not eat of the tree of knowledge of good and evil. Here we have freedom in terms of contingency. Man is created free, but he can only have that freedom (which is also freedom from death and dissolution to dust and therefore a freedom which includes immortality) as it is held from God. Man has his own identity and quality of nature, his own created integrity, but this is bestowed upon him by the loving-kindness of God. This loving-kindness of God is directed to the keeping of humanity within the sphere and condition where and how it is what it truly is and not something else. It is the handiwork of God who of His benevolence has granted to humanity this existence in relation to himself as loving Creator. It is humanity only within this existence.

The restrictions placed on humanity are to ensure its essential being as that humanity which is the handiwork of God. To depart from that sphere and to cast aside those conditions means that humanity denies itself for what it is in itself under God. Its freedom to be itself would therefore be compromised. It can only be free *towards* God: its freedom does not reside in itself. For humanity does not exist for itself, by itself and of itself. Its *self-control* consists in abiding by this and in perceiving that its freedom does not lie in any other allegiance or within itself by itself.

Here we are again faced with a relational and dynamic interpretation of terms. Expressions and values such as freedom and self-control are not statically fixed as formal concepts of natural attributes in themselves, but point beyond themselves to where they are grounded, wherein resides their validity and in reference to which they may be exercised. The double contingency of humanity's existence to and from God is the light in which these terms are to be understood in Irenaeus's employment of them.

The same is true of rationality. This is also to be viewed relationally. Rationality has been dealt with under the comments on Section 3 (see pp. 57ff.) where it was looked at in terms of κατα φυσιν thinking. Here we regard rationality as the direction of the mind towards, and informed by, objective realities. Thus the relational enters here again, this time between the mind and the objective reality whereby the mind is informed and to which the mind subjects itself. All notions of the autonomy of the mind, that is of judgmental ability being the prerogative of the mind itself of itself, are ruled out by the exercise of rational movement and relation.

The gathering together of Irenaeus's observations on 'image, likeness, freedom, rationality', applied to humanity is best summarized by way of general principle in this passage from *Adversus Haereses*:

> God is also truly perfect in all things, Himself equal and similar to Himself, as He is all light, and all mind, and all substance, and the fount of all good; but man receives advancement and increase towards God. For God is always the same, so also man, when found in God, shall always go on towards God. For neither does God at any time cease to confer benefits upon, or to enrich, man; nor does man ever cease from receiving the benefits, and being enriched by God.[24]

Irenaeus's vision of humanity's advancement towards God in the Word and Spirit, to its perfection in the fulfilment of the community of union between it and God into which Word and Spirit have led it, is the key to unlock the significance of his understanding of 'the image and likeness of God' and the whole estate and dignity and composition of humanity.

Notes

1 Irenaeus: e.g. *Adversus Haereses* IV:Preface:4; V:6:1.
2 *Ibid.* V:1:3.
3 *Ibid.* V:5:1.
4 *Ibid.* III:18:7.
5 *Ibid.* III:21:10.
6 Irenaeus: *Demonstration of the Apostolic Preaching* 32.
7 *Ibid.*
8 Irenaeus: *Adversus Haereses* III:21:5.
9 Irenaeus: *Demonstration of the Apostolic Preaching* 5.

10 Irenaeus: *Adversus Haereses* IV:39:2.
11 *Ibid.* IV:11:2.
12 *Ibid.* II:25:3; cf. Fragment XXIV.
13 *Ibid.* IV:11:2.
14 *Ibid.* IV:20:1.
15 *Ibid.* IV:38:1.
16 *Ibid.* IV:38:2.
17 *Ibid.* IV:38:1.
18 *Ibid.* IV:38:3.
19 *Ibid.* IV:38:4.
20 *Ibid.* IV:6:6.
21 *Ibid.* V:16:2.
22 Irenaeus: *Demonstration of the Apostolic Preaching* 22.
23 *Ibid.* 15
24 Irenaeus: *Adversus Haereses* IV:11:2.

Chapter 8

Sections 12 (cont.)–15: The Dominion, Place and Nature of Humanity

Irenaeus neither boasts of familiar knowledge with, nor indulges in speculation concerning, any detailed hierarchy or precise commission and office of angels, other than to remark on their service to creation (unspecified in Section 11) and that the angels in this world were set under 'the archangel' as 'steward'. He shuns any such claim or conjecture. To make such an assertion or to indulge in such speculation, even if they were within his theological priorities and approval, which they were not, would give opportunity for gnostic exploitation, the very tendency which he opposed.

There are some observations by Justin Martyr on the subject of angelic beings with which Irenaeus's comments agree. There are, however, in the full breadth of both theologians' treatment of the subject, fundamental differences. These are noted below. In common with some statements of Justin Martyr, however, Irenaeus is quite clear that angels and humanity are both the creatures of God and both under constraints imposed by God. However, unlike Justin Martyr who notes that humanity is under the care of angels – a hint that his doctrine of angels diverges fundamentally at certain points from that of Irenaeus – Irenaeus's view of the lordship of man over the angels puts a different emphasis on the relation of the two orders of creatures, angelic and human. Apart from this, Irenaeus agrees with those assertions whereby Justin Martyr at least says that angels and humanity both have their respective responsibilities in their appointed service by and of God *vis-à-vis* His creation. Thus Justin Martyr:

> God, when He had made the whole world and subjected things earthly to man, and arranged the heavenly elements for the increase of fruits and the rotation of the seasons, and appointed this divine law – for these things also He evidently made for man – committed the care of men and of all things under heaven to angels whom He appointed over them.[1]
>
> . . . He created both angels and men free to do that which is righteous, and He appointed periods of time during which He knew it would be good for them to have the exercise of free-will; and because He likewise knew it would be good, He made general and particular judgments; each one's freedom of will, however, being guarded.[2]
>
> . . . God, wishing men and angels to follow His will, resolved to create them free to do righteousness; possessing reason that they may know by whom they are created, and through whom they, not existing formerly, do now exist; and with a law that they should be judged by Him if they do anything contrary to right reason: and of ourselves, men and angels, shall be convicted of having acted sinfully, unless we repent beforehand.[3]

Apart from the statement about angels having the dominion of men and all things under heaven, Irenaeus's doctrine of angels, such as it is, agrees. There is a statement of the double contingency of created being in this, for angels and humanity in Justin's partial (and Irenaeus's total) view are created as entities with their own respective identities and are free to be so and act accordingly. But these angels and humanity can only hold this freedom in the context of the fact that it is God-bestowed, and this they contradict at their own peril. In the identity and nature and office of these angels and human beings, each has its existence *from* God (its freedom to be and act as itself) yet its dependence *to* God from whom alone it holds this existence and its attributes.

However, there are differences between Irenaeus and Justin Martyr in this area. Justin Martyr can also write in attempting to refute the charge that Christians are atheists

> But both Him (the Father) and the Son (who came forth from Him and taught us these things, and the host of other good angels who follow Him and are made like to Him), and the prophetic Spirit, we worship and adore . . . .[4]

In translation of this section of Justin's *First Apology*, only the most violent treatment of the text could remove the 'host of other good angels' from being with the Father, the Son and the Spirit that which 'we worship and adore'. With this sentiment of the adoration and worship of anything other than God Himself, Irenaeus would certainly part company and disown it.

Moreover, there is another assertion by Justin Martyr which is far removed from Irenaeus's treatment of angelic beings:

> so the Father, when he chooses, say they (Moses and the prophets), causes His power to spring forth, and when He chooses, makes it return to Himself. In this way, they teach, He made the angels. But it is proved that there are angels who always exist, and are never reduced to that form out of which they sprang.[5]

Again, this seemingly scriptural but debatable speculation as to the relation between angels and the being of God is an opinion which Irenaeus would repudiate. Both the dominion of angels theory and their relation to God as instanced from the writing of Justin Martyr have the potential and vulnerability for development into gnostic systems, and Irenaeus's approach to the subject of angels is much more circumspect than to allow such.

In arguing and safeguarding against various gnostic theories regarding angels both generally as to the nature of their being and particularly as agents of, or even creators in, the making of the universe, Irenaeus emphasizes that all creation is God's own possession and territory. Angels are under God's power and control, and He both views and knows them and their actions. All things are created by God, who does not need anything and certainly not assistance in creating the angels for and into their appointed place and apportioned office, in their own 'angelical' sphere of being and work, and everything felicitously likewise in its appointed office and estate.[6] All created beings serve God in the dispensation of His creation.

Whatever the provenance of *Fragments* LIII and LIV ascribed to the authorship of Irenaeus by some,[7] the role of the Word made flesh as the superior of all created orders is made clear therein. The Word is Lord and Author of all aspects of creation:

> He is All in all; Patriarch among the patriarchs; Law in the laws; Chief Priest among priests; Ruler among kings; The Prophet among prophets; the Angel among angels; the Chief also of the cherubim; the Prince of the angelic powers; God of God; Son of the Father, Jesus Christ.[8] . . . the Charioteer of the cherubim; the Leader of the angelic host.[9]

There is a marked difference between the muted approach to angels adopted by Irenaeus and some of the statements of Justin Martyr noted above, and as there is also with regard to a statement by the earlier Papias. In a fragment ascribed to him, Papias remarks of God that to some of the angels 'He gave dominion over the arrangement of the world, and He commissioned them to exercise their dominion well'.[10]

Irenaeus does not go beyond that, and indeed does not even approach anything so definite as angelic dominion. Dominion could imply territory, and territory ownership, and ownership that the holder had created that domain. Irenaeus deliberately removed himself from such a train of thought; it was too near the tenets of some of the gnostic systems. This is why the stress in the text towards the end of Section 11 is on the angels as the 'servants of that God who formed all things' and as those beings which had appointed 'tasks', even the archangel (unnamed) being but 'the steward' of his fellows. The implication is that they are related to the ὀιχονομια of creation, but Irenaeus insists that their function in this relation is that of serving the will of God. Angels would seem, according to Irenaeus, to serve God in their occupation of the seven heavens (as we have mentioned in regard to Section 9) and also to serve him in this world which is encompassed by these heavens, as he states in this section. On their dominion of creation, heavenly or earthly, even if it is apportioned out to them severally by God (a widely held conviction) he is silent. Concerning the angelic beings who are servants in this earth, even the archangel is regarded by Irenaeus as superior to the other angels concerned with this domain, by function. He makes no mention of hierarchical being.

With regard to the incarnation, Irenaeus remarks that the Word is supreme in the corporeal and visible creation 'as in super-celestial, spiritual and invisible things the Word of God is supreme'.[11] It is the supremacy and unquestioned ownership and authority over all creatures, heavenly, angelic and earthly, with which Irenaeus is concerned. Angels are referred to necessarily, but in a tempered fashion. It is this disinterest which singles Irenaeus out not only from Justin Martyr and Papias, but, for example, from Hermas and Athenagoras. In Hermas[12] and Athenagoras[13] there is the acceptance and indeed proclamation that angels are mediatorial functionaries of cosmic principles. We have noted that Justin Martyr speaks of angels as worshipped and reverenced by Christians and that he also seems to suggests that Christ is the head of the angels, but they are of similar eternal quality. Irenaeus's taciturnity on such matters was not only necessarily prudent in the face of gnostic speculations and innovations, but also more balanced by a stricter adherence to the constraints of scriptural references to angels.

He habitually mentions angels and humanity together, and here we have a view of creation in its totality as utterly distinct – however perfect the angels – from the Creator. So it is in these sections in their movement from Section 11. For Irenaeus creation is the place of angels and of humanity. It is, however principally the domain of the latter, for man is the lord of angels who are servants in creation. This designation of man as lord of the angels, however, is a *secret* one, the reason given for this observation being that angels were in their perfection while man was but a child who had to grow towards such excellence in his own nature as they already enjoyed in theirs.

The relation of humanity to angels, with regard to their respective significances within creation is set out at the opening of Section 12. Section 11 ('this great created world . . . was given to man as his place') suggests that the angels, too, being in 'this place', were given to man who, according to Section 12, is secretly appointed by God as lord over the angels who are servants in the earth. The man, as created, is not yet openly lord over the angels, because, as Irenaeus remarks, he was a child who had to grow and come to his perfection. Nevertheless, Irenaeus is quite clear as to Adam's precedence in the earth. This precedence is in the context of the purpose of creation, and one statement in *Adversus Haereses* more than all others makes Irenaeus's view on the matter succinctly and abundantly clear:

> In the previous books I have set forth the causes for which God permitted these things to be made, and have pointed out that all such have been created for the benefit of that human nature which is saved, ripening for immortality that which is of its own free will and its own power, and preparing it and rendering it more adapted for eternal subjection to God. And therefore the creation is suited to man; for man was made not for its sake, but creation for the sake of man.[14]

The unique being of humanity for which creation is made and which has this dominion over it all, is underlined throughout Sections 12 and 13 in three ways.

The first is: the place especially prepared for human dwelling by God. It is a place where development is fostered, man being carefully nurtured by the excellence of the provisions therein. Much conjecture has been stirred in the question raised by some as to where this place is deemed to be sited in Irenaeus's cosmology. I doubt if Irenaeus has any such cosmology. He is not interested in *place* as a primary concern, and certainly here, in the issue of the siting of Paradise, there is little that can be concluded as to his views. If he has that which can be deducted as at least a semblance of a cosmology, then I think we find that he is concerned primarily with the *quality* of existences, rather than *with quantifying* space as place. This may be drawn out of that which we have dealt with already, the seven heavens with which this world is surrounded. Rather than detail their quantifying extent, Irenaeus immediately on mentioning them goes on to describe them in terms of the virtues of the Spirit (cf. Chapter 6 and particularly pp. 97ff.). Irenaeus transfers interest and speculation away from cosmology to the analysis of the nature and qualities of Creator and creation.

J. Armitage Robinson, in his footnotes to his translation of the *Demonstration*, is of the opinion that for Irenaeus, Paradise was situated in a region outside this world. This opinion is formed for him by the import which he sees in the opening words of Section 17:

> And when they were put out of Paradise, Adam and his wife Eve fell into many troubles of anxious grief, going about with sorrow and toil and lamentation in this world.[15]

However, this does not necessarily mean the translation of Adam and Eve physically to a place and a location other than their first. This is not stated. What is declared is that their present quality of this wordly existence is far removed – again qualitatively – from that which they enjoyed as their prelapsarian existence. Thus the importance of the exclusion from the garden of Eden, which Irenaeus in common with the prevailing tradition equates to Paradise, is that Adam and Eve are removed 'far from the tree of life'.[16] The interest lies in the contrast of qualities of life rather than in the contradistinction of places.

In those sections of *Adversus Haereses* where Paradise is mentioned, no certain conclusion can be drawn as to Irenaeus's view as to where Paradise was situated. In I:5:2 he recounts the gnostics' assertions on the matter. The similarity to certain ideas, held as orthodox at the time, may be appreciated – for example, that seven heavens have been created, though by whom, of course, shows the heretical tenet. They are created by the Demiurge, who is an angel 'bearing a likeness to God' and who, in the last resort is ignorant of that which he has created, since, without realizing it, he created them in conjunction with the productive powers of Achamoth in the places of darkness and vacuity.[17] Moreover, these heavens are identified with angels – they are angelic existences – and Paradise for the gnostics is situated above the third heaven which is itself the fourth angel 'possessed of power, from whom Adam derived certain qualities when he conversed with him'.[18]

The danger of heresy lay not so much in those claims which were blatantly dissimilar to, and an obvious contradiction of, orthodox tenets, but in its confusing similarity to them and in its subtle misuse of them – ('Error is plausible and bears a resemblance to the truth'[19]). The heavens identified with the being of angels might not be so far from Irenaeus's emphasis on quality of existences being the determinatives of 'place', but here the similarity ends. For these heavens of the gnostics are part of self-determining existences locked in the bonds and feuds between conjectural beings constructed to explain the dualistic attitude which coloured the approach of such as the gnostics to the relation between creature and Creator, time and eternity, material and spiritual, darkness and vacuity and light and life. There is no concept of quality of existence as that which is determined by the relation between creature and Creator through the Word and Spirit.

Again, the gnostics' view that Paradise is beyond the third heaven, is not of itself a contradiction of any of Irenaeus's statements on the matter. But the identification of Paradise with an angel of the fourth rank in a series of dualistic emanations is. Irenaeus himself is ambivalent in his statements with regard to paradise being either beyond the third heaven or elsewhere. The section in *Adversus Haereses* to which J. Armitage Robinson also appeals in his view that Irenaeus did site Paradise out of the region of this world is not so clear as to draw any such definite conclusion.

In this part of the larger work, Irenaeus is writing of the translation of Enoch and Elijah. The burden of this passage is on the concept of the Word and Spirit as 'the hands of God'. The hands of God are capable of the translation of such righteous persons to where these hands will, for they had been accustomed to such activity in the creation of Adam and in the placing of him in Paradise.

> Where then was the first man placed? In Paradise certainly, as the scripture declares: and God planted a garden (paradisium) eastward in Eden, and there He placed the man

> whom He had formed. And then afterwards when proved disobedient, he was cast out thence into this world. Wherefore also the elders who were the disciples of the apostles tell us that those who were translated were transferred to that place (for Paradise has been prepared for righteous men, such as have the Spirit; in which place also Paul the apostle, when he was caught up, heard words which are unspeakable as regards us in our present condition) and that there shall they who have been translated remain until the consummation, as a prelude to immortality.[20]

The exact biblical phrase 'eastward in Eden' does not encourage us, or for that matter would hardly encourage Irenaeus, to think in terms of a placement of Paradise literally above the literal third heaven. Locating Paradise seems to be of little interest to Irenaeus – for he does not attempt to reconcile the apparently inconsistent sitings as suggested by the reference from Genesis that it is in Eden, and yet it is also the place of both Adam's original state in his intimacy with God and the place of the righteous who 'have the Spirit' and therefore are in another sort of intimate relation with God.

It is noteworthy that the words which St Paul heard in Paradise are 'unspeakable to us in our present condition', the last three words being the significant factor. We are not as yet of the condition required for domicile in Paradise.

We are left with the impression again that all that interests Irenaeus is the quality of creaturely existences in their integrities within their relation to the Creator which sojourning in Paradise suggests.

Certainly in Sections 12, 13 and 14 of the *Demonstration*, the importance of Paradise is that it is the setting for humanity's advance and development towards the perfection of the fullness of community of union with God, which is its purpose and destiny, and to that end it is the trysting place of the Word of God with the man as man is given the tutelage of the Word. It is the state of near perfection in obedience to the Word – hence the expulsion of Adam and Eve in their insubordination to the command of God. And, since it is the place of the near perfection of life, they are removed far from the tree of that life from which they have turned.

It is one of the idiosyncrasies of Irenaeus that Adam was created as a child, and likewise Eve in turn. This comes out of his twofold concern in theological emphasis: first, that life is an advance towards God and a tutelage in the knowledge of God, the perfect vision of whom is immortality: 'Men therefore shall see God, that they may live, being made immortal by that sight, and attaining even unto God'.[21] This idea of the potential growth of Adam from infancy to the fullness of human stature in the Word, and therefore in perfect community of union with God, whereby Adam will be made like unto God[22] points to an integral and characteristic feature of Irenaeus's theology; namely that humanity is given the opportunity to grow and advance in the knowledge of God. The whole lump of Adam, that is humanity of which Adam is not only the forefather but the recapitulation, after the fall, is still given that opportunity to progress towards God by sharing in the cutting forward of the Word made flesh as he advances from birth, through infancy into manhood and (according to Irenaeus) old age (another of this idiosyncrasies as to the age of Christ at his death[23]). He thereby recapitulated all the ages of man, summed up the whole of Adam in Himself, and giving, through His joining of Himself to us by the incarnation and us to Him by the outpouring of His Spirit, that community of union with himself whereby we join in his advance, his 'cutting forward' (προεκοπτε) in his re-creation of humanity as He moves towards His passion, cross and resurrection.[24]

Hopefully it will have been noticed throughout the sections upon which comment has been made already that this growth, or advance, or being led, in the Word by the Spirit towards God, is a constant theme of Irenaeus and a foundational tenet of his theology. Here in these sections, Irenaeus concerns himself with the growth that is offered to Adam from his formation onwards. Paradise is, as we have noted, the trysting place of the Word with the man. To this place the Word resorts from time to time, tutoring Him in the things of the coming fullness of God's relation with Him. This is elaborated in *Adversus Haereses*:

> Now this is His Word, our Lord Jesus Christ, who in the last times was made a man among men, that He might join the end to the beginning, that is, man to God. Wherefore the prophets, receiving the prophetic gift from the same Word, announced His advent according to the flesh, by which the blending and communion of God and man took place according to the good pleasure of the Father, the Word of God foretelling from the beginning that God should be seen by men, and hold converse with them upon earth, should confer with them, and should be present with His own creation, saving it, and being capable of being perceived by it, and freeing us from the hands of all that hate us, that is, from every spirit of wickedness; and causing us to serve Him in holiness and righteousness all our days, in order that man, having embraced the Spirit of God, might pass into the glory of the Father.[25]

The question may be asked: does Irenaeus think that the Word, talking in the garden to the first man, spoke of His dwelling with man, that is His incarnation, as an incarnation which would take place as the highlight of creation? This would seem to be the substance of the conversation, which has no mention of the fall, as interpreted here by Irenaeus. Put another way, the question which is provoked by this section is, more precisely: would there have been an incarnation if man had not fallen? The substance of the conversation, in its context, does seem to be that man, as a child, will have an even growth towards righteousness and perfection in the company of the Word dwelling with men. In other words, this section would seem to be a declaration that creation has its fulfilment in the union of God and humanity. Incarnation, therefore, is not only the conclusion of the work of creation, but the very initial purpose of it, the *terminus a quo* and the *terminus ad quem* of creation.

This question as whether or not the incarnation would have taken place if there had been no fall greatly exercised theological minds through the history of doctrinal thought. For example, in the early thirteenth century, Robert Grosseteste, who became the first Chancellor of Oxford and Bishop of Lincoln, in struggling with the concept of the necessity of a unifying factor in all creation, could write:

> By these and other arguments it seems possible to conclude that God would have become man even if man had never sinned. I confess I do not know if I am right, and I am afflicted by my ignorance in this matter . . . . I do not remember if any authority has come to this conclusion, and I do not wish to pronounce conclusively on so hard a question without express authority.[26]

The last observation is typical, generally, of medieval hesitation to proceed without the precedence of absolute patristic pronouncements at least pointing to a conclusion clearly, and particularly of Grosseteste's constant reluctance to come to a definitive conclusion on matters conjectural, however compelling the argument for that conclusion he may have constructed. It is perhaps not without note, however, that Grosseteste, like Irenaeus, believed that man was created without his potentiality fully developed.[27]

In the same vein as Grosseteste, however, it is better to leave such questions unanswered, for only conjecture upon conjecture would ensue. But in this particular section it may be said that the whole purpose of creation, and the growth of man towards God in the grace and loving-kindness of God's Word, is set before the first man, in Irenaeus's thought, as the declaration of the perfection of creation and the chief end of man which is to enjoy God and glorify Him for ever.

Adam is viewed by Irenaeus, therefore, in a somewhat different way than the heaping of opprobrium upon him as the one responsible for the fall of all humanity and the sorry state and woeful face of creation. That Adam is the high handiwork of God, created to progress and advance and be led into the perfection of community of union with God in the Word and Spirit, precludes Irenaeus from treating Adam in an ignominious way. This emphasis in Irenaeus's thought, that Adam is not regarded as being reprehensible primarily regarding the fall, is somewhat neglected or even passed over and unrecognized. It manifests itself in Irenaeus's theology in three ways. First, the constancy of God towards Adam; second, that the blame for the fall is apportioned by God to the serpent-tempter; and third, that Adam and Eve are the epitome of human repentance. These three emphases will be noted in the next chapter in commenting on Sections 16 and 17.

Here the special place occupied by Adam in the whole creative dispensation of God is indicated by the task to which he is summoned by God. Section 13 recalls Genesis II:19 in the Septuagint version. God brings before Adam every living thing that Adam may name them all as living souls. Irenaeus has caught the nuance of the Hebrew thought here through the septuagint text in the equation of 'soul' with 'name'. The name is the soul, and whatever Adam calls each living entity that is its nature and quality. Adam is regarded here as, as it were, the prophet of creation, in that he is concerned with the relation of words to life. In the necessary rationality and respect which this entails lies the nature of man's dominion within creation.

Irenaeus curiously reverses the sequence of the verses in Genesis, for he next notes that God determines to create a helper for Adam and goes on to note the making of Eve, whereas in the biblical narrative God's observation that man should not be alone comes before the bestowal of the prophetic vocation and office on Adam. This sequence, seemingly deliberately adopted by Irenaeus in reversing the biblical layout, heightens the fact that among all that lived upon earth, there was nothing like to Adam and suitable to be his helper, for all are named, catalogued and assessed in their nature already. Only that which is equal to, and comparable with, Adam can assist him in his estate and office. The rest of creation is therefore delineated from humanity, and particularly from humanity as a relational being, that is, not only as relational within itself, but, in that relation having a particular relation to the God after whose image this creature is. The male/female composition of humanity is the stamp of both its dignity of being and the nature of its dignity in the estate and vocation given to it by God.

Human being is construed as a rational existence which in its created rationality corresponds to the uncreated Rationality which God is as He exists in His relational being as the Triune God. The man is the surveyor, analyst, namer and cataloguer of all the order which God has created and brings before him. His naming corresponds to the nature of God's presented order. The correspondence to the triunity of God is reflected in the male and the female being bound together as one. The bond is recognized in the man seeing the woman and in the repetition of the biblical words 'This is now bone of my bone and flesh of my flesh'. The likeness to God which man is, is because he has been endowed with reason and is in rational relation with God the source and upholder of his being. He loses the likeness when he loses that rationality in his disobedience to God, and lives irrationally, opposing the righteousness of God.[28] The 'image and likeness of God' is very much bound with the consideration of both the being and the rationality of humanity in its relation to God.

There is one curious reference to Paradise in the way in which God provides the man with a helper. This is Irenaeus's observation following his noting of the biblical statement about God causing a trance to fall on the man in order to take one of Adam's ribs to create Eve from it: 'and that work might be accomplished from work, since there was no sleep in Paradise, this was brought upon Adam by the will of God'.[29] The meaning would seem to be that 'in order to bring like out of like, both being the work of God, it was the will of God which accomplished this, and He accomplished it by causing Adam to fall into a trance, since sleep had not yet been experienced by the man'. There are two considerations here: the first that the unity and diversity of humanity as male and female is the will and work of God and this nature of humanity has no other author: and the second – another emphasis of Irenaeus – that sleep was not yet known by the man in Paradise because this was still the sixth day of creation and the evening of that day had not yet come. 'Day', for Irenaeus, does not mean a day of twenty-four hours. The 'days' of creation are delineated, not by a temporal measurement, but by the particular work of God. The 'sixth day' is the day of humanity, and indeed, the day of the recapitulation of the whole epic of humanity's beginning, of its identity, estate and vocation, and of the purpose and nature of its fulfilment – and also, according to Irenaeus, of its fall and the consequences of that. This treatment of 'day' in the creative process of God, as a particular sort of 'day' – 'days of creation' – is seen when Irenaeus can say concerning the day when Adam and Eve ate the forbidden fruit:

> Thus then, in the day that they did eat, in the same did they die, and became death's debtors, since it was one day of the creation. For it is said; There was made in the evening, and there was made in the morning, one day. Now in this same day that they did eat, in that also did they die.[30]

Irenaeus then goes on to say that that day of eating and dying was the sixth day (when, since there was as yet no evening, man had not known sleep). This he deduces – with all his characteristic parallelism – from the fact that our Lord summed up the death of Adam by dying on the sixth day, the day preceding the sabbath:

> From this it is clear that the Lord suffered death in obedience to His Father, upon that day on which Adam died while he disobeyed God. Now he died on the same day in which he did eat. For God said: In that day in which ye shall eat of it, ye shall die by death. The Lord, therefore, recapitulating in Himself this day, underwent His sufferings on the day preceding the sabbath, that is, the sixth day of the creation, on which day man was created; thus granting him a second creation by means of His passion, which is that out of death.[31]

For Irenaeus the whole epic of Adam and Eve, from creation through to the fall, is the content of the sixth day of creation. But their state before the fall is that characterized by 'an innocent and childlike mind'. This state, according to Irenaeus, precluded any conception or knowledge of 'anything, of that which by wickedness through lusts and shameful desires is born in the soul'. The importance of the exact wording of this statement can be missed. What is determinative here is the phrase 'by wickedness'. Man, as created, is neither wicked nor cognizant of and familiar with wickedness. The wickedness to which Irenaeus refers is that which comes upon the first humans from without, and this is part of the consistent view of Irenaeus that the apportionment of blame for the fall has to be directed at the source of that wickedness primarily, and only in the second place – and this with reservations and qualifications – to Adam and Eve. This, again, will be considered in the comments on the following sections.

This state of childlike innocence is theirs because they are 'entire, preserving their own nature'. That is to say, they enjoyed the perfect integrity of human being, what it really is in itself as it is truly itself in its relation to God. That is why Irenaeus speaks next of the fact that they were such and had this, since the breath of life, breathed on them at their making by God, is that breath which knows no base thing, being so far removed from such. It is this breath which seems to be synonymous with 'spirit' in Irenaeus's thought, which, as we have noted already in the comments on Section 2,[32] is the bond between humanity and God, holding body and soul in their unity in a contingent relation to and from him as their Creator and preserving the integrity of human being in the creative purpose of God in that relation. Hence, wickedness has no part in this relation of humanity to God in that state in Paradise, and humanity can be unashamed in the purity it has in that undisturbed relation which it has both with God and within itself.

But because the creature, again as has been noted before, is less than the Creator, and has its integrity, that is, what it really is in the identity and character which God has given it, only within that contingent bond, the constraints of that bond have to be safeguarded. For this reason God gives his creature a commandment to preserve it as it really is in itself. The limitations imposed by that command reflect the limitations of the creature as creature, and therefore its need to observe that it holds everything from God in his grace and loving-kindness in creating and sustaining and fulfilling it in relation to him.[33] The command is given to preserve humanity from the consequences of thinking that it possesses an autonomy, destroying its true contingent relation to God whereby it lives and moves and has its being – the idea that it can thereby exist as, for, through and by itself. It is the source and consequences of that self-ascribed autonomy with which the following sections deal.

Notes

1 Justin Martyr: *Apology* II:V.
2 Justin Martyr: *Dialogue with Trypho* CII.
3 Justin Martyr: *Ibid.* CLXI.
4 Justin Martyr: *Apology* I:6.
5 Justin Martyr: *Dialogue with Trypho* CXXVIII.
6 Irenaeus: cf. *Adversus Haereses* II:2:1–5.
7 Cf. Melito of Sardis: *Fragment* IV *On Faith.*
8 Irenaeus: *Fragment* LIII.
9 Irenaeus: *Fragment* LIV.
10 Papias: *Fragment* VII.
11 Irenaeus: *Adversus Haereses* III:16:6.
12 Hermas: *Vision* III:4:1.
13 Athenagoras: *A Plea for the Christians* XXIV.
14 Irenaeus: *Adversus Haereses* V:29:1.
15 Irenaeus: *Demonstration of the Apostolic Preaching* 17.
16 Irenaeus, *Adversus Haereses* III:23:6.
17 *Ibid.* I:4:1.
18 *Ibid.* I:5:2.
19 *Ibid.* III:15:2.
20 *Ibid.* V:5:1.
21 *Ibid.* IV:20:6.
22 Cf. Chapter 4, comments on Sections 3 cont. and 4, especially pp. 75ff.
23 Cf. Irenaeus: *Adversus Haereses* II:22:4–6.
24 Irenaeus: *Adversus Haereses* II:22:4.
25 *Ibid.* IV:20:4.
26 Robert Grosseteste: *De Cessatione Legalium* I:viii:7–13.
27 *Ibid.* I:viii:7–13.
28 Cf. Irenaeus: *Adversus Haereses* IV:4:3.
29 Irenaeus: *Demonstration of the Apostolic Preaching* 13.
30 Irenaeus: *Adversus Haereses* V:23:2.
31 *Ibid.* V:23:2.
32 Comments on Section 2, Chapter 2, especially pp. 46ff.
33 Comments on Sections 11 and 12, Chapter 7, pp. 108ff.

Chapter 9

Sections 16–17: The Fall and its Consequences

In the last chapter we noted three emphases of Irenaeus regarding issues concerning the responsibility for the fall of Adam and Eve[1] – the constancy of God towards humanity; second, the apportionment of blame for the fall; and third, that Adam and Eve, for Irenaeus, are the very epitome of repentance. While only the second of these is explicit in Section 16 of the *Demonstration*, it can only be understood in its context of the other two with which it is invariably coupled in *Adversus Haereses* when Irenaeus is expounding more fully his interpretation of the fall. It is noteworthy that here Irenaeus merely, as it were, states the facts of the biblical narrative of the fall in a very condensed manner, leaving a fuller exposition of it to be undertaken in the light of his understanding of the person, event and work of the Word made flesh in Sections 31ff. However, he here emphasizes God's apportionment of blame concerning the fall, which he does not do later in the *Demonstration*. So this is now examined in the light of the other two emphases.

First, then, the constancy of God towards humanity. Irenaeus takes care to note consistently throughout his works that after the fall, the Word and Spirit are still present with humanity. We have already cited his declaration that 'never at any time did Adam escape the hands of God'.[2] The whole context of that part of *Adversus Haereses* in which this is stated is an exposition of the love and fidelity of God towards his creature. Hence, again for example, the consequences of the fall have to be dealt with in a way that would ensure that 'neither justice should be infringed upon, nor the ancient handiwork of God go to destruction'.[3] This loyalty of God towards humanity is emphasized by the constant repetition throughout *Adversus Haereses* that creation, and particularly humanity within it, is God's *own possession*. The whole dispensation of the Word made flesh is the love and constancy of God towards humanity.

Moreover, though man has been turned out of Paradise, God has provided that which is paradise-like, parallel in all its benefits to the first Paradise, but with these made appropriate to the present condition of humanity and its need.

> For the church has been planted as a garden (paradisium) in this world; therefore says the Spirit of God, Thou mayest freely eat from every tree of the garden, that is, Eat ye from every scripture of the Lord; but ye shall not eat with an uplifted mind, nor touch any heretical discord. For these men profess themselves to have the knowledge of good and evil; and set their own impious minds above the God who made them. They therefore form opinions on what is beyond the limits of understanding. For this cause also the apostle says: Be not wise beyond what is fitting to be wise, but be wise prudently: that we may not be cast forth by eating of the 'knowledge' of these men (that

> knowledge which knows more than it should do) from the paradise of life. Into this paradise the Lord has introduced those who obey his call, 'summing up in Himself all things which are in heaven and are on earth'; but the things in heaven are spiritual, while those on earth constitute the dispensation of human nature. These things, therefore, He recapitulated in Himself; by uniting man to the Spirit, and causing the Spirit to dwell with man, He is Himself made the head of the Spirit, and gives the Spirit to be the head of man: for through Him we see, and hear, and speak.[4]

The preparative for this paradise was the patriarchs, the prophets, the law, the whole epic of the old covenant. Irenaeus is insistent that both covenants, the old and the new, are 'of one and the same substance .... But one and the same householder produced both covenants, the Word of God, our Lord Jesus Christ, who spoke with Moses and Abraham'.[5] And again, he describes the old covenant as: 'a matter of the correction of man and the probation of all'.[6] The old covenant is inseparable from the new and is the indispensable background to the church as this paradise. The institution of the old covenant is the firm ground upon which the gospels rest,[7] and the hinge upon which the old covenant passes into the new in unbroken succession with regard to the substance of both, is the proclaimer of that substance, John the Baptist who 'himself did hold the place of both prophet and apostle'. For

> John did both announce (Christ's coming) beforehand, in like manner as did the other (prophets), and actually saw Him when He came, and pointed Him out, and persuaded many to believe on Him .... For this is to be more than a prophet, because 'first apostles, secondarily prophets'; but all things from one and the same God Himself.[8]

This paradise of God which is the church was prepared for, and foundationally set out, in God's dealings with the people of Israel, both Israel and the church pointing in their respective ways to their substance, of σκοπος, of the Word made flesh, the one in pointing towards the coming event under the presence of the Word and the prophetic Spirit, the other to the fulfilment of that in the incarnation of the self-same Word and in the power of that self-same Spirit. Much of Book IV of *Adversus Haereses* from the beginning is occupied with this theme.

That self-same Word who talked to Adam in the garden Himself provides this paradise where is His truth in the Spirit. And this self-same Word who talked to Adam in the garden is the voice of God who searched Adam out after his folly and still searches out humanity in its lost state. From the first man onwards, despite Adam's disobedience and the consequent state of the whole human race, God maintains faithfulness and loving-kindness towards his handiwork of all humanity.

> Wherefore also the scripture, pointing out what should come to pass, says that when Adam had hidden himself because of his disobedience, the Lord came to him at eventide, called him forth, and said Where are thou? That means that in the last times the very same Word of God came to call man, reminding him of his doings, living in which he had been hidden from the Lord. For just as at that time God spoke to Adam at eventide, searching him out, so, in the last times, by means of the same voice, searching out his posterity, He has visited them.[9]

The theme of the constancy of God towards Adam, and his regard for Adam, is further strengthened and underlined by Irenaeus's insistence that Adam himself is saved by Christ. It is this which is a fundamental point in his doctrine of recapitulation. Christ's saving act means that he sums up in himself the whole of the human race – without exception. His argument is unambiguous, and proceeds through clearly defined steps. These, forming Irenaeus's first emphasis on the constancy of God towards humanity, and the substance of the other two emphases with which we are dealing in these two sections, are set out in the third book of *Adversus Haereses*.

Had God turned his back on humanity after the fall, then the serpent would have triumphed. God had created man to live and therefore God does not abandon his handiwork to death. God, in that case 'would have been conquered, and the wickedness of the serpent would have prevailed over the will of God'.[10] God, states Irenaeus, is 'invincible and longsuffering', and thus establishes the old covenant as a preparation for the bringing in of the new man in whom the old man of our Adamic humanity is re-created. The new man is Christ, the Word (who made Adam) made flesh. But if all humanity should be so saved by its recapitulation and therefore transformation in and by Christ, it is necessary, Irenaeus insists, that the very recapitulation of the human race, Adam himself, should be saved.

Unless Adam is himself saved by Christ, he argues, then humanity in its totality is not saved, and some of the handiwork of God is lost and God thereby thwarted.

> It was necessary, therefore, that the Lord, coming to the lost sheep, and making recapitulation of such a comprehensive dispensation, and seeking after His own handiwork, should save that very man who had been created after His image and likeness, that is, Adam . . .[11]

Adam is 'the ancient formation',[12] the 'original handiwork'.[13] All humanity is bound in the lump of Adam, for he is the determinative of the whole race, the 'head' in whom all humanity is recapitulate. Thus, in his constancy towards humanity, the Word at his incarnation, comprises

> in Himself that original man out of whom woman was fashioned, in order that, as our species went down to death through a vanquished man, so we may ascend to life again through a victorious one; and as through a man death received the palm against us, so again by a man we may receive the palm against death.[14]

We have noted in the comments on Section 11 and 12 in Chapter 7 (pp. 101ff) the parallelism of Irenaeus between the virgin dust out of which Adam was formed and the virgin birth of our Lord as the second Adam. This parallelism, like the one of Mary and Eve, used by Irenaeus as a secondary attendant parallel merely to point to this primary one, heightens the recapitulative theme of the Word saving the humanity which first fell as a integral part of the constancy of God towards the total human race. In Irenaeus's theology, all humanity, which is only humanity in Adam the patriarchal recapitulation of the race, and therefore not excluding Adam in whom it is included, is the recipient of that faithful loving-kindness of God in and by and through and with the recapitulation of Adam by the Word made flesh. Adam recapitulates humanity, and Christ recapitulates Adam.

> For it is too absurd to maintain, that he [Adam] who was so deeply injured by the enemy, and was the first to suffer captivity, was not rescued by Him who conquered the enemy, but that his children were – those whom he had begotten in the same captivity. Neither would the enemy appear to be as yet conquered if the old spoils remained with him . . . . For God is neither devoid of power nor of justice, who has afforded help to man, and restored him to his own liberty.[15]

In the midst of this argument from *Adversus Haereses*, Irenaeus instances the illustration of a people conquered and led away captive, who, in their captivity, beget children. Should the captors in turn be conquered and the children born in that former captivity be released, their fathers' cause thereby being avenged, it would not be equitable, reasons Irenaeus, for only the children to be released and the parents who were captured originally, and suffered that act, to be left in bondage.

Irenaeus becomes more pointed in his argument that Adam is saved.

> Therefore, when man has been liberated, What is written shall come to pass, Death is swallowed up in victory. O death, where is thy victory? O death, where is thy sting?[16]

> This could not be said with justice if that man over whom death did first obtain dominion were not set free. For his salvation is death's destruction. When the Lord therefore vivifies man, that is, Adam, death is at the same time destroyed.[17]

So adamant is Irenaeus that the credibility of salvation depends on Adam's salvation in his recapitulation by the Word made flesh, that he is quite prepared to criticize Tatian in no uncertain measure and force:

> All speak falsely, therefore, who disallow (Adam's) salvation, shutting themselves out from life forever, in that they do not believe that the sheep which had perished has been found. For if it has not been found, the whole human race is still held in perdition. False, therefore, is that man who first started this idea, or rather, this ignorance and blindness – Tatian[18] . . . . Thus also do those who disallow Adam's salvation gain nothing except this, that they render themselves heretics and apostates from the truth, and show themselves patrons of the serpent and of death.[19]

Thus for Irenaeus, the decree of Adam's salvation is a fundamental necessity for the true understanding of redemption. Tatian on the other hand, was quite prepared to consign Adam, not only to perdition, but to the state of a demon. This, for Irenaeus would radically call into question the constancy of God towards creation and humanity, thereby detracting from the nature of the Being of God.

Of significance for the emphasis on the constancy of God in Irenaean thought, is the statement in Section 16 that Adam is removed by God out of Paradise but 'on the way to Paradise'. J. Armitage Robinson thinks that the phrase is suggested by Genesis III:24 which narrates the expulsion but speaks of the angel guarding 'the way of the tree of life'. Whether or not this is so – and if it is so it strengthens the point – it would suggest, bearing in mind Irenaeus's insistence that humanity advances towards God in his Word and Spirit, the goal of Paradise is therefore not out of sight, and in perhaps noting this in this way, Irenaeus introduces the fact of God's constancy towards humanity and the objective He sets before humanity in placing it so. God expels humanity from Paradise, but nevertheless places humanity towards Paradise and on the way to it. It is God who places Adam there, so Adam is still within the same hands of God, the Word and the Spirit, who placed him in Paradise at the first.

Second: the apportionment of blame for the fall. Adam is portrayed very much by Irenaeus in Section 17 as the victim of Satan's jealousy over the favoured position man enjoys in relation to the Creator. What is expanded here is not primarily the judgment of God on Adam, but the divine dealing with the serpent. It is, in Irenaeus's view, to the serpent that God foremostly directs his wrath, and on the serpent that he first pronounces his judgment. The serpent 'carried and conveyed the Slanderer', that is, was the vehicle of that jealous angel, 'the angel hidden and concealed in him, even . . . Satan'.

The recapitulation of Adam by the Word at his incarnation, and the salvation of Adam thereby, involves the recapitulation by the Word of 'that ancient and primary enmity against the serpent'.[20] This involves the fulfilling of God's promise to Adam that his seed would bruise the head of the serpent. Irenaeus construes this treading upon and crushing the serpent in terms of our Lord's active and passive obedience to the Father. His passive obedience is that in the Adamic flesh and nature He assumes at the incarnation, He does no sin. His active obedience, in this particular action, is his temptations in the wilderness whereby he cancels (in all the parallelism Irenaeus can muster) the stategy and events of the serpent in the garden. As we will see later, the active and passive obedience of the Word made flesh is exhibited above all on the cross. But here, Irenaeus is interested in the battle between the Word and Satan on behalf of humanity, and, it is clear, Irenaeus by this part of *Adversus Haereses*,[21] is laying the blame for Adam's fall, not on Adam primarily, but on Satan as the cause. Man is depicted, again, as being victimized. Thus, after the recitation of each step in the episode of the temptation by which our Lord cancelled out the work of the serpent in the garden –

> The Hebrew word 'Satan' signifies an apostate. And thus, vanquishing him for the third time [the last temptation], He spurned him from Him finally as being conquered out of the law [note that for Irenaeus, picking up our Lord's quotations from the law to parry Satan, Christ uses the law, the commands of God, as his instrument of conquest here]; and there was done away that infringement of God's commandment which had occurred in Adam, by means of the precept of the law, which the Son of man observed who did not transgress the commandment of God.[22]

The three steps of the progress of the Word in being tempted by Satan in this part of *Adversus Haereses* are undertaken by the Word not drawing the means of confounding Satan 'from any other source than from the words of the law, and made use of the Father's commandment as a help towards the destruction and confusion of the apostate angel'. The ὀιχονομια of the Word made flesh involves the assumption of the ὀιχονομια of the old covenant, the constraint of humanity by God as the constancy of God towards humanity within the consequences of the fall, as the strategy for the freeing of humanity and its restoration into the liberty of the children of God.[23] This is the fulfilment of the law by the Word made flesh.

The three steps in this fulfilment in the temptations of Christ are first: 'Man does not live by bread alone'.[24] The context of this in Irenaeus's account is our Lord hungering for forty days, after the pattern of Moses and Elijah. This showed that he was really man, and also gave Satan the opportunity to tempt him with that food that was not from God – stones into bread. The parallelism of Irenaeus comes into full play here, for it is noted that as our first parents corrupted humanity by eating the forbidden fruit, so our Lord overturned this by fasting.

The second is our Lord's rebuke out of the law 'Thou shalt not tempt the Lord thy God',[25] in reply to Satan's use of scripture ('thus concealing a falsehood under the guise of scripture as is done by all the heretics') to tempt him to cast himself down from the pinnacle of the Temple since the angels had charge over him. Satan produced such reasoning from himself – as indeed he had done with Adam and Eve and so infecting them likewise. This reasoning concerns the temptation to believe that the mind is autonomous, the measure of all. It consists in paying lip-service to God, an attitude which is manifested by treating God solely as a disinterested objective factor. So Irenaeus can remark about the devil's reasoning to Adam and Eve: '. . . in the garden of God he disputed about God, as if God were not there'.[26] This pride of reasoning, says Irenaeus, is countered by our Lord's humility, and by the fact that he is the very presence of God though here as man.

The third step is 'Thou shalt worship the Lord God and Him only shalt thou serve'[27] in reply to the attempt to have Christ fall down and worship Satan, the latter claiming to have the patronage of all the kingdoms of the world and the glory of them in his gift. This is that temptation which is in the same vein as that to Adam and Eve to be themselves as gods. It is answered, indicates Irenaeus by the words of the One who quoted the law that God was the only God worthy of worship and service, and thus revealed the devil's apostasy by calling him 'Satan', and showing that Satan did not recognize him as that very God.

Irenaeus concludes:

> And justly is he led captive, who had led men unjustly into bondage; while man, who had been led captive in times past, was rescued from the grasp of his possessor, according to the tender mercy of God the Father, who had compassion upon His own handiwork, and gave to it salvation, restoring it by means of the Word – that is by Christ – in order that men might learn by actual proof that he receives incorruptibility not of himself, but by the free gift of God.[28]

The judgment of God in apportioning blame for the fall is decreed as condemnation on Satan, but is manifested for humanity as the loving-kindness of God in the law of grace. Irenaeus regards Satan as the perpetrator of the fall, man as the fallen victim from whom, as God's handiwork, the Creator's constancy has never been turned.

Another facet of the glancing off man of the judgment of God is the fact that the curse of God is directed, not to man primarily or even secondarily, strictly speaking, but to the serpent first, the earth second, and only as at a tangent, but nevertheless there, to man.

> Immediately after Adam had transgressed, as the scripture relates, (God) pronounced no curse against Adam personally, but against the ground, in reference to his works . . . . Man received as the punishment of his transgression, the toilsome task of tilling the earth, and to eat bread in the sweat of his face, and to return to the dust from whence he

> was taken . . . . But the curse in all its fullness fell on the serpent who had beguiled them. And God, it is declared, said to the serpent: Because thou has done this, cursed art thou above all cattle, and above all the beasts of the earth. And this same thing does the Lord also say in the Gospel to those who are found on the left hand: Depart from me, ye cursed, into everlasting fire which my Father hath prepared for the devil and his angels; indicating that eternal fire was not originally prepared for man, but for him who beguiled man, and caused him to offend.[29]

That there is judgment for those who turn from the constant grace of God and are thus serpentine, Irenaeus does not deny. But it is a judgment primarily against Satan into which they have cast themselves. The constancy of God's loving-kindness to humanity is Irenaeus's first and foremost concern in this second emphasis of his in a consideration of the question of responsibility for the fall and its consequences. This, however, is a matter not of the withdrawal of God's loving-kindness, but the fact that it is that loving-kindness in freeing humanity from Satan's captivity by his Word made flesh which they have of themselves rejected.

The third emphasis of Irenaeus in the matter of responsibility for the fall, is the repentance of Adam and Eve. The sense of sin, the realization of having done wrong, says Irenaeus, leads to repentance. He sees this sense and realization, and therefore the hallmarks of repentance in the action of Adam and Eve clothing themselves with fig leaves. The argument is that these leaves are irritants, and they thus clothe themselves with the garments of penitence.

> For having been beguiled by another under the pretext of immortality (Adam) is immediately seized with terror, and hides himself; not as if he were able to escape God; but in a state of confusion at having transgressed God's command, he feels unworthy to appear before, and converse with, God. Now, The fear of the Lord is the beginning of wisdom; the sense of sin leads to repentance, and God bestows His compassion upon those who are penitent. For (Adam) showed his repentance by his conduct through means of the girdle, covering himself with fig leaves, while there were many other leaves which would have irritated his body in a less degree. He, however, adopted dress appropriate to his disobedience, being awed by the fear of God . . . . Inasmuch as, he says, I have by disobedience lost the robe of sanctity which I had from the Spirit, I do now also acknowledge that I am deserving of a covering of this nature, which affords no gratification, but which gnaws and frets the body.[30]

By these three emphases, Irenaeus shows the compassion of God upon hapless humanity, and these sections of the *Demonstration* are within this movement. Here begins in Section 17 onwards, the long recitation of the epic of the salvation history of humanity – the dispensation of God for its redemption. Irenaeus's theology is essentially philanthropic.

Notes

1 Chapter 8, p. 118.
2 Irenaeus: *Adversus Haereses* V:1:3.
3 *Ibid.* V:1:1.
4 *Ibid.* V:20:2.

5 *Ibid.* IV:9:1.
6 *Ibid.* III:23:1.
7 *Ibid.* III:11:7.
8 *Ibid.* III:11:4.
9 *Ibid.* V:15:4.
10 *Ibid.* III:23:1.
11 *Ibid.*
12 E.g. *ibid.* III:18:7; IV:33:4; V:1:2, etc.
13 *Ibid.* V:14:2.
14 *Ibid.* V:21:1; cf. Irenaeus: *Demonstration of the Apostolic Preaching* 31.
15 Irenaeus: *Adversus Haereses* III:23:2.
16 I Corinthians XV:54, 55.
17 Irenaeus: *Contra Haereses* III:23:7.
18 Tatian: e.g. *Address to the Greeks* VII.
19 Irenaeus: *Adversus Haereses* III:23:8.
20 *Ibid.* V:21:1,2.
21 *Ibid.* V:21:1:2,.
22 *Ibid.* V:23:2.
23 *Ibid.* cf. V:21:3; V:22:1.
24 Deuteronomy VIII:3.
25 Deuteronomy VI:16.
26 Irenaeus: *Adversus Haereses* V:23:1.
27 Cf. Exodus XX:5; Deuteronomy V:9, VI:13.
28 Irenaeus: *Adversus Haereses* V:21:3.
29 *Ibid.* III:23:3.
30 *Ibid.* III:23:5.

Chapter 10

Sections 18–42: The History and Fulfilment of the Blessings of God (1)

Sections 18–24: Adam's Seed to Abraham's Seed

The large remainder of the *Demonstration* seems to fall into four parts, each determined by its respective emphasis. This first part, comprising the sections enumerated above, is introduced by Section 18 with its theme stated in Sections 19, 20 and 21.

The introduction consists of the first and last comments in Section 18 – sin and death, entering through Adam's transgression, now show their collective face in the expansion of wickedness engorging the whole human race until only a remnant possessed 'a very small seed of righteousness'. Evil was rampant and righteousness 'diminished and enfeebled'. In the previous section, Irenaeus had noted that the same apostate spirit who tempted Adam and Eve was responsible for this expansion of evil, first infecting Cain with it by employing a similar strategy to that which he held before Adam, stirring up Cain with his jealousy, envy and malice.[1] Cain, as a result of the murder of his righteous brother, was cursed by God, and in this story of Cain, according to Irenaeus, is the pattern setting the future lamentable truth whereby righteousness can be persecuted and slain by unrighteousness. Thus, Cain's descendants were like him who begot them.

The primal sin, the result of which was the fracturing of humanity's contingent relation to and from God, that is, as it were, the primary and determinative vertical relation, now manifests itself horizontally in the sundering of relations within humanity itself. The relational aspect of human being, which is its determinative factor by which it is truly human being, is assaulted in all its dimensions.

In order to explain the expansion and success of wickedness introduced by Satan, Irenaeus traces this to the mingling of the apostate angels with humanity with what Irenaeus calls 'illicit unions'. This he no doubt gleaned from the book Enoch VII:1 and VIII:1 (as later did Tertullian who has the same observations). This tradition of later Judaism interprets Genesis VI:2 with its mention of the 'sons of God' taking wives of 'the daughters of men', and these 'sons of God' are interpreted by Irenaeus to be the apostate angels fallen from heaven in the judgment of God. In *Adversus Haereses*, Irenaeus contrasts the righteousness of Enoch with the state of the fallen angels, and is clearly making a reference to the contents of the book Enoch:

> Enoch, too, pleasing God without circumcision, discharged the office of God's legate to the angels although he was a man, and was translated, and until now stands as a witness of the last judgment of God, because the angels when they had transgressed, fell to the earth for judgment, but the man pleasing (to God) was translated for salvation.[2]

These fallen angels in their solidarity to Satan are the cause of the expansion of evil introduced at the fall of the first man in Irenaeus's view. What they bring to humanity are gifts which are designed to advance humanity's self-enhancement and autonomy, and therefore to drive it even further from its contingent relation to God. But what interests Irenaeus is the extent of evil and the subsequent history of the human race. This topic is his introduction.

The theme of this part, how he deals with this topic, is then developed. It revolves round the history of those whom God has respectively blessed and cursed, but particularly deals with the blessing of Shem and Japheth, the sons of Noah. This is put against the background of the cursing of Ham, the other son. In fact the cursing in the Hebrew text is clearly recorded to be that placed on Canaan, the son of Ham. Ham himself is not recorded as being so cursed by God. In Section 20 Armitage Robinson notes that Irenaeus used the Septuagint text, which, in some manuscripts renders a different reading from that of the Hebrew text. The Hebrew text of Genesis IX:25 reads: 'Cursed be Canaan; a servant of servants shall he be unto his brethren'. Some versions of the Septuagint read 'the child of Ham' (that is, Canaan) and others 'Ham the child'. The Armenian translator of the *Demonstration* here opts for 'Ham the child', and reflects in this the gist of Irenaeus's overall meaning in working out this general theme of those who are blessed and those who are cursed. The importance of this is that Irenaeus sees the subsequent history of the human race in its relation to God as the unfolding of the original blessing and cursing which determines the relations of the respective races descended variously from their favoured or rejected forefather. These three sons of Noah are the only surviving post-diluvian ancestors from which all succeeding generations spring. They are therefore determinally patriarchal, and in their state is the state of all mankind bound. There is an implicit recapitulation in Irenaeus's treatment of the three sons of Noah, here, in which all humanity is seen as, not only the physical offspring of the three, but having its significance throughout its subsequent history, bound up variously in their blessed state as forefathers of nations, or in the cursed state of Ham's children. That Ham should be regarded as the one cursed in the view of Irenaeus, I would suggest, is not a bare following of one version of the Septuagint text, but also because the three sons of Noah are taken together in the matter of blessing and cursing as a more expressive way appropriate to Irenaeus's general mode of thought. In this thought entities are gathered together to signify a recapitulative significance – in this case the treatment of them as recapitulative forefathers of the various races. To ignore Ham and introduce Canaan his son as the recipient of the curse throughout the generations of Ham's progeny, would upset the recapitulative personages in their collective balance.

Irenaeus gives a list of the races descended from Ham, drawn from the Old Testament narratives and from those noted in the recitation of nationalities who heard the Gospel first proclaimed at the outpouring of the Holy Spirit on the apostles at Pentecost in Acts II:9–11. This would seem to be a deliberate addition in support of his thesis regarding the working out of the original blessing and cursing, and how both are subsumed in the events of the Word made flesh. Even those long cursed (and he notes at the end of section 20 that 'the curse is of long duration for the ungodly') come under this resolution, and play their part finally in, the dispensation of God through the incarnation of the Word.

The initial importance of the blessing of Shem is set out in the opening part of the section and then its significance is developed. Shem's blessing is the blessing of Israel, and here Irenaeus magnifies it as the source of the blessing of Abraham, and so projects it into the significance of Israel's history. Japheth's blessing recorded in Genesis IX:27, is that 'God shall enlarge unto Japheth, and he shall dwell in the house of Shem, and Ham shall be his servant'. Again, Irenaeus uses the Septuagint version which replaces 'Canaan' in the Hebrew text with 'Ham' Japheth's blessing is centred on the Gentile nations and the Christian Church gathered from the peoples who are 'called'. In that calling of the Gentiles at the appearing of Christ, Japheth blossomed forth – that is, his blessing is fulfilled. Irenaeus's use of the text of Genesis IX:27 is significant in that the two blessings of Shem and Japheth are not separated into two distinct and unrelated entities in their respective fulfilments, Israel on the one hand and the Gentiles on the other. The citing of the text is commensurate with his insistence that the two covenants, the old and the new, Israel and the Church, are 'of one and the same substance',[3] for Japheth, that is the calling of the Gentiles in the Christian Church, dwells in the house of Shem, that is, the Church dwells in the inheritance of Israel as the blessing of the firstborn.

To this phrase 'the calling of the Gentiles', we will return shortly. But here we may note that Irenaeus's reasoning follows and differs from the reasoning of Justin Martyr on the same topic. Justin Martyr does not exhibit the same mode of thought as Irenaeus which formulates and finds in recapitulative patterns the significance of developments in the dispensation of God for the epic of the human race. Justin Martyr, in his treatment of the blessing of Shem and Japheth and the cursing of Ham, interprets the Septuagint version of Genesis to read 'the child of Ham', rather than 'Ham the child', the latter exposition being adopted, as has been noted, by Irenaeus. Justin is quite content to ignore the slight difficulty that it was Ham who, having committed the sin of being indiscreet about his father's nakedness, should earn a curse on himself, rather than it being pronounced on his child, as is suggested by the Hebrew text and some versions of the Septuagint text. He uses the somewhat strained device of pointing out that

> the Spirit of prophecy would not curse the son (Ham) that had been blessed by God along with (his brothers). But since the punishment of the sin would cleave to the whole descent of the son (Ham) that mocked at his father's nakedness, he made the curse originate with his son.[4]

Justin Martyr's main thrust here is to emphasize that even the curse of Canaan, the child of Ham, is removed by Christ, it clinging only to those who persist in idolatry, and who therefore are the spiritual descendants of Canaan so cursed.

He is more detailed than Irenaeus in spelling out the relation between the descendant races of Shem and Japheth in their respective blessings

> Now in what he (Noah) said, he foretold that the descendants of Shem would keep in retention the property and dwellings of Canaan: and again, that the descendants of Japheth would take in possession the property of which Shem's descendants had dispossessed Canaan's descendants; and spoil the descendants of Shem even as they had plundered the sons of Canaan. And listen to the way in which it has so come to pass. For you, who have derived your lineage from Shem, invaded the territory of the sons of Canaan by the will of

> God; and you have possessed it. And it is manifested that the sons of Japheth, having invaded you in turn by the judgment of God, have taken your land from you, and have possessed it . . . and as the offspring of Shem were decreed first to possess the dwellings of Canaan, and the offspring of Japheth were predicted as in turn receiving the same possessions, and to the two peoples there was the one people of Canaan handed over for servants; so Christ has come according to the power given Him from the Almighty Father, and summoning men to friendship, and blessing, and repentance and dwelling together, has promised . . . that there shall be a future possession for all the saints in this same land. And hence all men everywhere, whether bond or free, who believe in Christ and recognize the truth in His own words and those of His prophets, know that they shall be with Him in that land, and inherit everlasting and incorruptible good.[5]

However, the general pattern of developed argument is, in its conclusion, broadly the same for both Justin Martyr and Irenaeus: the two blessed and the one cursed are the progenitors of three races. Those cursed are swallowed up in service by Israel (from Shem) in covenant with God; Israel in turn, in the dispensation of God, is subsumed by the new Israel, the Church (from Japheth in the calling of the Gentiles). The cursed who still remain are those who resist the truth as it is in Christ, who offers repentance and redemption to all, bond and free.

'The calling of the Gentiles' is a phrase which Irenaeus uses at various points in several discussions or conclusions. It is found in Sections 28, 41, 42, 89, 91 and here where it appears in the form 'the calling from among the Gentiles'. Here it also appears in the context of the fulfilment of the blessing of Japheth, which Irenaeus sees as the fact that Japheth has 'blossomed forth' in the 'enlargement of the Gentiles'. In Section 28 the phrase is used almost as an *aide-mémoire* to keep the reader's mind fixed on the development of the contention still to be resolved. In Section 41 it is a foretaste of the conclusion of that argument which is fully stated in Section 42. In Sections 89 and 91 it is reintroduced as a summing up process for the final statement of Irenaeus on the whole matter of the faith.

Irenaeus sees a continuity of development and a recapitulation. The continuity of the acts of God, his mercy and his judgment, is spread throughout the history of the peoples. The recapitulation, where that continuity is fulfilled in all the apparent exigencies of history, is found in the advent of our Lord. It is this twofold usage of biblical texts as suggesting both this continuity and this summing up, and the search for them to do so, I would venture, which stamps the character of Irenaeus's biblical theology. The interacting strands of the acts of God in his relation to humanity, spread throughout the history of the nations, can only be appreciated in their divine logic, and ultimate sense made of them, when they are summed up in the personal interaction of God gathering up his own handiwork in the incarnation. This is both the deployment and the goal of Irenaus's theological way of working.

Both the particularity of the strands of that continuity, and their convergence in the incarnation of the Word, are reflected in the statement in Section 21, that the 'Father of all' should be to Shem (that is Israel) 'a peculiar possession of worship'. This is a preliminary statement of God's choice of Israel for universal purposes.

The universal purposes are stressed in the opening sentence of Section 22 that 'God made a covenant with all the world'. This is the reason for the blessings and cursings of the offspring of Noah. That this is a new era in the history of humanity, with three patriarchs of the human race, is signified by the comment that God

> changed the food of men, giving them leave to eat flesh: for from Adam the first-formed until the Flood men ate only of seeds and the fruit of trees, and to eat flesh was not permitted to them. But since the three sons of Noah were the beginning of a race of men, God blessed them for multiplication and increase . . . . According to this covenant the race of men multiplied, springing up from the seed of the three.[6]

This is a covenant in which the relation of humanity to the rest of creation is seen in terms of the fracturing of the created orders which occurred at the fall and of which God takes stock. It is with creation in this state, nevertheless, that God makes 'a covenant with all the world, even with every living thing of animals and of men, that He would no more destroy with a flood all that grew upon the earth'.[7] The lethal competition, as it were, within creation is noted. This is what it has become, but it remains, in this covenant, under the overarching scrutiny and containment of God. Thus, after the prohibition of consuming blood as the life with regard to animals as humanity's food in this covenant, God demonstrates the moral strictures concerning the whole question of life as seen within the estranged orders of creation in their shattered state, in that with regard to the blood of man, he 'will require (it) also at the hand of all beasts and at the hand of man. Whoso sheddeth a man's blood, in return for his blood shall it be shed'.[8] Then comes what appears to be a doctrinal interjection concerning the image of God. It is not Irenaeus would seem to revert to what he has written in Section 11, and here reminds that man is made the image of God, and that the image of God is the Son, after whose image humanity was created. He does so, first of all because the text of Genesis IX:1–6a, in the Hebrew version, but more emphatically so in the Septuagint, goes on to add the fact that the image of God is the pattern for the creation of man. That is, Irenaeus is following in obedient commentary the flow of the biblical text. The scriptural note of the image of God in the making of man in its account of this covenant of God, is the prompt for Irenaeus to use it in a particular way in his exegesis of the part this covenant plays in the whole sweep of God's acts towards and for creation.

But second, in the flow of Irenaeus's argument and development of the epic of this covenant with humanity in its beginning anew here in the three patriarchal figures of the sons of Noah, the mention of the original identity of man comes as a reminder that all this history, of which a new era here begins, is still linked inseparably to, and profoundly bracketed with, the one who, as the Son of God, is Himself the Image of God. This is underlined here, in terms of the fact that the Son will, at the end of all the times – of which this covenant is a significant and determinative part – demonstrate that humanity was made to be conformable to the image which the Son is.

The full significance of this, in terms of definite fundamentals concerning Christ's human nature, is set out in *Adversus Haereses*.[9] It is also expanded, but in terms of the mode and effect of the work of the Person of Christ, later in the *Demonstration* in Sections 32ff.

The argument in *Adversus Haereses* centres round the observation that our Lord recapitulates in his own Person the reality of humanity as the *original handiwork* of the Father. This has certain ramifications. Irenaeus follows that principle, later to be concisely formulated and applied in the Apollinarian controversy, as 'not assumed means not healed'. That is to say, the incarnation means the assuming by the Word of that which is indeed the reality of human existence in its totality, not only all that makes the human being a human being,[10] but also that which is the state of human existence in its need of redemption. The Word assumes human flesh and nature, body and soul, where it lies under the judgment of God, that is, fallen flesh and nature. In this, as Irenaeus points out,[11] our Lord did no sin nor was deceit found in His soul. This is how He breaks the mould of fallen Adamic flesh, but to do so the Word has to take it to himself at His incarnation that He might re-create it in his active and passive obedience to the Father.

> But now the case stands thus, that the Word has saved that which really was humanity which had perished, effecting by means of Himself that communion which should be held with it, and seeking its salvation.[12]

This argument in *Adversus Haereses* is worked out in the context of a comment on St Paul's observation[13] that 'flesh and blood cannot inherit the kingdom of God'. Irenaeus points out that the apostle is not talking about the *substance* of flesh and blood. These are indeed the substance of human being and the object of God's redeeming act in the incarnation. This is why the Word assumes them, that there may be a transformation whereby what is

> mortal and corruptible becomes immortal and incorruptible, not after its own proper substance [that is, not of its own nature and ability], but after the mighty working of the Lord who is able to invest the mortal with immortality and the corruptible with incorruption.[14]

The Word assumes flesh, for that is what needs to be saved, otherwise, Irenaeus notes, He would not have become flesh. Likewise,

> if the blood of the righteous were not to be inquired after, the Lord would certainly not have had blood. But inasmuch as blood cries out from the beginning, God said to Cain when he had slain his brother, 'The voice of thy brother's blood cries out to Me'. And as their blood will be inquired after, He said to those with Noah, 'For your blood of your souls will I require, [even] from the hand of all beasts', and again, 'Whoever will shed man's blood, it shall be shed for his blood'. In like manner, too, the Lord did say to those who should afterwards shed His blood, 'All righteous blood shall be required which is shed upon the earth .... Verily, I say unto you, All these things shall come upon this generation'. He thus points out the recapitulation that should take place in His own Person of the effusion of blood from the beginning, of all the righteous men and of the prophets, and that by means of Himself there should be a requisition of their blood. Now this [blood] could not be required unless it also had the capability of being saved; nor would the Lord have summed up these things in Himself, unless He had Himself been made flesh and blood after the way of the original formation, saving in His own Person at the end that which had in the beginning perished in Adam.[15]

The recapitulation of Adam by the Word assuming flesh and blood means the assumption of the whole human race in its condition. That condition is its Adamic condition, that is, its fallen state with all the attendant woes which characterize the plight of human existence. The post-fall condition of humanity has, as one of its tragedies, the fact that righteousness is persecuted by unrighteousness. It is this tragedy which our Lord assumes at his incarnation and manifests in his crucifixion in the totality of his recapitulative aim and end. The blood of the righteous crying out is acknowledged by God in this covenant with Noah and his patriarchal sons; it is this, as a hallmark of fallen human nature, which the Word takes to himself as part of the reality of his human nature.

Hence the taking up by Irenaeus of the biblical text with its mention of the image of God, and his comment here which ties this 'covenant with all the world' into the Being of the Word made flesh as its resolution and fulfilment. It introduces the framework of the epic of Israel leading into the Church in which he is engaged in this part of the *Demonstration* as that which moves under the compulsion of the Word made flesh. That framework he expands and fills out later.

In section 23, he continues his narrative of this epic, recounting the megalomania of humanity, aided by everyone having one language and therefore capable of inculcating the whole race with myth concerning itself as to its glory and ability, the sign of which was the building of the tower of Babel.

> They sought means thereby to go up to heaven, and to be able to leave their work as a memorial to those men who should come after them . . . . And the boldness of their audacity went forward as they were all of one mind and consent, and by means of one speech they served the purpose of their desire.[16]

The true unity of humanity lies not in itself, nor can it be maintained by itself. It lies, in the view of Irenaeus, in humanity's relation with God. It is as humanity is in a 'community of union' with God through and in His Word and thereby partakes of the image according to which it was made and in which it finds its identity, that it finds its unity of origin, of nature and of purpose and fulfilment. The episode of the Tower of Babel is an attempt by humanity to establish, safeguard and proclaim a false unity which has no ground but which it has sought to establish out of itself and in its self-awareness. In so doing, it can only thrust itself and break itself against the dispensation of God.

This is what happens. But the subsequent scattering of humanity and its division into 'groups and companies' based on the respective languages by which God had confounded their common speech, and the arising of distinctive tribes as a result, is still overarched by the blessing on the two sons of Noah and the cursing of the third as a more fundamental and determinative identification of more general human groupings.

What Irenaeus is doing here is beginning with the broad sweep of all humanity under the delusion of Adam. He now begins to narrow it down in terms of the sons of Noah. Their respective blessing and cursing from God forms a contrapuntal movement in all that follows. But the *cantus firmus* in this movement, as we shall see, is the image of God as expressed in the Word made flesh and humanity's relation to this image, as the fulfilment of this blessing and cursing. It is this constantly repeated and heard theme which gives direction and meaning to the whole movement of this unfolding history.

Irenaeus begins first with Shem and his blessing as he was the first son to be blessed. He notes that the race of Shem dwelt in the east 'and held the land of the

Chaldeans'. By this mention he swiftly narrows down the whole story for by it he is able to introduce Abraham in Ur of the Chaldees. The immensity of what he has mentioned already – the 'Father of all' and the covenant made 'by this God with all the world' – is now concentrated, but not annulled, for it is the same God and the same divine will, in the intensity of God's dealings with Abraham and Abraham's relation to this God as the recipient of His promises.

Abraham sincerely seeks for God, but he is only able so to feel and do because in the blessing of his ancestor Shem God gave Himself to be to Shem and His posterity, as Irenaeus previously points out in Section 21, 'a peculiar possession of worship'. This is not a search initiated in the piety of Abraham. Rather, Irenaeus perceives the righteousness of Abraham to be a result of his binding into the blessing of Shem and God's gracious self-giving therein. Even this is not enough and Irenaeus underlines the fact that God takes pity on Abraham and appears to him, making himself known by the Word 'as by a beam of light'. Abraham, and the blessing of Shem, is enlightened within the light of God, and that blessing begins to unfold towards its fulfilment.

The blessing does so in its relation to the cursing of Ham. The land to which God leads Abraham, later to be named Judaea, is occupied, it significantly is noted by Irenaeus, by the descendants of Ham. Their land God promises to Abraham and his posterity. Thus, in Irenaeus's eyes, the blessing of Shem and the cursing of Ham begin to be worked out in the dispensation of God in his calling of Abraham and in the promises given. This is further interpreted by the swift movement in Irenaeus's treatment of the biblical narrative to the introduction of the sojourn in, and exodus from Egypt, and the permanent settlement of Abraham's progeny in the land promised to him. This he introduces in the conversation he sees God having with Abraham foretelling all this. He concludes this introduction by saying, regarding the progeny of Abraham, 'that God would judge that race which brought his seed into bondage'.

The significance of this is that the Egyptians are regarded by Irenaeus as the children of Ham.[17] This last comment is set over against the exaltation of the seed of Abraham in Irenaeus's statement on the biblical account of God bringing forth Abraham to view the night sky and to see that his seed will be as the immeasurable multitude of the stars. That is, Shem in his blessing triumphs over Ham the accursed, and does so in a threefold manner. First, the Egyptians as children of Ham are judged and routed; second, the seven tribes, likewise of Ham's descent, occupying the land to be called Judaea, the land of Abraham's promise, are despoiled and displaced; and third, the seed of Abraham will fulfil Shem's blessing in a particular way. As we will see later, Irenaeus interprets them as doing so in their relation to the blessing of Japheth, the two blessings intermingling in the one purpose of God in bringing into being the one true Israel which will be vindicated over against all who oppose that purpose and that end as the children of Ham. The fulfilling of the promise made to Abraham regarding his seed which would be as the stars of heaven is in the universality of Christ's recapitulation of all humanity and his constitution of those who are 'lights in the world'.[18]

Abraham therefore, in Irenaeus's biblical theology, stands as a pivotal patriarch who both sums up and dispenses the blessing of Shem. Hence 'the original blessing of Shem reached to Abraham, and from Abraham to Isaac, and from Isaac to Jacob, the inheritance of the Spirit being imparted to them'. That 'inheritance of the Spirit' is interpreted in *Adversus Haereses*. It is the substance of what Abraham saw in prophecy, that which he

> saw in the Spirit [namely] the day of the Lord's coming, and the dispensation of His suffering, through whom both he himself [Abraham] and all who, following the example of his faith, trust in God, should be saved.[19]

This is the Day which Abraham saw and in it rejoiced. In this passage in *Adversus Haereses*, Irenaeus specifically links 'the stars of heaven' with 'the lights of the world',[20] that is, all who believe in, and trust, and are led to, the Word made flesh. The blessing of Shem is clarified and interpreted in the covenant of God with Abraham, as a constituent part of what will be fulfilled in the Person and event of the Word made flesh, and as a then present part of the movement towards that recapitulation of all things in the incarnation. This universality is stressed by Irenaeus in repeating the biblical report of Abraham's words acknowledging the nature of God: 'I will stretch forth my hands to the most high God, who made the heaven and the earth'.[21]

Notes

1 Cf. for the exegesis of Cain's act of fratricide, Irenaeus: *Adversus* Haereses III:23:4.
2 *Ibid.* IV:16:2.
3 *Ibid.* IV:9:1.
4 Justin Martyr: *Dialogue with Trypho* CXXXIX.
5 *Ibid.*
6 Irenaeus: *Demonstration of the Apostolic Preaching* 22.
7 *Ibid.*
8 *Ibid.*
9 Irenaeus: Adversus Haereses V:14:1–4.
10 E.g. *ibid.* III:22:1; V:1:1.
11 *Ibid.* V:14:3.
12 *Ibid.* V:14:2.
13 I Corinthians XV:50.
14 Irenaeus: *Adversus Haereses* V:13:3.
15 *Ibid.* V:14:1.
16 Irenaeus: *Demonstration of the Apostolic Preaching* 23.
17 *Ibid.* 20.
18 *Ibid.* 35.
19 Irenaeus: *Adversus Haereses* IV:5:5; cf. IV:7:1–3.
20 *Ibid.* IV:7:3.
21 *Ibid.* IV:5:5.

Chapter 11

Sections 18–42: The History and Fulfilment of the Blessings of God (2)

Sections 25–29: Moses

With a few broad strokes, Irenaeus indicates the framework of the events of Israel's history from the circumcision given to Abraham as a sign of the 'excellency of his faith' in Section 24, through the mention of the begetting of twelve sons by Jacob, and into Egypt with exodus from that land in Section 25. Irenaeus sees the institution of the Passover as 'revealing in a mystery the sufferings of Christ'. It is here that a parallel may be seen between Irenaeus and Melito of Sardis.

There is indeed much that is common and much that is complementary in the writings of both theologians. Eusebius of Caesarea took it for granted that the works of both were familiar and commonly juxtaposed in the church of his day: 'Who does not know the books of Irenaeus and Melito which proclaim Christ as both God and man?'[1] We may note that it is primarily for their common Christological emphasis that these two writers are regarded as significant in the early church. In this particular passage from the *Demonstration of the Apostolic Preaching*, the parallel between them is an instance of an accentuation derivative from their Christology – their insistence that Christ is not only found in the Old Testament in a paradigmatic way – that he is pointed to by the giving and observations of the law, the lamentations and rejoicings of psalmists, the example and rule of upright kings, the exhortations and warnings of prophets, the sacrifices offered and made in priestly rituals, as the coming fulfilment of all these – but that he is actually present in the directing and events of the epic of Israel as this moves and unfolds. It is, the writings of both Irenaeus and Melito suggest, under the compulsion of the Word and Spirit that this movement and development take place. But even more than this, the Word and Spirit are present and active in such a way that it is the revelation of the incarnate Word yet unborn to the flesh which is unveiled, and in this sense Christ is personally and dynamically present in the particular events of the Old Testament. It is in the context of this cognition that Sections 44–51 of the *Demonstration* should be read and interpreted.

In *Adversus Haereses* we find certain passages which mention that the Word is both always present with his handiwork[2] and also intervenes personally in a particular way in certain events. Thus

> . . . He who has brought in the end has also wrought the beginning: and it is He who does Himself say to Moses, I have surely seen the affliction of my people which is in Egypt, and I have come down to deliver them; it being customary from the beginning with the Word of God to ascend and descend for the purpose of saving those who were in affliction.[3]

In such a manner, Irenaeus (and Melito after his style) emphasizes that there is a dynamic presence, intervention, guidance and control by God in the working out of his dispensation for humanity and creation. The presence of the Word at the Passover, and the relation of the Passover and Exodus to his subsequent fulfilment of it in his own body and blood, his passion and resurrection and ascension, is one of the undergirding themes of this working out which Irenaeus stresses.

Both in our Lord's own timing of his instituting the new covenant of his body and blood, and in the matter of the interpretation of it, there is a profound relation with the events and interpretation of the old covenant with the Passover and the Exodus as the redemption of Israel out of Egypt. The early church saw this with clarity and this relation between the old and new covenants formed an integral part of its varied theology concerning the redemption by the Word made flesh. This is certainly obvious in the theology of Melito and Irenaeus.

Thus, apart from his insistence that the two covenants, the old and the new, are of 'one substance; and that the Word of God, our Lord Jesus Christ, . . . spoke with both Abraham and Moses',[4] Irenaeus clearly states in the *Demonstration*:

> It is He who spoke with Moses in the bush, and said, I have seen the affliction of my people that is in Egypt; and am come down to deliver them. It is He who came forth and came down for the deliverance of the oppressed, bringing us out of the power of the Egyptians, that is, from all idolatry and impiety; and delivering us from the Red Sea, that is, delivering us from the deadly confusion of the Gentiles and the grievous vexation of their blasphemy . . . .[5]

and so on in like vein. It is to be noted that the identification of the Egyptians of the narrative of the old covenant with the reprobate and relentlessly unbelieving Gentiles of the new, is founded on Irenaeus's identification of the Egyptians with the children of Ham in the context of Ham's cursing and Shem and Japhet's blessings by God.

Irenaeus's presentation of the Passover and Exodus by way of exegesis and theological interpretation is in distinction of form, but not of substance, from that of Melito of Sardis. In the writings of Melito of Sardis there is a clear, implicit echo of the distinction found in the *Mishnah*[6] where the Passover is given a double treatment by interpreting it in terms first of the event itself on the night before the Exodus ('the Passover of Egypt') and second, the memorial of this to be kept for ever ('the Passover of the Generations' or 'the Passover of the Future'). This distinction is found in the Gospel narratives regarding the institution of the sacrament of Christ's body and blood. While it is not explicit in Melito of Sardis's work, it obviously constitutes the fabric of his interpretation of the Eucharist, referring, as his analysis does, to the saving events of Christ's death and resurrection in the light of the redemption of Israel from Pharaoh's tyranny and the eternal memorial of both that event and that of the new covenant.

It must be emphasized that Melito's main concern in his works is not liturgical form, but that which gives rise to the shape of the liturgy – the 'mystery of salvation'. This mystery is the mystery of the 'Pascha' which is Christ Himself,[7] for he bluntly states 'The Mystery of the Pasha is Christ himself'.[8] The Fundamental of the Eucharist and the entrance to the understanding of the fulfilment of the

Passover, and therefore to the true significance of the Passover itself, are, for Melito of Sardis, Christological – the mystery of the Word made flesh for the redemption of humanity and the recreation of all things which are.

It is likewise, but stated in a variant way, with Irenaeus. The similarity of theological content and emphasis, yet the difference in approach, has also its parallel in the diverse technique stating the same message in Judaism between exposition of the biblical writings and the dramatic rehearsal of the events of redemption. The first is represented by the Torah, the interpretative application of the ordinances and statutes of God to the existence and practice of the people of Israel, and the second to the dramatic narrative of the redemptive acts of God in the Exodus as set out in the rite of the Passover. In the early Church the same distinction with the same aim is found respectively in the various expositions of Christian doctrine as in the *Demonstration of the Apostolic Preaching* and the Paschal Homilies or preaching such as that represented by the *Pascha* of Melito of Sardis. The distinction in the early Church, however, must not be exaggerated. As has been pointed out, Irenaeus is concerned that his presentation is a *Demonstration*, because the Word made flesh of which he writes is not a theoretical but a dynamic truth, and Melito is concerned that his dramatic style and presentation should convey the Christological truth of the saving events of the crucifixion and resurrection of our Lord which is determinative of all Christian doctrine. It would be stretching the parallel between the practice of Judaism and Christianity too far to state that there is a similar clear distinction in presentation of belief, as typified by the *Halakah* mode of interpretation and the *Haggadah* dramatic presentation, in Judaism. However, there is a similarity somewhat discernible between them, which in the early Church is more a matter of emphases in presentation than a clear-cut differential of approaches.

The dramatic emphasis of Melito is echoed here in this section of the *Demonstration* by Irenaeus in his statement that in the Passover, God 'saved the children of Israel, revealing in a mystery the sufferings of Christ by the sacrifice of a lamb without spot . . . . And the name of this mystery is *Passion*, the source of deliverance.'[9] The same is found in *Adversus Haereses*:

> Of the day of His passion, too, he (Moses) was not ignorant; but foretold Him, after a figurative manner, by the name given to the passover; and at that very festival, which had been proclaimed such a long time before him by Moses, did our Lord suffer, thus fulfilling the passover. And he did not describe the day only, but the place also, and the time of day when the sufferings ceased, and the sign of the setting of the sun, saying: Thou mayest not sacrifice the passover within any other of thy cities which the Lord God gives thee; but in the place where the Lord thy God shall choose that His name may be called on there, thou shalt sacrifice the passover at evening, towards the setting of the sun.[10]

It is not to be thought that Irenaeus (who was well acquainted with Hebrew) used the word πασχα – *pascha* – for the sufferings of Christ, the word being the Greek equivalent for the Hebrew or Aramaic word for 'passover' (as in, for example, I Corinthians V:7; 'Christ our passover is sacrificed for us'), by limiting it as if it were derived from πασχειν – to suffer. This supposed derivation was common in the early Church. Gregory Nazianzen later pointed out the mistaken view which so confined the full interpretation of πασχα

> . . . we say a few words about the word Pascha itself . . . . This great and venerable Pascha is called Phaska by the Hebrews in their own language; and the word means 'passing over'. Historically, from their flight and migration from Egypt into the land of Canaan; spiritually, from the progress and ascent from things below to things above to the Land of Promise. [We may note the self-same distinction between the Passover of Egypt and the Passover of the Future.] And we see that a thing which we find often to have happened in scripture, the change of certain nouns from an uncertain to a clearer sense, or from a coarser to a more refined, has taken place in this instance. For some people, supposing this to be a name for the holy Passion, and as a result Grecianizing the word by altering Phi and Kappa into Pi and Chi, called the day Pascha. And custom took it up and confirmed (this usage) of the word, assisted by the ears of most people to whom it had a more pious sound.[11]

Gregory is noting that the word-change, and therefore the restricted meaning, occurs through both common ignorance of the Hebrew language and the temptation to 'spiritualize' meanings. Neither charge can be laid upon Irenaeus.

Undoubtedly it is in the sense of suffering that it is so used here by Irenaeus in the above quoted section of *Adversus Haereses* – but where he is concentrating on the passion of Christ in relation to the blood of the Passover. For the suffering of Christ is never treated by Irenaeus as a factor by itself. Its significance has a context, and that setting is the full sweep of the redemptive act of God in the incarnation of the Word through to his resurrection and ascension. In the same way, Irenaeus always injects into his observations on the Passover a note of triumphant deliverance – as here in this section of the *Demonstration*: '. . . the name of this mystery is Passion, the source of deliverance'. He also writes, later, in the *Demonstration* 'His sufferings are our ascension on high'[12] and with regard to the sufferings of Christ dwelt upon in *Adversus Haereses*, the same context of the victory of Christ on the cross in resurrection and ascension is obvious. His sufferings are the means whereby, recapitulating in himself the plight of humanity's bondage under the tyranny of Satan and the sentence of death, he penetrates to the heart of that sorry estate in order to vanquish the powers which have bound the handiwork of God and be victorious over them in liberating humanity and leading it to its promised place.

The sufferings of Christ are never disengaged from the whole work of redemption in the thought of Irenaeus. They are part of a Passover/Exodus movement by the Word of God made flesh fulfilling the heart of the old covenant. Nor does Irenaeus vest the wounds and afflictions of Christ with an aura of glory in themselves. He is insistent on the reality of them in all the stark materiality of Gethsemane, Gabbatha and Golgotha, for in that reality, the reality of the Adamic flesh of the Word within the historical exigencies and iron necessities of this creation, lies the reality of resurrection and the bestowal of immortality.

This stress on the reality of the flesh of the Word and the reality of our redemption as creatures of flesh is set out in *Adversus Haereses* V:1–4. In that section there is also introduced the reality of the creaturely elements of bread and wine, which, when they receive the Word of God 'the Eucharist of the body and blood of Christ is made . . . the Eucharist which is the body and blood of Christ'.[13] The natural elements, so conjoined to the Word of God, as the body and blood of Christ, are the pledge, provision and sustenance of God whereby partakers of them are nourished and

> shall rise at their appointed time, the Word of God granting them resurrection to the glory of God, even the Father who freely gives to this mortal immortality and to this corruptible incorruption, because the strength of God is made perfect in weakness in order that we may never become puffed up, as if we had life from ourselves, and exalted against God, our minds becoming ungrateful; but learning by experience that we possess eternal duration from the excelling power of this Being and not from our own nature, we may neither undervalue that glory which surrounds God as He is, nor be ignorant of our own nature, but that we may know what God can effect, and what benefits man receives, and thus never wander from the true apprehension of things as they are, that is, both with regard to God and with regard to man.[14]

It may be noted in passing that in this part of *Adversus Haereses* how faith and godliness, God's Self-revelation and giving and κατα φυσιν thinking underlie and undergird implicitly the thought of Irenaeus.

Here also we have the same implicit pattern of the Passover in its dual nature of the Passover of the 'Passover of Egypt' and the 'Passover of the Generations' or 'of the Future' in the argument of these first chapters of Book V of *Adversus Haereses* – the once and for all event of Christ's passion and resurrection and the memorial whereby we become partakers throughout the ages of that event. In Irenaeus's view, this is the event which creates the community of union between God and man, and the sacrament by which we partake of that community of union through the reality of the humanity of the Word. The observation Irenaeus makes in this section regarding the sufferings of Christ as the fulfilment of the Passover is not to be taken as a statement sufficiently capable of interpretation as it stands here by itself. The passion of Christ is, as Irenaeus's wider interpretation of the delivering and liberating and triumphing substance of these sufferings in *Adversus Haereses* suggests, the mode of the exultant victory of the Word for his own handiwork as he descends in all the reality of his incarnation to the depths of human misery to lead his humanity out of that bondage into the freedom of its fulfilment in the dispensation of God.

The Passover itself is set within a context of that to which it points, in Irenaeus's treatment of it. Its significance lies in the fact that

> the whole exodus of the people out of Egypt, which took place by the divine guidance, was a type and image of the exodus of the church which should take place from among the Gentiles; and for this cause He leads it out at last from this world into His own inheritance, which Moses the servant of God did not, but which Jesus the Son of God shall give for an inheritance.[15]

Moreover, the Passover is also within the context of how Irenaeus describes this liberating of humanity by the Word, in the anticipation of the old covenant and its record in the new, in terms of the working out of the respective blessings by God of Noah's sons, Shem and Japheth. We noted the importance which Irenaeus accords to these blessings in the comments of the last section, and, as we will note later, the way in which Irenaeus works out their fulfilment. In *Adversus Haereses*, the work of Christ is described in terms of these blessings as their fulfilment:

> He . . . the head corner-stone, appearing in these last times, has gathered into one and united those who were near and those who were far off; that is the circumcision and the uncircumcision, enlarging Japhet and placing him in the dwellings of Shem.[16]

We have already seen (Section 20) how Irenaeus regards the Egyptians as 'children of Ham'. It is the progeny of Ham who tyrannizes and reduces into bondage, and who symbolize therefore the despotism and the fetters of evil from which our Lord, in the fulfilment of the Passover, rescues and restores humanity in the exodus of the progress of faith in community of union with him, the Lamb slain and the Lamb reigning.

Hence it is that Irenaeus remarks at the end of this section that in the Passover the judgment of God has fallen on those who oppressed the seed of Abraham, Abraham being the line through which the seed of Shem, and therefore the blessing of Shem, descends. The Passover for Irenaeus is an integral and determinative part of the working out by God of the dispensation of his blessings on Shem and Japhet in their relation to the accursed children of Ham. These blessings and their fulfilment as the directive of history are the framework in which Irenaeus places the whole dispensation of redemption. As such, they are determinative for an understanding of these sections of the *Demonstration* and a key to the understanding of Irenaeus's theological method in seeing the patterns of history as the working out of the decrees and dispensations of God in terms of the faithfulness of his promises from which faithfulness faith itself is evoked and progress made within the οἰκονομια of God's creative and redemptive purposes.

It is to further that progress in a particular way that God gives the dispensation of the law as set out in Section 26. This is the next stage in the unfolding of the epic of Israel under the working out of God's promises. Irenaeus significantly notes that the Law from God is received by Moses as

> the Ten Words on tables of stone, written with the finger of God (now the finger of God is that which is stretched forth from the Father in the Holy Spirit); and the commandments and ordinances which he delivered to the children of Israel to observe.[17]

Three points may be made here. The first is Irenaeus's deliberation in almost underlining that the 'ten words' are written on 'tables of stone'. I think that he is intentionally juxtaposing this by way of contrast with the second, the equally deliberate emphasis that they are written by 'that which is stretched forth from the Father in the Holy Spirit' – namely, 'the finger of God'. The first is the basis on which he describes the law-centred worship of Israel as 'stoney religion or stoney worship'[18] – that is, that the worship of Israel is centred on tables of stone, the law. In the passages in which Irenaeus so describes Israel's worship, the stoniness of the law is always contrasted with the faith of Abraham. In *Adversus Haereses* IV:25:1, the substance of the text of Matthew III:9 and Luke III:8 – our Lord's words concerning raising up children to Abraham out of stones – is used to indicate that faith, as typified by Abraham, the father of faith, the forerunner of our faith, has precedence over the giving of the law and over the divine institution of the rite of circumcision, Abraham pre-dating Moses and being yet uncircumcised when his faith was kindled. Irenaeus uses 'stones' here to describe the law, that is, he would see these Gospel texts as meaning that in them John the Baptist is saying that it is possible even out of the law for God to raise children of faith as the true seed of Abraham. In *Adversus Haereses* IV:25:1, he is contrasting the 'stones' typifying the dead law with Christ as the chief Corner Stone, who sustains all things, and gathers

> into the one faith of Abraham those who from either covenant are fitted for God's building. But this faith which is in uncircumcision, as joining the end to the beginning, has been made the first and the last. For, as I have demonstrated, it existed in Abraham before circumcision, as it did also in the rest of the righteous who pleased God. And in these last times it sprang up again among humanity through the coming of the Lord. But circumcision and the law of works occupied the intervening era.

In *Adversus Haereses* IV:7:1–2, Irenaeus explicitly centres faith – whether it be the faith of Abraham or the faith of the church – on Christ. Abraham's faith descends on those who, like Mary at the annunciation and Simeon holding the infant Christ in his arms, rejoice to see Christ's day as Abraham did 'through the Spirit of prophecy'. And, on the other hand, Irenaeus notes, there is a 'reciprocal rejoicing' which passes backward from the children of faith to the father of faith, because the substance and goal (the 'scope) of faith is Christ Himself who gathers it all together in Himself.

This faith, as it were, overarches the 'intervening era' when the injunctions of circumcision and the law were given. This leads to the second point to be noted, that this 'intervening era' indicates that for Irenaeus, the old covenant is not typified by the ordinances of circumcision and the statutes of the law of Moses, but by that faith of which Abraham, in the line of the blessing of Shem, is the patriarch and exemplar for the faith of those who are the 'enlargement of Japheth' standing in the line of that blessing. The pattern for Irenaeus is that these are seen to be one in Christ, He gathering in one the faithful Gentiles and the faithful of Israel, the first as the 'fruit of the blessing of Japheth' into the second as the 'dwelling of Shem'[19] thereby accomplishing the 'enlargement of Shem' in, as we have seen in the preceding chapter, the one land. The significance of the law is not that it characterizes and forms the substance of the old covenant, but that it is given as a temporary expedient for the period 'intervening' between the eras of faith. The whole *raison d'être* of the law standing at the centre of its attendant institutions and rituals, is, as this section mentions, that it was given as 'the visible form on earth of those things which are spiritual and invisible in the heavens, and a figure of the form of the Church, and a prophecy of things to come'.

The law in its external dictates and material injunctions is temporary and in nature paradigmatic. It is in this way, and only within this significance, that it furthers the progress of faith within the faithfulness of God's creative and redemptive purposes, and, in so doing is related to faith tangentially. This brings us to the third point, which is that the law is given in the context of the understanding that God is 'long-suffering in the matter of the correction of man and the probation of all'.[20]

Irenaeus's view of the significance of the law, and the part it plays in the pattern of the dispensation of God in creation and redemption may be appreciated in certain key phrases in the chapters of *Adversus Haereses* where he enlarges on this,[21] all his observations being under the general observation determinative of his stance that the two covenants are 'of one and the same substance'.[22] The old covenant and therefore the law of Moses is fulfilled in the new which is *greater* than it. But, as Irenaeus notes, the terms 'greater and less' are not used of things which have nothing in common and are

> of an opposite nature and are mutually repugnant; but are used in the case of those which are of the same substance and which possess properties in common, but merely differ in number and size; such as water from water, and light from light, and grace from grace.[23]

This argument anticipates that of the Nicene theologians in their insistence that God is beyond comparison and cannot be approached by quantitative reasoning, which way of thinking would merely be to project created values and nature to whatever vast degree into the divine and blur the qualitative distinction between Creator and creature.

In the same section he argues that the new covenant is 'greater' in this light in several ways. The first might seem to contradict his overall thesis that the substance of the two covenants is qualitatively the same, the disparity being that of only quantitative difference: 'Greater, therefore, is that legislation which has been given in the dispensation of liberty than that in the dispensation of bondage'.[24] However, the subsequent argument makes it clear that for Irenaeus the two dispensations equally are 'of one and the same substance' for they are part of the creative and redemptive dispensation 'of one and the same God', the content of which dispensation, as we have seen elsewhere, is the Word make flesh. The one covenant is peculiar and particular to Israel; the new covenant is general and universal in that the

> same Lord, who is greater than the temple, greater than Solomon, and greater than Jonah, confers gifts upon men, that is, His own presence and the resurrection from the dead; but He does not change God nor proclaim another Father, but the very same one who always has more to mete out to those of His household. And as their love towards God increases, He bestows more and greater.[25]

This is taken up in the second way in which Irenaeus looks at the significance of the law. The law of the old covenant is of 'one and the same substance' with the new, because it is part of the development and progress of faith. It belongs to a stage in that development within the dispensation of God towards his handiwork. This also means that the old was not without knowledge of the new, for it is shot through with the new as its fulfilment. Thus

> . . . the new covenant having been known and preached by the prophets, He . . . was also preached who was to accomplish it according to the good pleasure of the Father, having been revealed to men as pleased God; that they always might make progress through believing in Him, and by means of the covenants should gradually attain to perfect salvation. For there is one salvation and one God; for the precepts which form man are numerous, and the steps not few which lead man to God.[26]

The old covenant plays its distinctive and necessary role in the dispensation of redemption by the one God and Father.[27] It is 'a course of discipline and a prophecy of future things'.[28] That is to say, it both has the validity and suitability for the particularity and necessities of its own time and yet also has a paradigmatic function as to its full purpose within the context of that dispensation of the one God and Father for all humanity. Irenaeus points out that this dispensation of God – in the establishing of the patriarchs, the giving of the law, the construction of the tabernacle, the building of the temple in Jerusalem, the instituting of the Levitical priesthood – is that which takes into consideration particular historical estates and conditions, and adapts itself to them, making itself appropriate to the lot of the people therein. All this is for the end that the people were to be instructed that they might eventually be sharers in the glory of God, and it is all, as Irenaeus constantly underlines, a matter not of necessity on God's part, but of the freedom of God's grace and loving-kindness towards His people.[29] This adaptation by God to the particular circumstances of the people is stated by Irenaeus. Humanity was in bondage to death until the resurrection of Christ. Therefore that which answers to, and is fitting for, the estate of bondage is given to the people for their instruction – namely, the bondage of the law. The law draws by its bonds those in bondage to death to teach them of coming liberty, for it is the bond which binds them to the service and knowledge of God whose Word accomplishes freedom for humanity so that 'the bonds of slavery should be removed to which man had become accustomed, and he should follow God without fetters'.[30]

The law is the pointer to Christ. It is that which 'prepares . . . for the coming of Christ'.[31] For this purpose, its essential nature is that of love. Here Irenaeus makes a twofold distinction. The law proper is that given by Moses, and at the heart of this is the double commandment to love God and neighbour. This is distinct from the 'tradition of the elders' which not only is added to the true nature of the law but indeed contradicts it. He bluntly points out that this 'tradition' was at variance with the law as it really was. Appealing to Isaiah I:22 – 'thy dealers mix the wine with water' – Irenaeus observes.

> that the elders were in the habit of mixing a watered tradition with the simple command of God; that is, they promulgated a specious law contrary to the law; as also the Lord made plain when He said to them: Why do ye transgress the commandment of God for the sake of your tradition? For not only . . . did they set the law of God at nought, mixing the wine with water, but they also set up their own law in opposition to it . . . they suppress certain things, add others and interpret others as they see fit . . . .[32]

The second part of the distinction is that even in the scrupulous acknowledgement of the precepts of the law, there were those who paid lip-service but who were without love in their observation of these precepts. Thus, notes Irenaeus,

> [The Lord] does not cast blame on that law which was given by Moses when He exhorted it to be observed, Jerusalem being in that time secure; but He did pronounce censure upon those persons because they indeed repeated the words of the law, but were without love.[33]

The law of Moses, therefore, in Irenaeus's estimation, has its time, its place, its reason both historical and paradigmatic. Its suitability for its time and circumstances is God's accommodation of his precepts to the estate of humanity then, but it performs a wider function in teaching of freedom found in the love of God and neighbour, which freedom and which love is Christ Himself. Christ, then, is the substance or the σκοπος of the law. Our Lord's interpretation of the law, as reported at various times in the Gospels, penetrates to the essential nature of love in the law, the love to which it pointed. Thus, penetrating to the fullness of meaning in the law, He forbids even concupiscent thoughts rather than only adultery; anger than bare killing; generosity to the poor than mere tithing.[34] He, as the 'Liberator', sets us free to thus fulfil the law, and this freeing is a matter of His grace alone which evokes yet more and more love the more it is extended to us. The law, then, is the beginning and origin of this progress; the fulfilling of it the 'receiving of growth and completion'[35] towards the one and same God who gave the law and is his own Word.

> For to yield to assent to God, and to follow His Word, and to love Him above all, and to love one's neighbour as one's self (now man is neighbour to man) and to abstain from every evil deed, and all other things of a like nature which are common to both [covenants], do reveal one and the same God. But this is our Lord, the Word of God, who in the first instance certainly drew slaves to God, but afterwards set those free who were subject to Him, as He declares to His disciples: I will not now call you servants, for the servant knoweth not what his lord doeth; but I have called you friends, for all things which I have heard from my Father I have made known . . . . He indicates in the most emphatic manner that it was Himself who originally appointed men for that bondage with respect to God through the law, and then afterwards conferred upon them freedom.[36]

The law, then, in Irenaeus's thought, is that which is a necessary stage of tutelage in the progress of humanity in the knowledge of God and towards community of union with the divine life. It is a phase in the progress towards freedom in that community of union which points to the necessity of that faith and love which is Abraham's and the church's, which faith and love rejoice in the day of Christ.

Because of their common substance, horizon and goal, their σκοπος, Christ Himself, Irenaeus can apply the term 'greater' not by indicating the formal and material aspects of the old, but in the way of comparing the respective modes of witnessing to that common scope. Clearly, Christ himself is 'greater' than the paradigmatic role of the old covenant pointing to him.

The trinitarian content of Irenaeus's exposition as to the significance of the law at this stage of progress towards the knowledge and love of God, is seen in an emphatic way in his introduction in this Section 26 to his observations on the institutions of the old covenant. The law is written by 'the finger of God (now the finger of God is that which is stretched forth from the Father in the Holy Spirit)'. It will not do to equate here (as for example Armitage Robinson does) the 'finger of God' barely with 'the Holy Spirit'. It can surely only mean the Word here, the Word, the inner content of the law writing the words of the law which witnesses to him. While the 'finger of God' is applied in the Gospels to the Spirit,[37] with which application Irenaeus must have been cognizant, there is here an implicit interchange of the attributes of the Spirit with the Word – a theological device which Gregory Nazianzen was later to bring out and extend boldly[38] in terms of the unity of the

Trinity. This is in line entirely with Irenaeus's general observations regarding the relation between Word and Spirit.[39]

It may be asked here if Irenaeus is indicating, in his observations about the giving of the law, a parallel to the incarnation, the Word accomplishing what He does in taking flesh by the will of the Father in the power of the Spirit.

In Section 27, the emphasis on the awareness of Christ in the old covenant is heightened by the remarks on the events when the people of Israel were near to the promised land and Moses sent out men to spy it out.

> At that time God revealed to Moses the Name which alone is able to save them that believe thereon; and Moses changed the name of Oshea the son of Nun, one of them that were sent, and named him Jesus; and so he sent them forth with the power of the Name, believing that he should receive them back safe and sound through the guidance of the Name; which came to pass.[40]

Irenaeus probably picked up Justin Martyr's interest in this change of name,[41] for the latter expands on this in the context of the same argument of the essential Christocentricity of the old covenant, and the instances in the epic of Israel where, in accordance with the exegetical method of the early church, Christ's presence may be deduced. This 'Jesus', Joshua, brings good tidings of the promised land to the people, but in their disbelief the people incurred the wrath of God in their rejection of the good news, and were condemned to desolation in the desert for forty years.

Irenaeus, with ever an eye for parallelism in order to heighten the whole concept of the working out of the dispensation of God, points out that the forty years stems from the forty days which were spent by Joshua and the others sent by Moses in spying out the land. In *Adversus Haereses*,[42] Joshua is regarded as a type of believer. He had seen the fruition of the promised land, and he, as is noted both in this part of *Adversus Haereses* and this section of the *Demonstration*, continued faithful in this knowledge of God's promise. These two alone, of the original multitude at the Exodus, together with the children who had grown up in the wilderness and were therefore not part of the unbelievers, entered the promise of that land. Irenaeus enlarges on these children, noting only in *Adversus Haereses* that they were 'innocent' but here that 'they knew not the right hand and the left' – appealing, presumably, to the similarity with the state of the Ninevehites on whom God had compassion and saved.[43]

There are differences between Irenaeus and Justin in this account of the change of the name of 'Oshea' to 'Jesus'. Irenaeus links him with Caleb the son of Jephunneh both here and in *Adversus Haereses*, and also with the innocent children of the Israelites, as he recounts the circumstances of the composition of Israel as the people entered the promised land. Justin does not. In this, Irenaeus is following the biblical account more thoroughly than Justin, but their respective aims in using this episode from the biblical narrative are different. Justin is concerned with a sort of typology; Irenaeus is concerned with the sameness of belief evidenced in the two covenants. Hence Joshua is both a pointer to Jesus and an exemplar in the companionship of those who companied with Him, as instanced by Caleb, and of those who were not disbelievers in the sureties of the dispensation of God and who required instruction.

This instruction is given, Irenaeus notes in Section 28, and again, the whole tone is Christocentric. It is a matter of recapitulating all the law and its intent afresh towards 'fashioning and preparing those who had grown up in the wilderness to fear God and keep His commandments'.[44] This recapitulation is thoroughly Christocentric and sets out the paradigmatic purpose of the law of the old covenant. For in this new giving of the law, which Irenaeus sees as Deuteronomy, there is contained by way of addition and clarification 'many prophecies concerning our Lord Jesus Christ and concerning the people, and also concerning the calling of the Gentiles and concerning the kingdom'.[45] In *Adversus Haereses*,[46] Irenaeus underlines the whole Christological interpretation of this second giving of the law. The significance of this recapitulation of all that had gone and been given before is precisely that it is the words of Christ.

> But since the writings of Moses are the words of Christ, He Himself declares to the Jews, as John has recorded in the Gospel: If ye had believed Moses, ye would have believed Me: for He wrote of Me ... He thus demonstrates in the clearest manner that the writings of Moses are His words.[47]

As in all instances of his doctrine of recapitulation, Irenaeus here sees even this minor formulation and use of it as Christological. Christ is not the agent of recapitulation; his person and words and works are, by their very nature, recapitulative.

The sections on Moses and the significance of the old covenant with the law at its heart end, therefore, with a strong statement of the σκοπος of the law, its very *raison d'être*, as Christ Himself. It is in this light that Section 29 notes that 'when Moses had finished his course ... he died according to the word of the Lord; and Jesus the son of Nun succeeded him'.

Notes

1 Eusebius: *Hist. Eccl.* V:25:5.
2 E.g. Irenaeus: *Adversus Haereses* III:16:6; 18:1; IV:6:2; 6:7.
3 *Ibid.* IV:12:4.
4 *Ibid.* IV:9:1.
5 Irenaeus: *Demonstration of the Apostolic Preaching* 46.
6 Mishnah: *Tractate Pesahim* 9:5.
7 Melito of Sardis: *Homily on the Pascha* 10, 65, 396.
8 *Ibid.* 448
9 Irenaeus: *Demonstration of the Apostolic Preaching* 25.
10 Irenaeus: *Adversus Haereses* IV:10:1.
11 Gregory Nazianzen: *Oration* XLV:10.
12 Irenaeus: *Demonstration of the Apostolic Preaching* 45.
13 Irenaeus: *Adversus Haereses* V:2:2,3.
14 *Ibid.* V:2:3.
15 *Ibid.* IV:30:4.
16 *Ibid.* III:5:3.
17 Irenaeus: *Demonstration of the Apostolic Preaching* 26.

18 Irenaeus: *Demonstration of the Apostolic Preaching* 93; *Adversus Haereses* IV:7:2, cf. IV:8:1; IV:25:1.
19 Irenaeus: *Demonstration of the Apostolic Preaching* 42; cf. *Adversus Haereses* III;5:3.
20 Irenaeus: *Adversus Haereses* III:23:1.
21 *Ibid.* cf. esp. IV:9:1ff.
22 *Ibid.* IV:9:1; cf. Chapter 3 above.
23 *Irenaeus:* Adversus Haereses IV:9:2.
24 *Ibid.*
25 *Ibid.*
26 *Ibid.* IV:9:3.
27 Cf., e.g., *ibid.* III:12:11, 12; III:12:15; III:15:3; IV:9:1; IV:12:3, 4, 5;
28 *Ibid.* IV:15:1.
29 *Ibid.* IV:14:2–IV:16:5.
30 *Ibid.* IV:13:2; cf. IV:4:1.
31 *Ibid.* IV:12:1.
32 *Ibid.* IV:12:1.
33 *Ibid.* IV:12:4.
34 *Ibid.* IV:13:3.
35 *Ibid.* IV:13:4.
36 *Ibid.* IV:13:4.
37 Cf. Matthew XII:28 with Luke IX:20.
38 Gregory Nazianzen: 5th *Theological Oration* (On the Holy Spirit) III.
39 Cf. Comments on Sections 5–8, Chapter 5.
40 Irenaeus: *Demonstration of the Apostolic Preaching* 27.
41 Justin Martyr: *Dialogue with Trypho* LXXV, CXIII.
42 Irenaeus: *Adversus Haereses* IV:28:3.
43 Jonah IV:11.
44 Irenaeus: *Demonstration of the Apostolic Preaching*, 28.
45 *Ibid.*
46 Irenaeus: *Adversus Haereses* IV:2:1; cf. 2:2 and 3.
47 *Ibid.* IV:2:3.

Chapter 12

Sections 18–42: The History and Fulfilment of the Blessings of God (3)

Sections 29–42: The Pre-eminence of the Word

The death of Moses, the settlement of the promised land by Joshua or Jesus and the establishment of Jerusalem as the place of the name of God, are set out swiftly in Section 29. I am sure that there is deliberation on the part of Irenaeus to revert to what he sees as the pattern of the events of the person and work of the Word made flesh whenever he compacts episodes of Israel's history. Here is perhaps discernible the pattern, underlying his choice of brief terminology, of the death, resurrection, ascension and intercession of Christ. Moses, the very epitome of the old covenant, is death, having 'died according to the word of God'. Jesus (Joshua)

> divided the Jordan and made the people pass over into the land [the resurrection of our Lord and the opening of immortality in the promise of God. Jesus (Joshua) having] overthrown and destroyed the seven races that dwelt therein [a reference to the seven heavens which the ascending Christ passes through] assigned to the people the temporal Jerusalem, wherein David was king, and Solomon his son, who builded the temple to the name of God, according to the pattern which had been made by Moses after the pattern of the heavenly and spiritual things.[1]

There seems to be urgent deliberation in this contracted episode. It may be that the seven races suggest the seven heavens, peopled (though Irenaeus is not interested in angelic orders – cf. comments on Sections 9 and 10, Chapter 6) by the principalities and powers and dominions. These acknowledge Christ's triumph over all things in heaven and earth as he ascends and passes through the seven heavens, all things in heaven and things in earth bowing before him. He ascends to the place of the name of God, the dwelling place of God, which this 'temporal Jerusalem', with the appointment of its temple, signifies. So Israel, in the tutelage of similitude, having vanquished the seven nations, comes to the place of the Name of God, the holy of holies of the temple. It would be unwise to read too much into this, save to acknowledge it as a pattern to which Irenaeus reverts in order to show that the events which he so swiftly notes, have nevertheless an integral part in the overall pattern of the Christ-centred and determined dispensation of God. For Irenaeus is indeed imbued with the idea that the pattern of the salvation events at every stage, takes its form and content as an appropriate paradigmatic witness to the reality and accomplishment of the Word made flesh, in the old covenant prophetically signifying this as the actual form and content of the dispensation of God. In all this, the treatment by the early Church, through such figures as Justin Martyr, of the interpretation of the scriptures of the old covenant, is gathered up and developed in a more theologically interpretative, rather than a bare typological, way. Irenaeus stands, with his own kerygmatically emphatic presentation, side by side with the dramatic presentation of Melito of Sardis of the saving events of Christ – Melito's emphasis being that they are graphically prefigured in the annals of Israel which are in strict accord with the nature and accomplishment of these events.

Section 30 notes that the prophets are sent by God through the Holy Spirit to this place of the name of God. This, of course, is not historically valid. But Irenaeus's intent is to focus on the place of revelation of God. The place, Jerusalem itself, of itself, has no significance, except that it is the trysting place of God with humanity. The place is only such a place because it is the place which is not other than the humanity of the Word made flesh and what is wrought out there. The significance which God makes for himself in the midst of creation by assuming human flesh and nature creates place where and when this happens.

This is why the prophets, with regard to Jerusalem, according to Irenaeus are 'hither sent through the Holy Spirit' to become 'heralds of the revelation of our Lord Jesus Christ'. Their specific role is to 'instruct' the people and to place before them 'the God of their fathers'. What Irenaeus is doing here is to portray the prophets as those who recall the people to the fundamental essence of the law given by Moses – to remind them and school them in its essential nature and content. Hence, the burden of their prophecies is that our Lord as 'the Son of God' takes His human flesh and nature from the line of the true inheritance of Israel. Irenaeus sees this line stretching from Solomon, who built the temple 'according to the likeness of the tabernacle which had been made by Moses' through David to Moses whose original tabernacle was 'after the pattern of the heavenly and spiritual things'.[2]

David himself was descended from Abraham, who is the patriarch of the faithful. The overall interpretation of Irenaeus with regard to the incarnation of the Word is that there is a twofold assumption of human flesh and nature. The Word takes, as has been discussed already, Adamic, that is fallen flesh. But while all flesh is Adamic, the Word confirms and establishes the direction which Adamic flesh should take – that is, the way of Abraham's faithfulness, in order, as the conclusion of these sections in Section 42 of the *Demonstration* points out with regard to the faithful person, that the blessing to which Abraham was in turn an heir, may be fulfilled:

> This is the fruit of the blessing of Japheth, in the calling of the Gentiles, made manifest through the Church, standing in readiness to receive its dwelling in the house of Shem according to the promise of God.[3]

What we have to take into consideration here is the way in which Irenaeus conceives a pattern in the dispensation of God's creative and redemptive purposes. It is his employment of these brief strokes, graphically encapsulating what for him is the meaning of Israel's history, which exhibits his intent. These are parts of the broader canvas of all creation. It is as though his perception of this is both a motion from the centre out to the circumference and a motion from the circumference into the centre, and these two dynamic impulses, in the thought of Irenaeus, are entirely in harmony and are mutually bound in one in complementarity.

In the outer limits, so to speak, we have creation. Yet immediately in Irenaean thought, this creation is harnessed and referred to the Word in His relation to the Spirit and the Father, by whom all things were created. In the next circle we have God's judgment upon His world in the narrative of Noah and his sons. There we have the blessing of Shem and Japheth and the cursing of Ham. Humanity is divided according to the dispensation of God. The next narrowing circle is the body of those who are clustered around the figure of the patriarch Abraham upon whom the blessing of Shem descends. The faith of Abraham, which is focused on the promise of God to be his people's God and they to be his people, rejoicing in its fulfilment in seeing the day of Christ, finds expression in the integrity of the law of Moses in its instructive and paradigmatic functions, the next narrowing circle. This law, in the same way in which the first man made the fruit of the tree of the knowledge of good and evil his own, despite the already declared divine decree as to what was good, is made to meander off into the traditions of men, and, so dissipated, needs to be recalled to its basic purpose and aim. The prophets, again an even narrower circle within the people of Israel, fulfil this function. They are, in Irenaeus's understanding, centred in Jerusalem as 'heralds of the revelation of our Lord Jesus Christ the Son of God', and the burden of their message is, in turn, in this place, centred in the place where God makes his personal tryst with humanity. This is the axle on which all creation turns, and round which the whole epic of humanity, with Israel as its epitome and as the exemplar of its direction towards God, revolves. The axle is the recapitulative Word made flesh, who spreads out to the circumference of all creation, gathering up all these ever-widening circles, the prophets, the law, the faith of Abraham, the blessing of Shem and Japheth, Adam and the entirety of all things that are. This totality, through the particularity of the passion and crucifixion of Christ, is expressed in Section 34. Irenaeus, in Sections 31ff, begins to draw out the implications of why this particularity of the Word made flesh should embrace the sum of all creation.

He begins in section 31 with a statement concerning the incarnation as the establishment of a 'community of union' between God and man (cf. comments on Section 1 in Chapter 1 above). The union of human flesh and nature with the divine nature is the ground, and indeed as is emphatic in Irenaeus's thought, the sum, of this. Christ himself is recapitulation and in Him all things are gathered up in union with God. Before he expands on this in Sections 32ff, Irenaeus follows his introductory remark in Section 31 with a brief statement in terms of our 'participation in incorruption' in order to demonstrate the incarnation to be the only way in which this could be achieved. This is construed in terms of revelation and reconciliation bonded inseparably.

It is to be noted that 'incorruption' for Irenaeus is not some quality of and in and by itself. 'Incorruption' is the personal revelation and reconciliation of God. This is set out in *Adversus Haereses*:

> For by no other means could we have attained to incorruptibility and immortality unless we had been united to incorruptibility and immortality. But how could we be joined to incorruptibility and immortality unless, first, incorruptibility and immortality had become

what we also are, so that the corruptible might be swallowed up by incorruption and the mortal by immortality, that we might receive the adoption of sons?[4]

Incorruptibility (and indeed, importantly, immortality) are not independent qualities. They are the Word – and it is this Word who assumes corruptibility and mortality, the whole bundle of Adamic humanity, in order in this 'royal exchange' to grant us incorruptibility and immortality in a 'community of union' with Him through His humanity in its union with the Word in His relation to the Father and the Spirit.

As long as God, who is incorruption, remains invisible and unrevealed, 'it helped us not at all'. So, he continues, 'therefore it became visible'. Here we have another declaration of the oft-repeated theme that the Invisible became visible, the Incorruptible became corruptible, the Immeasurable became measurable, the Inexpressible became expressible, etc. That is, God accommodates Himself in His Word by the Spirit to the necessities of the limitation of our senses as created entities over against the incomparability of Himself (see again comments on Section 1 in Chapter 1 above).

Irenaeus expands this thought in various sections of *Adversus Haereses*, but attention may be drawn to one comment he makes there in particular.[5] Here we have a statement that the Word assumes the totality of human being and poured out the Spirit, in this twofold way creating a 'union and communion' of God and man.[6] But this appearance of the Word as flesh is not a 'seeming'; it is actuality, for the reality of God and the reality of human being in its totality are involved in the incarnation of the Word.[7] Only as really man, argues Irenaeus, could the Holy Spirit have rested upon him – that is, the incarnate Word is the place of the Spirit, the outpouring of whom is necessary for the establishment of this 'union and communion' of God and man. The reality and significance of 'place' regarding the relation of Creator to creation is therefore stated. The incarnate Word is the 'place' of the Creator in the midst of creation. There is the 'place' in the redemptive dispensation of God which he has made for himself in creating. Irenaeus notes importantly, otherwise 'the Spirit is invisible'.

The essential Word-centred theology of Irenaeus is made clear here. The Word is 'the visible of the Father'[8] because his humanity is that which is the accommodation of God to our limitations, making His divinity appreciable, in measure as befits our creaturely-strictured senses. The fact that the Word is 'the visible of the Father' does not imply a subordination within the Triune being of God. Humanity is called to be the bearer of divine glory, and here is God's humanity in which we may, in this 'union and communion' or 'community of union' established by the Word made flesh and the Spirit in the will of the Father, participate, and so be the bearers of such. Hence: 'The glory of God is a living man; and the life of man consists in beholding God'.[9] Christ is God's 'living man' who alone has beheld the Father, and in him the integrity of humanity is found and its fulfilment, in the 'community of union' which He and the Spirit bestows upon us.

This is further dwelt upon by Irenaeus when he points out that humanity is acceptable to the Father because it is the humanity of his Son. The visibility of the 'image of God' was not shown until the Word became flesh, thus humanity was at a disadvantage in not having the fulfilment of its creative purpose before its eyes. The full proof was not before the human senses, thus it was easy for humanity to fall from its creative purpose and to lose the 'similitude' to the 'image of God'. The 'image', which Christ is, is now in our sight. For Christ, as the Word made flesh

> confirmed both of these [that is, the 'similitude' and the 'image']: for He both showed the image truly, since He became Himself what was His image; and He re-established the similitude after a sure manner, by assimilating the man to the invisible Father by means of the visible Word.[10]

But here in *Adversus Haereses*,[11] Christ is seen as also the visible of the Spirit, since the Spirit is 'invisible'. I suggest that here in Irenaeus's distribution of the attributes – the invisibility of Father, Word and Spirit, but the visibility opened out of the Word Himself by assuming flesh, and of the resultant visibility of the Father and the Spirit – we have the embryonic doctrine of *perichoresis*, that the respective Persons of the Trinity 'make room' for each other in their mutual indwelling, this indwelling, the interpenetration of the Persons yet sustaining their own integrity, being seen in the visibility which the Word made flesh makes possible. And because it is the Word made flesh, the Trinity makes room for itself in creation.

For Irenaeus there is no disjunction between the doctrine of the Incarnation and that of the Trinity, the two being bracketed together in a substantial and interpretative way. This is set out in section 47 of the *Demonstration* where the Being of God, as He is in Himself, is stated:

> So then the Father is Lord and the Son is Lord, and the Father is God and the Son is God, for that which is begotten of God is God. And so in the substance and power of His being there is shown forth one God; but there is also according to the economy of our redemption both Son and Father [we may note the order of Persons here, the Son coming first in the economy of our redemption]. Because to all created things the Father of all is invisible and unapproachable, therefore those who are to draw near to God must have their access to the Father through the Son.[12]

It is the role of the Holy Spirit, who can only be co-equal to the Father and the Son in order to be competent to do so, to name both Father and Son as Lord.

The doctrine of the Trinity is not a matter of perceiving first an 'economic' Trinity – that is, that in the appreciation of the works of the redemption events, argument may be made that these works are of necessity accomplished by the Persons of the Trinity, the argument from works to the Persons variously accomplishing the works. This doctrine for Irenaeus is rather a matter of perceiving the actuality of the Persons in their dynamic activity and there from seeing the significance of the works. To put it simply the work of redemption is because the Word in his relation to the Father and the Holy Spirit became flesh – not that there is a work of redemption and therefore the Word must be involved in the flesh.

When Irenaeus says in section 31 that 'we could not in any other way participate in incorruption, save by His coming among us', this is not an argument of the necessity of sequence from effect to cause, but of the fact that the need is humanity's and that this need is only shown and acknowledged in the light of the visible presence of God as the Word made flesh. It is a matter of the fact that there is only that which requires *saving* because the Word is His essential being is not only the one by whom all things are made, but who simultaneously with this is their *saviour*. God has made humanity in His dispensation of creation to be that which progresses towards God, and therefore requires a *saving* process. He has created humanity to *advance* towards Him in perfect correspondence with His Being and involves His whole Being as Father, Word and Spirit in that work. Hence creation and redemption for Irenaeus are bound together inseparably. That God said 'let us make man after our image' is coterminous with the fact that 'the Word was made flesh and dwelt among us and we beheld His glory'. Thus humanity receives 'advancement and increase towards God. For as God is always the same, so also man, when found in God, shall always go on towards God'.[13] As has been set out part by part in comments in former chapters, the gist of this is that the overall plan of God in creating, his dispensation, the working out of this ὀικονομια, is that the creative act, for Irenaeus, is also the revealing and saving act centred on the Word made flesh.

What may be said of all this is that Irenaeus had a clear view that the dispensation of God in the work of creation takes into account that that which is created is made with respect to the fact that it is *created* and is not as the *Creator*. Creation, therefore, in the very act of creation, requires nurture in a community of union with the existence of the triune God, and that this nurture is already present in the very existence of God as Father and Word, bound in the bond of eternal love who is the Holy Spirit.

What might be deemed to be the necessity of the Word becoming flesh in order to save humanity is dealt with by Irenaeus in Section 33 of the *Demonstration*. Here we have to read this in the context not of circumstances which happen outwith the grasp of God, but of the whole dispensation of creation. When he writes that 'it was necessary that Adam should be summed up in Christ, that mortality might be swallowed up and overwhelmed by immortality', he does not mean that God had made some mistake in creating and that this had to be rectified, but rather that, in the dispensation of God, provision was made for the nature of creation in the very act of creation because God is as He acts and acts as He is. There is no discrepancy between the being and the acts of God. The 'it was necessary that Adam should be summed up in Christ' refers to God as Father and Creator in His Word and Spirit so creating, rather than the creation imposing dictates upon God out of the difficulties into which it had haphazardly fallen.[14]

In Section 32 (for the commentary on this see Chapter 7) this is emphasized by Irenaeus's comment that 'to show forth', that is to demonstrate, 'that which was written in the beginning, man after the image and likeness of God', the Word recapitulated anew this man by being born 'from the Virgin by the Will and Wisdom of God'. That is to say that the 'image and likeness' of God resides in the Word primarily, and that this prime image and likeness is established in the incarnation in order to 'show forth the likeness of Adam's entry into flesh'.[15] There then follows in the subsequent sections a detailed parallelism between the act and following events of creation and the act and achievement of re-creation in the Word made flesh, backed up by reference to Isaiah's prophecy and the intent of prophecy in Israel in general as to the foreseeing of that which was to come. This perception of the role of prophecy is meaningless unless it is appreciated that Irenaeus was trying to say that that what was to come was already established in the dispensation of God, and that the parallelism was within the dispensation of God already established in His Word and through His Spirit.

This parallelism is centred on the roles of Eve and Mary respectively and the significance of 'the tree of obedience' (the cross) and the tree of good and evil in the garden of Eden. Again, this must not be seen in terms of cause and effect – as though God had to act summarily to repair His supposed oversight and negligence, the state into which creation had fallen so dictating. To think so would be to deem God necessarily contingent upon creation, and devising appropriate methods of rectification *de nouveaux*, rather than perceiving that this is the pattern of God's creative and redemptive dispensation. So, within the latter perception it is clear that it is equally necessary in the creative and redemptive dispensation of God that Eve be 'summed up in Mary, that a virgin should be a virgin's intercessor, and by a virgin's obedience undo and put away the disobedience of a virgin'.[16] Likewise the cross is paralleled to the tree in the garden by which came the fall. The comments of Irenaeus are full of implicit parallelisms; thus, in this Section 34, we read that the Son of man was nailed to the cross, which is the tree of obedience, because he was

> hearkening unto God . . . thereby putting away the knowledge of evil and bringing in and establishing the knowledge of good: now evil it is to disobey God, even as hearkening unto God is good . . . . He put away the old disobedience which was wrought in the tree.[17]

What is obvious in parallel is the disobedience of Adam and the obedience of Christ. But implicit here, in the light of what is one of Irenaeus's favourite descriptions of humanity in Adam in Section 33, 'the sheep that was lost',[18] is God's search for the man in Christ, just as he searched for the man in the garden. Thus 'just as at that time God spoke to Adam at eventide, searching him out; so in the last times, by means of the same voice, searching out His posterity, He has visited them'.[19]

So, too, there is the more than implied parallelism between the knowledge of good and evil, which the fruit of the tree bestowed on Adam and Eve – that is, the concept of free-will and autonomous judgment of the will – and the obedience of Christ. This implication is brought out in the statement that Christ by his obedience on the cross 'put away the old disobedience which was wrought in the tree'. The freedom of humanity is now a freedom *for* God, and not a freedom *from* God. This reminds us of double contingency; that the freedom given by Christ is found in participation, in the 'community of union' with him, in his obedience to God. Yet it is our freedom, for it has been won on our behalf – we, who, as the lost, are unable to find it for ourselves.

All this work of Christ is then set out in its full significance by Irenaeus in the conclusion of Section 34. Here we see the 'cosmic' Christ. But caution must be exercised here. The time and place of the cross is particular in all its historical reality as the place where the redemption of all things is wrought. What makes this event and this place significant for all time and every place is that the humanity of this crucified man is the humanity of the Word. The whole creation is 'encompassed' by the Word, for by Him Himself it is 'ordered and disposed'. The Word comes into his own possession – an important facet of Irenaeus's insistence that the world was not made, as the heretics think, by angelic or other agencies, and one which is emphatically stated in *Adversus Haereses* V:18:1,2 just before we find a passage in V:18:3 which is the same in content as this part of Section 34 of the *Demonstration*. The humanity of Christ only has being because it is in union with the Word, that is, it is that which the Word assumed and to which he gave existence in that assumption, in union with himself, for outwith this union the humanity has no existence. It is because it is such a humanity grounded in and given existence by the Word, that what happens in the crucifixion affects the whole universe which is related again contingently to the Word for its beginning, upholding and course. The passage does not suggest that in some way the humanity of Christ is extended throughout creation; Irenaeus is too insistent on the reality of the Word's humanity in the face of heretical interpretations to postulate this. We have to note that it is the unseen Word who, with regard to creation, 'is universally extended in all the world, and encompasses its length and breadth and height and depth', and in the midst of this sweeping panorama – 'in it is crucified the Son of God, inscribed cross-wise upon it all'. It may be that Irenaeus takes the phrase 'crosswise upon it' from Justin Martyr,[20] though in this particular passage from Justin Martyr the reference is accredited to Plato's *Timaeus*[21] where the philosopher is speaking about the soul of the universe which is impressed upon the creation in the form of the letter X. The argument in Justin Martyr, trying to salvage what he can from Plato's supposed reference, may have contributed something to Irenaeus's thought here, even if only the phraseology; that of Plato's would not. The relation of creation to the Creator Word in the thought of Irenaeus is one of double contingency – that it holds its beginning and upholding and course as bestowed by the Creator (its contingency *to* God), yet the identity it has is its integrity precisely as creation – it is not the Creator, and certainly not related to him through any Platonic conception of Logos or Word-soul, and this is its contingency *from* God. The relation of creature to Creator for Irenaeus is one of sheer grace in which its created nature is upheld by the Creator.

The historical particularity of the cross is made effective for the universe because it is the cross of the Word made flesh. The second 'cosmic' utterance of Irenaeus in this section with which he continues can only be understood in terms now of the Word made flesh, and crucified flesh, as opposed to his first 'cosmic' reference earlier in the section which is to the unseen Word in His creative work. It is because the Son of God has been crucified that He

> illuminates the height, that is the heavens; and encompasses the deep which is beneath the earth; and stretches and spreads out the length from west to east; and steers across the breadth of north and south; summoning all that are scattered in every quarter to the knowledge of the Father.[22]

The Word has always held fellowship with his creatures,[23] co-existed with his creatures,[24] was present with his own handiwork from the beginning.[25] But now, as the Word made flesh, the Son of God crucified, He calls the whole of creation to a knowledge of the Father.

This is the fulfilment of the promises made in the working out of the blessings of Shem and Japheth – first, in Section 35, to Abraham, the patriarch of faithfulness and the faithful. The virgin of whom Christ was born was of the seed of Abraham, and thus Christ stands in the line of the seed of Abraham, fulfiling the promise that his seed would be as 'the stars of heaven'. This Irenaeus picks up in remarking that Christ 'constitutes' the faithful, the true inheritors of Abraham's faith, as 'lights of the world'. He Himself is light and God spoke to Abraham 'making Himself known by the Word as by a beam of light'.[26] The same God who so called and conversed with Abraham brings the promise to fruition through the same Christ, who 'prepares lights in the world, those who believe from among the Gentiles. And He says; Ye are the light of the world; that is, as the stars of heaven';[27] thus raising up Abraham's seed as 'the stars of heaven' from among the Gentiles.

Section 35 which speaks of the fulfilled promise to Abraham is centred around the fulfilled faith of Abraham in the universal accomplishment of the Word made flesh. It is this faith, the self-same in the old and new covenants, to which in the old the law and the prophets bear witness – again the insistence on the paradigmatic role of the law and the prophecy pointing to their proper substance – and which in the new the Word now 'presents to us'. Here, J. Smith's translation makes this passage clearer, where he renders the last sentence in this section, that we are justified 'through the faith of Him to whom witness was borne by the law and the prophets whom the Word of God brought to us'.[28] That is, faith is Christ's alone, He being the embodiment of the faithfulness of God, whom the Word presents to us in being made flesh.

It is to be noted that faith is not an achievement of human endeavour or piety, but a gift 'presented', its substance in its presentation and reception being not other or less than the Person and completed work of the Word made flesh. Faith, whether it be the faith of the old or the new covenants – which faith is the same in both for it is of 'one substance', being variously centred on the Word made flesh either in promise or fulfilment – rests primarily on the faithfulness of God. The looking forward to the faithful of the old covenant, epitomized and recapitulate in Abraham, stands in the sequence of faith, for their expectation and prophecy was concentrated on the Word made flesh.

The prophets called the people of Israel to a recognition of the proper substance of the law, its paradigmatic content. It is in this respect of that content, our Lord Himself, which, Irenaeus explains, shows that the teaching of Christ is not 'the utterance of one undoing the law, but of one fulfilling, extending and affording greater scope to it'.[29] This is the substance and fulfilment of the law, the faith which undergirds it and gives it its proper validity, and he, of course, is that substance of the law and therefore the law's fulfilment.

The prophets, too, point to this enlarging and fulfilment of the substance of their respective prophecies. Each of them point to a particular facet of the accomplishment of the Word made flesh, but together all these prophecies exhibit 'the entire system of the work of the Son of God, knowing always the same God and acknowledging always the same Word of God'.[30] Section 36 then emphasizes the promise to David. Just as Section 35 has spoken of the nature and universality of believers, and the fulfilment of faith, so now the development of Irenaeus's observations turns to the nature, universality and establishment of the kingdom of which the faithful are the denizens. The fulfilment of the promise of God to David the king that 'of the fruit of his body' he would raise up 'an eternal King, whose kingdom should have no end', is succinctly stated by Irenaeus – 'And this King is Christ, the Son of God, who became the Son of man.'

The phrase 'eternal king' is employed in *Adversus Haereses* by Irenaeus in this particular context of the promise to David: 'the fulfilment of God's promise made to David, that from the fruit of his body there should be an eternal king'.[31] It is repeated in Sections 56, 66, 93 of the *Demonstration*, where again it is employed within the explicit or implicit terms of this Davidic promise, as it is in all instances of its use in *Adversus Haereses*. The same phrase is found in Justin Martyr's *Dialogue with Trypho*, but in these instances it is not applied to the promise made to David. In these it is used respectively to contrast Solomon with Christ,[32] as the content of the prophecies of Christ's ultimate glory,[33] of Ezekiel's prophecy,[34] and of Christ's constant kingship over Israel from the beginning.[35] Irenaeus does not so indiscriminately apply it.

This is one of the instances where supposed dependence on sources scented out by those on the constant search to make individual's theology little more than an amalgam of previous thoughts, is exaggerated. The phrase 'eternal king' is deployed by Irenaeus for a specific purpose. He could well have followed Justin Martyr slavishly in its wider use, but he does not. There is not the slightest shred of evidence that he coined it from Justin Martyr and that therefore this shows yet more of his conjectural dependence on the latter. The phrase itself is scarcely the preserve of any one theologian, and it should not be used for scenting out breaches of copyright, plagiarism and lack of original thought.

The 'eternal king' whose 'kingdom shall have no end' is the declaration of the triumphant Christ in his universal rule, but, in keeping with Irenaeus's theological method, it is anchored in the particular (in this instance the monarchy of Israel) in the dispensation of God of which this universal kingdom is the completion, and to which all historical factors point in their particularity. Again this particularity is underlined in that Christ is born of the virgin as 'the fruit' of David's body, she being descended from David. As the promise to Abraham regarding his seed extends out into the number and nature of the faithful being 'as the stars of heaven', so here the kingship of David expands through his seed into the universal and everlasting rule and dominion of Christ. Thus it is that Irenaeus in Section 37 can speak of Christ as 'perfecting and recapitulating' Abraham and David.

Having introduced this cosmic sweep of the triumph of the Word made flesh as the fulfilment of the dispensation of God, Irenaeus characteristically descends to a consideration of the particular yet again. From the full circumference he moves to the centre. He does this in Sections 38 and 39 by concentrating on the necessity of the actuality of the birth, death, resurrection and ascension of our Lord.

He does this principally by necessarily linking the birth and resurrection – simply it is a matter of both or neither. In so asserting this inseparable consideration, Irenaeus is firmly anchoring the whole work of redemption by the Word as a tangible event and a complete process, in which the reality of the flesh assumed by the Word is bounded and identified in its actuality by these two events. Identified by such, and only by such, is the incarnate and resurrected Christ the guarantor of redemption. Hence

> God the Father was very merciful: He sent His creative Word, who in coming to deliver us came to the very place and spot in which we had lost our life, and brake the bonds of our fetters.[36]

These 'bonds and fetters' typify our whole existence, being of the stock of Adam, as one of disobedience the end of which is death. Therefore it is necessary, as we have seen,[37] for the Word to assume every aspect and age of our life from birth to death in order to break these shackles and grant us freedom and immortality.

> Wherefore also He passed through every stage of life, restoring to all communion with God.[38]

> For He came to save all through means of Himself – all, I say, who through Him are born again to God – infants and children and boys and youths and old men. He therefore passed through every age, becoming an infant for infants, thus sanctifying infants; a child for children, thus sanctifying those who are of this age . . . youth for youths . . . . So likewise was He an old man for old men . . . . Then, at last, He came to death itself, that He might be 'the first-born from the dead, that in all things He might have the pre-eminence', the Prince of life, existing before all and going before all.[39]

> Wherefore also the Lord Himself gave us a sign, in the depths below and in the height above, which man did not ask for, because he had never expected that a virgin could conceive, or that it was possible that one remaining a virgin could bring forth a son, and that what was thus born should be 'God with us', and descend to those things which are in the earth beneath, seeking the sheep which had perished, which was indeed His own peculiar handiwork, and ascend to the height above, offering and commending to His Father that human nature which had been found, making in His own Person the first-fruits of the resurrection of man.[40]

Here in all these considerations we have an example of how Irenaeus does his theology. It is a matter of the presentation of circles of thought expanding through the Word made flesh to cosmic dimensions and touching that which is incomprehensibly and invisibly beyond, the very triune existence of the eternal God, and circles of thought contracting from that Being beyond comparison through the Word made flesh down to the particularity of 'the very spot' of human existence – or, with regard to the prophetic nature of the old covenant, as is found in Section 45, the Word of God comes and stands 'in a very small space' for the specific reason of speaking to Abraham.

These circles meet and pass and pass and meet in their outward and inward motions. Every aspect of Irenaeus's theology is so formed – again, for example, in the redemption of man the Word seeks Adam, the recapitulative patriarch, and expands the assumption of Adamic flesh, as an individual, into universal redemption. From the re-creative and redemptive ordering of all things by the triune God, we pass with the Word from this down to, again, 'the very spot' where we lost life. From our baptism into the incarnate and crucified and risen life of Christ we pass again into the expanding circle into this cosmic redemption. Again, so it is with the hinterland of the coming of the Word as man, the history of Israel. This goes from the original promise to Shem and Japheth, whereby the redemption of Adam's fall takes its first step, out into the whole panorama of law and prophets, and coalesces again in the birth of Christ out of the womb of Israel and from there out into the 'fruit of the blessing of Japheth, in the calling of the Gentiles, made manifest through the Church, standing in readiness to receive its dwelling in the house of Shem', as Section 42, in gathering up Irenaeus's argument in these sections, states.

All this is why the doctrine of recapitulation in Irenaean thought is the handmaid, or the consequence, of this Christocentric theology, and not its determinative. It is also why all doctrines, particularly that of baptism and redemption, are firmly anchored to the truth and actuality of the Word made flesh, and have no significance independent of this.[41]

Sections 40–42 exhibit just these circles of expanding, contracting and meeting thought, all with the Word made flesh as their content and horizon.

Notes

1 Irenaeus: *Demonstration of the Apostolic Preaching* 29.
2 *Ibid.* 29.
3 *Ibid.* 42.
4 Irenaeus: *Adversus Haereses* III:19:1.
5 *Ibid.* V:1:1,2,3.
6 *Ibid.* V:1:1.
7 *Ibid.* V:1:2.
8 *Ibid.* IV:6:6.
9 *Ibid.* IV:20:7.
10 *Ibid.* V:16:2.
11 Irenaeus: *Demonstration of the Apostolic Preaching* 47.
12 Irenaeus: *Adversus Haereses* IV:11:2..
13 *Ibid.* IV:11:2.
14 Irenaeus: *Demonstration of the Apostolic Preaching* 33.
15 *Ibid.* 32.
16 *Ibid.* 33.
17 *Ibid.* 34.
18 E.g. Irenaeus: *Adversus Haereses* III:19:3; 23:1; V:12:3; 15:2.
19 *Ibid.* V:15:4.
20 Justin Martyr: *First Apology* LX.
21 Plato: *Timaeus* 36BC.
22 Irenaeus: *Demonstration of the Apostolic Preaching* 34.
23 Irenaeus: *Adversus Haereses* II:32:5.
24 *Ibid.* IV:6:2.
25 *Ibid.* IV:6:7.
26 Irenaeus: *Demonstration of the Apostolic Preaching* 24.
27 Irenaeus: *Adversus Haereses* IV:7:3.
28 Irenaeus: *Proof of the Apostolic Preaching*, p. 70.
29 Irenaeus: *Adversus Haereses* IV:13:1; cf. 13:2.
30 *Ibid.* IV:33:15.
31 *Ibid.* III:10:3; cf. III:16:2; 21:5,9.
32 Justin Martyr: *Dialogue* 34.
33 *Ibid.* 36.
34 *Ibid.* 118.
35 *Ibid.* 135.
36 Irenaeus: *Demonstration of the Apostolic Preaching* 38.

37 Cf. comments on the *Demonstration*, Sections 3 and 4 in Chapters 3 and 4.
38 Irenaeus: *Adversus Haereses* III:18:7.
39 *Ibid.* II:22:4.
40 *Ibid.* III:19:3.
41 Cf. comments on the *Demonstration*, Section 3. Chapter 3.

Chapter 13

Sections 43–51: The Pre-existence of the Word

The necessity of believing 'God in all things' – referring to 'all' that Irenaeus has set out in the preceding sections – is that in all this he has demonstrated that 'in all things God is true'. The rehearsal of all these things is the dispensation of God in preparing humanity for its redemption. Irenaeus's argument is stated in the closing sentence of section 42:

> what was an impossibility to our nature, and therefore ready to cause incredibility to mankind, this God caused to be made known beforehand by the prophets; in order that, through its having been told in times long before, and then at last finding effect in this way, even as it was foretold, we might know that it was God who (thus) proclaimed to us beforehand our redemption.

We are forced back here to the third section of the *Demonstration*, to the assertion that

> faith rests on things that truly are. For in things that are, as they are, we believe; and believing in things that are, as they ever are, we keep firm our confidence in them.[1]

Faith does not spring naturally from human ability, for it concerns that which lies beyond the created limitations and proficiencies of the creature. It is a matter of thinking, not out of a centre of the capability of the mind as though standards of analytical ability and final judgment were resident in a supposed autonomy of the mind, but out of a centre in the things which confront the mind that the mind may be informed by their light. That is, according to Irenaeus here, we judge the things of God which have been now demonstrated, not by the credulousness of the mind as the measure of them, but by the very things themselves which in fact are incredible to the natural motions and conclusive abilities of the mind. The presence of 'incredibility to mankind' is a factor in fact necessary for such κατα φυσιν thinking, resulting in the apprehension of objective knowledge particularly here in the things of the Creator who is beyond comparison, becoming possible in faith and cutting through the limitations of our minds.

In the exegesis of the early Church, the fact that an event happened as prophesied beforehand was regarded as a necessary proof of the validity of that event. That the prophets foretold, and the whole old covenant anticipated, Christ,[2] is for Irenaeus indubitable proof that this is the working out of the dispensation of God in a manner in which humanity so confronted, has the possibility of entering into the process of believing in order to understand. The status and significance of the prophets in this is that they prophesied in such a compelling way that 'He who was not come as yet was present'[3] for he was present indeed with them, as we have noted already in Irenaeus's view of the old testament's relation to the Word.

What is compelling for belief is that in the whole sweep of the history of Israel, and therefore of the movement of the old covenant, and into the existence of the Church in the new,

> the Word of God always preserves the outlines, as it were, of things to come, and points out to men the various forms, as it were, of the dispensations of the Father, teaching us the things pertaining to God.[4]

Moreover, Christ

> at that time indeed, by means of His patriarchs and prophets, was prefiguring and declaring beforehand future things, fulfilling His part by participation in the dispensation of God and accustoming His inheritance to obey God and to pass through this world as in a state of pilgrimage, to follow His word, and to indicate beforehand things to come. For with God there is nothing without purpose and due signification.[5]

God is his own interpreter, and the 'dispensations' of God are not independent of the Word by whom God is known. Indeed, the 'dispensations' of God concern the component historical events and institutions and personages which together, from the creation and Adam and in the old and the new covenants are employed in the whole creative and redemptive dispensation which is the Word made flesh. Thus it is the demonstration of this dispensation that God is to be believed 'in all things, for in all things God is true'.

Irenaeus now works out the relation of this dispensation to the Being of the Triune God. He makes the entrance into this via the pre-existence of the Word, that is, that the Word, and by implication the Holy Spirit, is *semper co-existens* with the Father. He refers to Genesis I:1 in a curious way, namely claiming that its meaning in the Armenian language (the literal translation of the phrase which Armitage Robinson here renders 'our language') from the Hebrew text is 'The Son in the beginning; God established then the heaven and earth'. There is undoubtedly a problem here as to why this should be so stated. It may be that this is an attempt to conflate the Hebrew of Genesis I:1 (though Irenaeus here puts forward a corrupt version) with the statement in John I:1 – 'In the beginning was the Word'. Certainly the contemporary Clement of Alexandria would tend to the same in his phrase linking the Son with 'beginning'[6] – ὅτι ἀρχη ὁ ὑιος. Irenaeus shows his avowed intent to conflate Genesis with John's Gospel at the end of Section 43. This is centred round the other intent of Irenaeus expressed in this section which is to establish that the Word is the Son, so that any misconstruing by gnostics heretics of the term 'begetting' in the relation of Father to Son is confuted, for 'begetting' is not different from the term 'was with' in the eternal relation of the Word to the Father.

That the Son was in the beginning with the Father, before the creation, is put forward by Irenaeus in his equally curious citation and assigning of a composite quotation from the psalms.[7] This he ascribes to Jeremiah. Armitage Robinson,[8] in support of his thesis as to the extent of the debt owed to Irenaeus to Justin Martyr, makes much of the fact of the interplay in composite quotations commonly used by both Irenaeus and Justin Martyr, though not necessarily word for word. I do not see this as conclusive proof (and neither, it must be said does Armitage Robinson, though he does suggest what he sees as the likelihood of dependence on Justin Martyr by Irenaeus in this matter) of such indebtedness. Armitage Robinson does say that Irenaeus's lapse in assigning the quotations to Jeremiah is 'serious' – for it must be pointed out that Justin Martyr does not make this mistake. It is more likely, as is hinted at by Armitage Robinson, that these quotations in these forms came from a book or books of proof texts against the Jews, the existence of such long ago advocated by Rendel Harris.[9] If the form of such possible proof books were the same as that of the later medieval patristic proof text books, authorship was either not mentioned or indifferently apportioned.

Whatever the explanation, Irenaeus's intent is there, to equate the Son with the Word and show that the generation of both is the same. This explains the observation in this section (again using a text curiously attributed to Jeremiah – apportioned similarly by the later Lactantius[10] as Rendel Harris noted,[11] and thereby suggesting a common, careless source):

> Blessed is he who was, before he became a man. Because, for God, the Son was (as) the beginning before the creation of the world; but for us (He was) then, when He appeared: and before that He was not for us who knew Him not. Wherefore also His disciple John, in teaching us who is the Son of God, who was with the Father before the world was made, and that all things that were made were made by Him, says thus: In the beginning was the Word . . .

What Irenaeus is arguing here is that before the Word appeared to the fathers of the old covenant pointing to the fact that He would become flesh, and walk and converse with humanity, He was the Immeasurable, the Invisible, the Incomprehensible, one with the Father as the God beyond comparison. It is only as we see Him as Son, *for us*, in his accommodation of Himself to creatureliness, that we appreciate Him and know Him as this Word/Son.

We may note in the following sections how Irenaeus emphasizes this by his usage of 'Son' primarily and 'Word' secondarily as compared with his tendency to refer to 'Word' and 'Son' secondarily in the corresponding parts of *Adversus Haereses*. Hence here in Section 44 he points out that the Son spoke with Abraham, and in Section 45 that the Son speaks with men, and that same who speaks is the Word who 'came and stood in a very small space and spake with Abraham'. In the larger and earlier work,[12] Irenaeus is also at pains to underline the fact that the Word is the Son. The Father is known 'by the Son, that is the Word' and God is ministered to by 'the Son and the Holy Spirit, the Word and Wisdom'.[13]

What is being stressed here, too, is that God is known in his relations *in se*, as Father and Creator through the Son made a Son of man, the incarnation of the Word. It is clear, as we have remarked before,[14] that Irenaeus gives priority to the title 'Father' – an anticipation of Athanasius's insistence that God is known essentially through the Son as Father, and that he always has been Father, the Father of the Son,[15] signifying the very essence of God. 'None should imagine God the Father to be other than our Creator, as the heretics imagine', states Irenaeus emphatically in

Section 98 towards the conclusion of the *Demonstration.* This is in accord with the place he accords to the title Father in Sections 4–8, and in the way, throughout both works, that he constantly calls the 'dispensation' of God towards his creation 'the dispensation of the Father'. He never writes of God as 'Creator' alone whenever he discusses the redemption of the creature and its relation to the Creator. The triune Being of God as the internal and eternal Personal relations of the Godhead is that to which creation and humanity are related – not to some impersonal concept, however properly stated, of the Creator primarily. For God is never in the works of Irenaeus only considered as Creator. God is Creator because He is Father, and this is the emphatic order which is found in the theology of Irenaeus.

Is there an anticipation of Athanasius's further argument as to God's begetting being primary and His creating secondary to Him?[16] We have to note that in both Irenaeus and Athanasius, the incarnation and creation are bracketed together in a profound way. They both concern the Son and Word, who is *semper co-existens* with the Father, and therefore concern the very Being of God. Yet both incarnation and creation involve a beginning. The Word takes what He had not before, namely human flesh and nature, and brings into being that which has a beginning and which did not exist as co-eternal with God, namely creation. It is the will of God that such should take place.

Therefore a problem opens out. While both Irenaeus and Athanasius are clear that creaturely concepts, measurement and characteristics are not to be projected into God in his essential Being, nevertheless there is the question of the will of God accomplishing something that was not 'before'. The creation and the human nature of the Word are not coterminous with the eternity of God, which has no 'before' or 'after'. Therefore their respective bringings into being point to an ineffable 'beginning' in the will of the Being of God, which lies beyond and is not of the same temporal quality of their beginnings of being. To speak of a 'beginning' within God is not the same as speaking of a 'beginning' when the latter is applied to the created dimension. The two applications are different, the latter temporal and spatial, the former indefinable and transcendent. If this is not appreciated, as Athanasius notes,[17] then the heretical statement of the Arians, that there was a time when the Son was not, must follow. Athanasius continues in this vein, noting that behind the beginning of creation, there is a 'beginning' 'preceding their coming into being; but the Word, not being of things which come to be, rather comes to be Himself the framer of those things which have a beginning'.[18] The Word has no beginning with regard to His essence, for He is one with the Father who eternally begets Him, yet He 'becomes the framer of things which have a beginning'.

I suggest that this same sort of problem existed in the mind of Irenaeus regarding the word 'beginning' and its relation to the Creator and to creatures, lying behind, even in an embryonic, unspoken perception, the need for him to state in Section 43 here,

> The Son in the beginning; God established then the heaven and earth . . . . Because, for God, the Son was [as] the beginning before the creation of the world; but for us [He was] then, when He appeared.[19]

Indeed, the whole section would seem to be a wrestling with this question of 'beginning', centring strongly round the incarnation as the entrance into it. Again, in the full thought of Irenaeus, in both his extant works, the fact that the Son or Word remains what He was but assumes that which He had not before, is the entrance into the understanding that through the Son or Word, existing with the Father in all eternity, there is brought about a beginning, namely creation, which was not before, and that both of these are 'new' acts by the freedom of the grace and loving-kindness of God's will. The essence of God does not change in incarnation and in creating; the will of God is the 'beginning' which begins and accomplishes them.

The question Irenaeus now addresses is that of the relation of things which are made and have a beginning to the Son of God, the framer of those things which have a beginning, and through whom they were made, and how they are affected by his incarnation. Section 45 continues the vision of the Son of God in the old testament. Having spoken of our Lord's epiphany to Abraham, Irenaeus now turns to the Genesis XXVIII account of Jacob and his dream at Bethel, though Irenaeus places the patriarch in Mesopotamia. This is of itself significant in that it accords with Irenaeus's 'universal' view of the opening of the heavens for believing humanity. The 'tree' is the ladder 'which was set up from earth to heaven'. It is noteworthy that here Irenaeus does not follow Justin Martyr's observations[20] on this incident, in that the latter identifies the pillar set up by Jacob and anointed by him with Christ being anointed by the Father. It may be wondered why, for the interest of both Irenaeus and Justin Martyr is centred here, not on the identification of the ladder with the cross (neither theologian so identifies it specifically here, despite the assertion by Armitage Robinson[21]), but on the Person of Christ. Each approaches this in different ways; Justin Martyr by the anointing of the stone pillar, Irenaeus by the movement on the 'tree'.[22]

Irenaeus's concern is with the ascension of our Lord and our subsequent ascension. He asserts that 'His sufferings are our ascension on high', having noted that the 'tree' is that whereby 'they that believe on Him go up to heaven'. The tree, therefore, takes on more significance than being merely identified with the cross. There is a play on ascent and descent. Jacob in vision sees the Son of God 'standing upon the ladder, that is, the tree, which was set up from earth to heaven'.[23]

Here we have the ascended Christ, who is the one who has descended in his sufferings and through these sufferings opens up our ascension with him. Irenaeus seems to be identifying the 'tree' here with the sufferings of the Person of Christ and the recapitulation of us through these. While the tree in the thought of Irenaeus is the cross on which the obedience of Christ works out our redemption (in parallelism to the tree in the garden as the instrument of the fall on which our disobedience is centred), nevertheless, his emphasis is not on the cross as a static symbol, as though it had significance in and by itself, but on the Person and work of Christ. The passing reference to the fact that the cross is this tree in Section 79 hardly allows any suggestion of a veneration of the cross as the cross. The way in which he briefly comprehends the redemption wrought out for humanity by Christ here demonstrates his main interest on Christ himself and his sufferings. Thus, in Section 46, the deliverance afforded humanity, 'bringing us to the kingdom of the Father', typified by the deliverance of Israel from Amalek, is 'by the expansion of His hands'. The same phrase is found in *Adversus Haereses*[24] in the context of Christ gathering 'two peoples', that is the peoples of the old and new covenants, together to one God. He cites this as originating from 'A certain man among our predecessors', but this source is neither named nor is discoverable.

> Through the extension of the hands of a divine person [thus the Greek text; the Latin omits 'of a divine person'], gathering together the two peoples to one God. For there were these two hands, because there were two peoples scattered to the ends of the earth; but there was one head in the middle, as there is but one God, who is above all, and through all, and in us all.[25]

This comes at the end of a strange passage where the finding of the lost axehead (used by the prophets in Elisha's company in the hewing of the wood to build a tabernacle) by Elisha's casting of wood into the water wherein it had fallen, is seen as a prophetic action pointing to the restoration of that which humanity had lost, namely the 'sure word of God'. It would appear that Irenaeus is meaning that by the very cutting of wood the axehead was lost (the tree of the garden), so by Elisha's wood (the cross) the axehead was retrieved. But again, the emphasis is on that which the axehead signifies, the 'sure word of God', and the 'divine person' with the action of the 'extension' of His hands. That is the substance of redemption; the cross is but the instrument. It is, however, an instrument which itself is paradigmatic of the redemption wrought on it, and the Person by, and way in, which this was accomplished. He writes here that what was made manifest was by means of a tree 'showing the height, the length, the breadth, the depth in itself'. This seems to suggest that Irenaeus uses the shape of the cross to point to the nature of the saving Person and event. Hence, as we have seen in Section 34, the Son of God is 'inscribed crosswise' upon the whole universe – the universe which the self-same Word 'orders and disposes'. This means that the whole universe, in every direction and dimension, is affected by the cross, for it is the cross of the Son of God, and the dimension it also affects is that of the relation between heaven and earth, for through it earth is bent up to heaven and heaven down to earth, as it were.

Just as we saw in the previous chapter that Section 35 spoke of the universality of believers and the fulfilment of faith, and that Section 36 then turned this into a discussion of the nature, universality and establishment of the kingdom into which believers were received, so here there is the same turning between the universality of, and the effect of redemption fulfilled by, the cross, and, at the end of Section 46, the consideration of that kingdom in terms of the eternal relations of the Father and the Son and the Holy Spirit.

The flesh, sufferings and cross of Christ are universal in their effect because they are the flesh, sufferings and cross of the Word made flesh. 'By the expansion of His Hands', He 'brings us into the kingdom of the Father'. It may be as well here not to lose sight of Irenaeus's constant reference to 'hands' as the Word and the Spirit. Is there an underlying statement in this use of the 'expansion' or 'extension' of hands to the fact that the cross is the focal point of the redeeming work of Word and Spirit in the will of the Father, and therefore a linking of the sufferings of Christ to the divine existence of the triune God, a linking which is centred on the stretching out of the hands and the universal work which these hands accomplish?

Section 47 gathers this work together in that all that has been demonstrated before regarding the sufferings of Christ and their universal and revelatory effect, now demonstrates that, 'So then the Father is Lord and the Son is Lord, and the Father is God and the Son is God; for that which is begotten of God is God.' This is the essential and eternal Being of God – God *in se* – demonstrated in 'the substance and power of His being'. This is demonstrated in the 'economy of our redemption', for as God is, so He acts. There is no disjunction between God *in se* and God as He works *ad extra*. What God is eternally in Himself, so He is as He works our redemption in our midst.

Irenaeus underlines this fact, for there is 'according to the economy of our redemption both Son and Father'. This economy of our redemption has been set out in the previous sections, and here it is linked inseparably with revelation. Revelation and reconciliation are one. For as being and act are one so are act and knowledge. The Father is 'invisible' and 'unapproachable'. We cannot grasp God as He is in Himself, but He Himself has made a way for us to know Him and have access to Him. This way is 'through the Son' and in the revelation and reconciliation He Personally brings. The oneness of the Son with the Father, the co-existence of the Word and the Father, is the ground of this. For it is the Son in that relation to the Father who is born a Son of man. Here is our access to the divine life, the community of union which is brought about for us through the unchanging oneness of the Son with the Father and the oneness of the Son with us in His incarnation. Having access to the Father through the Son means both revelation and reconciliation, for we not only know the 'invisible' Father through the Son as the 'visible' of the Father, but we are able to 'draw near' to the 'unapproachable' Father in that same Son. The work of the Son is one in which we, in our darkened and alienated humanity, find knowledge of, and communion with, the divine existence.

Irenaeus's insistence on the establishing of a 'community of union' for humanity with God is the outcome of his understanding of the inseparable bracketing together of the work and Person of the Son of God born the Son of man and the Triune existence of the eternal God. It is in this context, too, that his equal insistence that 'faith and godliness', revelation and reconciliation, knowing and being, are one. For in and by and through the Son of God born the Son of man, our being is related to the divine Being. The 'royal exchange', the incarnation of the Word and the 'deification' of humanity by the grace and loving-kindness of Word and Spirit, our humanity now being capable of bearing the Holy Spirit because of assumption by the Word and His 'accustoming' our humanity to the Spirit, is the pivot around which all these factors inextricably revolve. Here again is this pulsating pattern of Irenaeus's theology – circles of theological thought going out from a point, overlapping, intermingling and returning again to the centre to be strengthened.

The incarnation and the eternal existence of God as Father, Word and Spirit are bound together in Irenaeus's description of the bestowing of the kingdom by the Father upon the Son and His 'coronation', His 'anointing' by the Spirit, in this Section 47. The Son receives the kingdom, which, it must be noted, is 'the everlasting kingdom', from the Father, and the seal of this enthronement is the 'oil of anointing', that is, as Irenaeus makes clear, the Holy Spirit Himself. This is found in expanded form in *Adversus Haereses*:

> In the name Christ there is implied: He that anoints, He that is anointed, and the very unction with which He is anointed. And it is the Father who anoints, and the Son who is

> anointed by the Spirit who is himself the unction, as the Word declares by Isaiah: the Spirit of the Lord is upon me because He has anointed me – pointing out the anointing Father, the anointed Son and the Spirit which is the anointing.[26]

And elsewhere in *Adversus Haereses*,[27] the same is found and again in the context of the dominion over all creation given to the Son by the Father. Here we have the convergence and interlocking of the existence of the triune God, the dominion of the Father, who rules over all having created by the Word, the pre-existence of the Word, and the completion of creation in the triumph and declaration of that rule in the victorious work of that Word incarnate, through His sufferings and cross, who is then given all power and dominion by the Father. Hence, at the end of Section 48, Irenaeus understands David prophetically in Psalm CX to proclaim 'the exaltation with glory that followed on His humanity and humiliation and ingloriousness'.

Justin Martyr treats of the same psalm. He applies the same meaning to the words quoted here by Irenaeus to indicate the humbling and exaltation of Christ.

> And that He shall first be humble as man and then exalted, these words at the end of the psalm show: He shall drink of the brook in the way, and then, Therefore shall He lift up the head.[28]

Justin Martyr also writes in a section[29] which is only vaguely paralleled in strength of interpretation, rather surprisingly, if Irenaeus is as beholden to Justin Martyr as is often stated, to that in *Adversus Haereses*.[30] Here Justin Martyr writes of the failure of the angelic hosts to recognize Christ in his ascension:

> For when the rules of heaven saw Him of uncomely and dishonoured appearance and inglorious, not recognizing Him they enquired Who is this King of Glory? And the Holy Spirit, either from the Person of the Father or from His own Person answers them, The Lord of Hosts, He is this King of Glory.[31]

Here, too, he is applying the same meaning to the words of the psalm quoted here by Irenaeus to indicate the humbling and the exaltation of Christ, and that that triumph is only on the grounds of abasement.

The curious thing with regard to their respective uses of Psalm CX, regarding the humbling of Christ being signified by the drinking from the brook in the way, and his exaltation being the lifting up of the head, is that Irenaeus – bearing in mind his main thrust as to the universality of Christ's redemption and what he is to write in subsequent sections concerning the rule of Christ over the Gentiles – does not (if he were slavishly or even closely following Justin Martyr) take up and repeat the point which Justin Martyr makes in commenting on Psalm CX in the *Dialogue with Trypho* regarding Melchisedek's priestly/kingly nature and role, which were patterns of Christ's office.

> Melchisedek . . . was a priest of the uncircumcision and blessed the circumcised Abraham who brought him tithes, so God has demonstrated that His everlasting Priest, called also by the Holy Spirit, Lord, would be Priest of those in uncircumcision.[32]

Irenaeus is more interested in the kingly office of Christ, though recognizing the essentially priestly nature of that in making even if but passing reference to it in Section 48 of the *Demonstration*. This is because he wishes to underline the interpretation of the sacrifice on the cross as an act of triumphant victory and a vindication and fulfilment of the claim that God has the dominion over creation as the sole God in the very act of creating all things out of nothing. It is equally strange, as has been stated, that he does not enlarge on Justin Martyr's interpretation of Psalm XXIV as an antiphonal between the angelic host and the Spirit regarding the acknowledgement of Christ's triumph through his sufferings. Even in Section 84, where Irenaeus takes up at greater length the same theme of the ascension of Christ prophetically put forward in the antiphon of Psalm XXIV, he does not portray the Spirit as answering the questioning angelic hosts, but puts an entirely different interpretation on the matter. He is concerned here with the invisibility of the Word who is made visible in the flesh, and therefore visible in his ascension. The angels below the firmament recognize the Word in the flesh as he ascends and call out to the angels in the firmament that the everlasting gates are to be opened to 'the King of glory'. When those higher angels saw him they asked 'Who is this' and those who had already seen and recognized him answered and testified to him that he is 'the Lord strong and mighty, he is the King of glory'. There is little reflecting Justin Martyr's interpretation here – merely a text applied to the ascension but now singularly interpreted by Irenaeus. Those parts of texts where similarity to Justin Martyr is found and the assumption of Irenaeus's dependence upon him laboured, are the very places where dissimilarity becomes obvious and where Irenaeus should be permitted to speak for himself by himself.

What now interests Irenaeus in Sections 49 and 50 is that the pre-existence of the Son is perceived by the fact that the Father 'spoke with Him'. This Irenaeus does by interpreting Psalms II, CX and Isaiah XLV, which read respectively: 'The Lord said unto me, Thou art my Son . . . The Lord said unto my Lord . . . God saith to my Anointed the Lord . . . – all bestowing kingship on the one addressed.

> The promise is the same by the two prophets [David and Isaiah] that He should be King: so that the speech of God is addressed to one and the same, I mean to Christ, the Son of God . . . . It is not a man who speaks the prophecies, but the Spirit of God, assimilating and likening Himself to the persons represented, speaks in the prophets and utters the words sometimes from Christ and sometimes from the Father.[33]

Irenaeus makes clear here his view of the nature, role and status of the old testament prophets, that they are the mouthpiece of the Spirit – the 'Spirit of the mouth of Christ',[34] the Spirit who articulates God and His Word.[35] Here again we move out swiftly in Irenaeus's theological movement of thought from old testament prophecy to the conversations within the triune Being of God.

This conversing concerns a transaction within the triune Being of God which involves the completion and establishment of the work of creation in its sure relation, its community of union, with that Being. This conversation and transaction is further set out by Irenaeus in the following sections in terms of the names bestowed upon the Word, and these will be considered shortly.

Irenaeus gathers all his preceding argument up in Sections 50 and 51 and also introduces that which he elaborates later, that is, the passive and active obedience of Christ as 'servant'. He sums up his argument in Section 51:

> Here, first of all, is seen that the Son of God pre-existed, from the fact that the Father spake with Him, and before He was born revealed Him to men; and next that He must needs be born a man among men.

But already in Section 50, quoting Isaiah XLIX:5f, Irenaeus has sounded the note of the servanthood of Christ, and does so here in Section 51:

> thus saith the Lord, who formed me as a servant from the womb . . . . And He said; a great thing shall it be to thee to be called my servant . . . that thou shouldst be for salvation unto the end of the earth . . . . The Son of the Father calls Himself servant, (that is) on account of His subjection to the Father: for among men also every son is the servant of his father.

What Irenaeus is doing is to introduce the whole work of Christ as a work of triumphant obedience, and to this we now turn.

Notes

1 Cf. comments on Section 3, Chapter 3.
2 Irenaeus: *Adversus Haereses* e.g. IV:20:8,11; IV:25:3, IV:32:10ff; IV:34:2–4.
3 *Ibid.* IV:20:8,11.
4 *Ibid.* IV:20:11.
5 *Ibid.* IV:21:3.
6 Clement of Alexandria: *Ecl. Proph.* 4.
7 Psalms CX:3 and LXXII:5.
8 J. Armitage Robinson: Introduction to the translation of the *Demonstration*, pp. 19ff; cf. pp. 12 and 13 for other questionable examples of Irenaeus's direct dependence on Justin Martyr.
9 Rendel Harris: *Testimonies* (Cambridge, 1916) – cf. p. 15 for these particular texts.
10 Lactantius: *Divin. Inst.* IV:8.
11 Rendel Harris: *Testimonies* pp. 15ff.
12 E.g. Irenaeus: *Adversus Haereses* IV:5:3ff; 7:1, etc.
13 *Ibid.* IV:7:3,4.
14 Cf. comments on Section 1 of the *Demonstration*, Chapter 1.
15 Athanasius *De Decretis* V:22; *Contra Arianos* 1:34.
16 Athanasius: *Contra Arianos* II:2.
17 *Ibid.* I:11,13.
18 *Ibid.* II:57.
19 Irenaeus: *Demonstration of the Apostolic Preaching*, 43.
20 Justin Martyr: *Dialogue with Trypho* LXXXVI.
21 J. Armitage Robinson: Introduction to the translation of the *Demonstration* p. 13.
22 E.g. Irenaeus: *Adversus Haereses* V:16:3; 17:3.
23 Irenaeus: *Demonstration of the Apostolic Preaching* 45.
24 Irenaeus: *Adversus Haereses* V:17:4.
25 *Ibid.*

26 *Ibid.* III:18:3.
27 *Ibid.* III:6:1.
28 Justin Martyr: *Dialogue with Trypho* 33.
29 *Ibid.* 36.
30 Irenaeus: *Adversus Haereses* IV:33:13.
31 Justin Martyr: *Dialogue with Trypho* 36.
32 *Ibid.* 33.
33 Irenaeus: *Demonstration of the Apostolic Preaching* 49.
34 Irenaeus: *Adversus Haereses* III:7:2.
35 Cf. *Ibid.* IV:1:1.

Chapter 14

Sections 52–66: The Names and Places of the Word in His Obedience

In these sections it becomes clear that Irenaeus links inseparably and in substance the incarnation of the Word and our redemption. That redemption is the incarnation of the Word; it is to be sought and found in the Person of Christ, in His oneness with the Father and in His oneness with humanity. Redemption is not a transaction of which Christ is the agent; He is redemption embodied, for it is worked out and fulfilled in His Person and particularly through His active and passive obedience to the Father. Humanity attains its redemption by participation in Him. This, as has been examined in earlier sections, is a matter of the 'royal exchange' and a 'community of union' established by the Word made flesh and by his Spirit.

Irenaeus begins this section with a summary of this: the Son, being with the Father before all things were created, is also 'nigh and close and joined' to humanity. It is in this double union that He is both declared and is King and Saviour. What is of importance here is the fact that the Son is ever with the Father even in his incarnation. Strongly implicit in this is the later maxim that 'what God is towards us in Jesus Christ He is eternally in Himself'. That is, Irenaeus is underlining the fact that the incarnation does not involve a change in the divine essence as it is in itself. The Word takes to Himself that which He had not before, namely human flesh and nature, but remains the Word by whom all things were created. He is still *with* the Father when yet held by the virgin.

In other words, we have the rejection of any Aristotelian 'container' theory of space here, that the Word was 'poured' into and limited by the confines of the human frame and nature. Equally there is rejected the later Arian idea of the Word made flesh as a *tertium quid*, a third thing between God and humanity. The Word remains the Word, Immeasurable, Invisible, but takes to Himself that flesh and nature which is measurable and visible. In this sense, and only in this sense, are Irenaeus's oft-repeated phrases such as 'the Invisible became visible', 'the Incomprehensible became comprehensible', 'the Immeasurable became measurable' and so on, to be understood. The Word did not turn into anything else, but assumed into His divine existence that which He had not before. That assumption is of that which is truly human. This is why Irenaeus emphasizes the real humanity of Christ in Section 53, even if the manner of His birth from a virgin was singular. In Section 53, He notes that in prophecy (Isaiah VII:14ff) that which the virgin was to bring forth would 'eat' and would be given 'a name'. These two considerations Irenaeus uses to indicate the real humanity, its necessity for sustenance and its identification as an individual. We have looked at already the oneness of the humanity of the Word with the realities of needy, fallen, Adamic flesh and nature.[1] It is Irenaeus's thesis that if God himself does not save, and if that is not assumed which requires saving, then there is no redemption. This is found in his continual insistence that, for example, the Word of God.

> did through His transcendent love, become what we are, that He might bring us to be what He is Himself[2]

> . . . the mighty Word and very man . . . thus has redeemed us by His own blood, giving His soul for our souls, and His flesh for our flesh . . . attaching man to God by means of His incarnation . . .[3]

> But how could we be joined to incorruptibility and immortality, unless, first, incorruptibility and immortality had become what we also are[4]

> . . . revealing God indeed to men, but presenting man to God.[5]

> The union of the Word of God with His own workmanship.[6]

The integrity of both God and man, and of the divinity and humanity of Christ at the incarnation, is thus stressed by Irenaeus. Here are the foundations for so much of the Christological development which was to take place particularly in the works of the Nicene fathers and their immediate successors in the east. 'Not assumed is not healed', the whole question of ἀνυποστασις and ἐνυποστασις – that the humanity of Christ only has no being outside its union with the Word, and that it has being within that union – and the whole direction of later Christology within the eternal and unbroken co-existence of the Word with the Father, are all present in latent or embryonic, and sometimes explicit, form in Irenaeus's works.

Irenaeus is clear in this Section 52 that the considerations of the relation of Son to Father and of the Son to humanity, are biblical. They are there in the prophets. The very names to be given to the Word made flesh are foretold regarding the offices of the Word made flesh and the nature and significance of the incarnation. In Sections 53ff these names are seen to reflect both the twofold relation of the Son to the Father and to His creaturely handiwork and the 'works actually wrought'. Act and being, work and existence, with regard to the Son of God in the flesh are not only complementary, they are one. Thus he is called 'Christ', because there is a twofold anointing involved – the one whereby the Father 'anointed and adorned all things', and the other because in His coming as man, He is 'anointed with the Spirit of God and His Father'. He is also called 'Saviour' because he is both the *cause* and the *author* of it. In such observation, Irenaeus indicates that the Word made flesh is the beginning and the end, the form and the content, of salvation. The astonishing fact of His birth is indicated by the appellation 'Emmanuel', which Irenaeus sees as 'a yearning cry' (or, perhaps, as Armitage Robinson notes, 'a cry of augury') conveying utter amazement that 'With us shall be God'.

This astonishment and amazement is in the fact that none other than God should be with us, but it is elaborated in Sections 70 and 71 also in terms of the fact that He, being God, should undergo such sufferings. He whose 'Father is undeclarable and unspeakable' descends to this. But here Irenaeus applies the 'astonishment' not only to the sufferings of Christ, but, interpreting 'His generation who shall declare?' from Isaiah LIII:8 as his 'descent', His 'undeclarable generation', being born into these sufferings. The 'astonishment' is applied here to the birth from the virgin, in the same way as he writes. 'God giving the sign, man not working it out'.[7] Hence, in Section 54, Irenaeus cites Isaiah LXVI:7 – 'Before she that travailed gave birth, and before the pains of travail came on, she escaped and was delivered of a man-child'. Thus, writes Irenaeus, 'His birth from the virgin was unforeseen and unexpected'. He is ascribing 'astonishment' not only because this birth was from a virgin, but here to the very manner of the birth itself, which, in turn, is a little sign of the greater sign. One is reminded of St Basil of Caesarea's later observation regarding the raising of Lazarus, that each miracle contains a little and attendant miracle within itself – in this case the fact that Lazarus emerged from the tomb yet was still bound hand and foot.

In the extended interpretation of Isaiah's prophecy of the birth from a virgin in *Adversus Haereses*, the same emphases are found centring around the three aspects of the divinity of the Word, the humanity of the Word and the mode of the union of the divinity and the humanity.

> Carefully then has the Holy Spirit indicated by what has been said [by the prophet] His birth from a virgin, and His essence that He is God (for the name Emmanuel indicates this), and He shows that He is a man when He says: Butter and honey shall He eat; and He terms Him a child also [by the words] Before He knows good and evil; for these are all marks of a human infant. But that: He will not consent to evil that He may choose that which is good – this is proper to God; that by the fact that He should eat butter and honey we should not understand that He is a mere man only, nor, on the other hand, from the name Emmanuel should think of Him to be God without flesh.[8]

Irenaeus determines here that the prophetic names and attributes of the Word made flesh should be held together in order that in their conjunction the truth should be apparent and not one-sided, which would lead to heretical interpretations of an adoptionist tendency on one count of treating the humanity only or an ebionite fallacy in considering solely the divinity. The sign itself, the birth, indicates just such a necessary juxtaposition and joint consideration, for, he continues:

> He [the Spirit] performed the part of one indicating that He whom God promised David that He would raise up from the fruit of his belly an eternal King, is the same one who was born of the virgin, she being of the lineage of David. For on this account also, He promised that the King should be: Of the fruit of his belly: this being appropriate to a virgin conceiving, and not: Of the fruit of his loins: nor: Of the fruit of his reins: which term is applicable to a man generating and a woman conceiving by the man. In this promise, therefore, scripture excluded all virile influence . . . .
>
> What Isaiah said: From the height above, or from the depth beneath: was meant to indicate that: He who descended was the same as ascended. But in this that he said: The Lord Himself shall give you a sign, he declared an unexpected thing with regard to His generation which could have been accomplished in no other way than by God the Lord of all, God Himself giving a sign in the house of David . . . . Since an unexpected salvation was to be provided for men through the help of God, so also was the unlooked-for birth from a virgin accomplished; God giving this sign, but man not working it out.
>
> . . . Joseph taking no part with regard to it, but Mary alone co-operating with the already determined plan . . . . So then we understand that His advent in human nature was not by the will of man, but by the will of God.[9]

There is therefore astonishment on three counts – the divinity of Christ, the humanity of Christ, and the sign of the birth from the virgin, and the names applied to Christ in prophecy embrace all three. It is to be noted how Irenaeus necessarily co-relates sign and thing signified, and distinguishes between them. The sign of the birth from the virgin is the exact pointer to the substance of the incarnation, the God-man, God with us, in the integrity of his divinity and the integrity of our humanity. Yet it is not because of the sign, that is, it is not because there was a birth from a virgin, that this came about. The pre-determined plan is that God will be with us, and the sign is chosen as an appropriate witness to this.

Irenaeus continues with prophecies from Isaiah, in this instance Isaiah IX:6. There is a misplacement in the quotation in Section 54 which is rectified in its repetition within a longer quotation in section 56: 'Unto us a son is born, and unto us a child is given: and his name is called Wonderful Counsellor, Mighty God.' 'Son' and 'Child' have become transposed here. Armitage Robison in the footnotes to his translation points to the same transposition in Justin Martyr,[10] but remarks that transposition in Irenaeus seems to be an oversight. There may, however, be deliberation in it, for Irenaeus goes on to expound the two titles accorded in prophecy to Christ here. The first, 'Wonderful Counsellor', concerns the Father, for the Son is the counsellor of the Father. There is a conversation between them, as is understood according to Irenaeus, from the account of the making of man in Genesis I:26 – 'And God said, let us make . . .'. The same title with 'Mighty God' is noted in Section 40 previously, referring then to the competence of Christ to draw humanity to God since He is that Word who has the 'pre-eminence in all things', having this relation with the Father. Here it is employed to elucidate the Genesis reference, for here 'there is seen the Father speaking to the Son, the Wonderful Counsellor of the Father'.

This title, then, refers to the dynamic and rational relations within the triune Being of God and indicates the relation of the Son to the Father in the working out of the dispensation of creation. This is elaborated in *Adversus Haereses* again in terms of the conversing within the triune Being of God. It may be noted here that the Spirit seems to be included in that conversation.

> Now man is . . . moulded by His hands, that is by the Son and Holy Spirit, to whom also He said: Let us make man . . . .[11]
>
> For with Him were always present the Word and Wisdom, the Son and the Spirit, by whom and in whom, freely and instantly, He made all things, to whom He also speaks, saying: Let us make man after our image and likeness.[12]

'Counsellor' is applied to the Son in His eternal existence and relation with the Father. But, continues Irenaeus, the Son is also our Counsellor. Here Irenaeus does two things; first he notes that the Son's relation to us is in correspondence with His ineffable relation to the Father. As He is eternally, so His relation and conversation towards and in creation accords with that divine status and office. As 'Counsellor' he gives 'advice' to us. The second thing Irenaeus does is to bring together the two titles in such a way that in his interpretation their juxtaposition heightens an understanding of the work of the Son towards us. Though he is 'Mighty God', yet as our 'Counsellor' as he does not compel us through might, but persuades us, 'giving us advice that we should forsake ignorance and acquire knowledge, and depart from error and come to truth, and put away corruption and receive incorruption'.

Theology is a matter of persuasion, rather than compulsion, in faith and godliness. This theme of gentle persuasion is set out in *Adversus Haereses* in the context of the advance of humanity towards God and in terms of the 'royal exchange'. For humanity is created and not uncreated, and therefore requires growth towards God.

> For this cause our Lord, having summed up all things into Himself, in these last times, came to us not as He might have come, but as we were capable of beholding Him. He could have come to us in His immortal glory, but the greatness of the glory we never could have endured. And therefore it came about that He, who was the perfect bread of the Father, offered Himself to us, as infants, as milk. He did this when He appeared as man, that we, being nourished as it were from the breast of His flesh, and by having such a course of milk-nourishment, become accustomed to eat and drink the Word of God, and may be able also to contain in ourselves the bread of immortality, which is the Spirit of the Father.[13]

Redemption is, for Irenaeus, very much an ontological matter. For it is brought about primarily by the union of the Word with us in our estate, and on this ground brings our existence, in the totality of our human being as individuals and in the recapitulative totality of humanity in Christ, into a 'community of union' with the divine existence. Within this determining context of redemption seen as the personal involvement of Christ as the One who takes our cause upon Himself for our sake, we being incapable ourselves – the *goel*, the kinsman-contender, of the old testament, as for example Job's crying out for 'redeemer', or the blood kinsman avenging a cause – there are other aspects of redemption interwoven into this prime one by Irenaeus. There is the 'kingly' aspect of redemption – God's victorious act by an outstretched arm and a mighty hand in the Exodus, to instance the one used by Irenaeus, and reflected here in his constant reference to Christ as the declared King of all, and the priestly aspect of redemption obtained through sacrifice and intercession. All these interpenetrate in the theology of Irenaeus, and involve, in that interaction, a mutual effect. Thus though the Son is 'Mighty God', and is declared so to be in his successful acts, he is 'not compelling as God', but rather persuades and counsels and advises. Likewise, the might acts of God are the sufferings of Christ. But all these are accomplished in terms of the ontology of Irenaeus's basic view of redemption, the identity of the Son of God with us as Son of man, the Word's assumption of our flesh and nature and therefore of Adam's lost cause. All these three aspects, with the ontological foremost, come together clearly in his comments on redemption in *Adversus Haereses*.[14] The persuasive aspect, the counselling and advice, mentioned here is to be understood in terms of the Word and the Spirit leading humanity in increase and growth into the knowledge of God and towards the fulness of the 'community of union' which Christ has established by means of the 'royal exchange'. Section 56 is quite clear, however, that this persuasiveness also has its judgmental side, for there will be no excuse, because of the way in which redemption has been so lovingly worked out by God in such a costly way to Himself, for those who have turned their back on that loving-kindness and counsel. This is applied also to those who died before Christ appeared, and who, in their fear of God, were bearers of the Spirit who pointed to Christ as the fulfilment of the old covenant.

Again in Section 56, there is the mixing of modes of redemption. The 'government, being a sign of the kingdom', is that which Christ carries on his shoulder, that is his cross, 'on which He was nailed back'. The same thought is found in Justin Martyr. In his work we read

> . . . and the government shall be upon His shoulders, which is significant of the power of the cross, for when He was crucified He applied his shoulders to it.[15]

The phrase 'nailed back' is a typical Irenaean usage. Again, there is little evidence that Irenaeus is indebted word for word to Justin Martyr, and in any case this would be a common interpretation of the instrument of Christ's government. This government is exercised by Christ as the 'Angel of great counsel', writes Irenaeus appealing to Isaiah IX:6. The same thought is expressed in *Adversus Haereses*, in the context of Christ being the 'Just One' born of the House of David to 'establish' a 'testimony in Jacob', and for the appointment of

> a law in Israel, that another generation might know [Him], the children which should be born of these, and they arising shall themselves declare to their children, so that they might set their hope on God and seek after His commandments.[16]

The phrase has to do, therefore, with the quality of rule in the kingdom, the Son being the counsel of the Father embodied and the establishment of that law of the knowledge of God. In other words, Christ himself is the Legislator and legislation of the kingdom which he establishes, and the quality of that government is found in his Person. Again, redemption is not a bare and static legal transaction – for

> He would not send back the redeemed to the legislation of Moses – for the law was fulfilled in Christ – but would have them live in newness by the Word, through faith in the Son of God and love.[17]

It is dynamic because it is centred on, and indeed is, the Person of Christ.

Section 57, however, does indeed bear much in common with the observations of Justin Martyr.[18] Much has been made of this particular section as a proof of the indebtedness of the former to the thought of the latter. Armitage Robinson in his introduction to his translation of the *Demonstration* offers a persuasive argument for such literal dependence, placing this section side by side with Justin Martyr's *Apology* I:32 by way of comparison. For ease of comparison this part from the *Apology* is set out here as Armitage Robinson reproduces it.

> Moses then, who was the first of the prophets, speaks expressly as follows: 'There shall not fail a prince from Judah, nor a leader from his loins, until he shall come for whom it is reserved: and he shall be the expectation of the Gentiles; binding his colt to the vine; washing his robe in the blood of the grape'. It is your part then to make careful enquiry and to learn up to what point the Jews had a prince and king of their own. It was up to the appearing of Jesus Christ, our teacher and the expounder of the prophecies which were

> not understood, namely how it was foretold by the divine holy prophetic Spirit through Moses that there 'should not fail a prince from the Jews until he should come for whom is reserved' the kingdom. For Judah is the ancestor of the Jews, from whom also they obtained that they should be called Jews. And you, after His appearance took place, both ruled over the Jews and mastered their land.
>
> Now the words 'He shall be the expectation of the Gentiles' were meant to indicate that from among all the Gentiles men shall expect Him to come again – which you yourselves can see with your own eyes and believe as a fact; for men of all races are expecting Him who was crucified in Judaea, immediately after whose time the land of the Jews was conquered and given over to you.
>
> And the words 'Binding his colt to the vine' and 'Washing his robe in the blood of the grape' were a sign to show what would happen to Christ, and what was to be done by Him. For the colt of an ass was standing at the entrance to a village, tied to a vine; and this He commanded His disciples at that time to bring to Him; and when it was brought He mounted and sat on it, and entered into Jerusalem, where was that very great temple of the Jews, which afterwards was destroyed by you. And after these things He was crucified, that the remainder of the prophecy might be accomplished. For 'Washing his robe in the blood of the grape' was the announcement beforehand of the passion which He was to suffer, cleansing by blood those who believe in Him. For what is called by the divine Spirit through the prophet (His) 'robe' means the men who believe in Him, those in whom dwells the seed from God, (that is) the Word. And that which is spoken of as 'blood of the grape' signifies that He who is to appear has blood indeed, yet not from human seed, but from a divine power. Now the first power after God, the Father and Lord of all, is the Son, the Word; of whom we shall presently tell after what manner He was made flesh and became man. For even as the blood of the vine not man hath made but God; so also is it signified that this blood shall not be of human seed, but of the power of God, as we have said before.
>
> Moreover Isaiah, another prophet, prophesying the same things in other words, said thus: 'There shall rise a star out of Jacob, and a flower shall spring up from the root of Jesse, and on his arm shall the Gentiles hope'.[19]

Armitage Robinson puts forward nine points from this part of Justin Martyr's *Apology* I to indicate what he sees as Irenaeus's dependence on this work. These are:

1 The well-known Blessing of Jacob is cited as the prophecy of Moses, who is called 'the first of the prophets'.
2 The quotation is abbreviated and Justin Martyr comments on it in its abbreviated form.
3 The statement that Judah was the father of the Jews from whom their name is derived is indicative of Justin Martyr's concern to explain such things for the sake of his Roman, non-Jewish, readers.
4 In the same vein, the point that the Jews had no ruler of their own after the time of Christ, but were subjected to Roman over-lordship, was a device of apologetic which would have been understood by his readers.
5 It is surprising that 'the expectation of the Gentiles' should be applied to the second coming of Christ.
6 The statement that the ass's colt was tethered to a vine does not appear in the Gospels.

7 'Washing his robe in the blood of the grape' suggests our Lord's passion; but that the identification of His robe with those who believe seems to Armitage Robinson 'far-fetched'.
8 Equally dubious and strange is the idea that the blood of the grape signifies blood not of human origin but from God.
9 The conjunction of Balaam's prophecy with the words of Isaiah, and the attributing of the whole to Isaiah, Armitage Robinson says, 'strikes us as a strange piece of carelessness'.

Armitage Robinson then treats these points one by one in a comparison of this text with Section 57 and the beginning of Section 58 in the *Demonstration*, believing that there is 'an intimate connection'. We must be aware, however, that even in Armitage Robinson's thesis, there are statements which themselves cast some doubt on such a close literal link. These we take up.

1 Certainly Irenaeus cites the Blessing of Jacob as a prophecy of Moses, but it must be asked if this were such a peculiarity in the exegesis of the early church. For example, Clement of Rome gathers him into the prophetic office: 'Moses, a faithful servant in all his house, recorded in the sacred books all the directives given to him, and when the other prophets followed him . . . .[20] Moreover, the point appealed to here, that Moses was 'the first that prophesied', as evidence that Irenaeus is indebted to Justin Martyr, is not used by Irenaeus here in Section 57, but in an earlier section (43) as Armitage Robinson admits, and in, as we have seen in the comments on that section, a vastly different context.

2 While Irenaeus does use, initially, part of the abbreviated quotation as presented here by Justin Martyr, he goes on to use the same reference quoted in full as in the Septuagint. This again Armitage Robinson notes. Morever, Irenaeus omits the non-Gospel phrase about the colt being 'tied to the vine', which is surprising; for, if he were leaning so heavily on Justin Martyr's observations as is suggested, in view of his contention in Section 57 'in what land and among whom of mankind He was to be born', why has he not employed it, especially bearing in mind the connotation of the vine with Israel.

3 Armitage Robinson's objection that the repetition in Irenaeus of the mention of the name Jew as a patronymic derived from Judah, is superfluous to Irenaeus's aim in writing the *Demonstration* for 'a fairly well-instructed Christian', seems to miss the point as to its inclusion here. Again, it seems to be a commonplace of exegesis, and it does suit Irenaeus's purpose and mode of thought here, for it highlights the particularity of the descent of the Jewish monarchy and leadership until the coming of Christ. He points out in Section 58 (appealing to Numbers XXXIV:17) that the promised one 'shall be raised up out of Israel'. He is to be born 'from Jacob and the tribe of Judah', but as 'King of all the redeemed'. It is only on the basis of the particular, that the 'dispensation of His coming in the flesh should be among the Jews', that he is 'King of all the redeemed', thereby fulfilling the promise to Israel's monarchy into the wider range of the redemption of all humanity. Again we have this movement out from the centre to the perimeter and back again to go out in yet more interpretative ways in Irenaeus's thought. This appealing to Judah and the Jews in the context of the Jewish monarchy and its redemptive significance is an entirely suitable tool for this as the grounding of the statement

that this king is 'the expectation of the Gentiles, of those who hope in Him; because we expect that He will establish the kingdom'.

4 Armitage Robinson thinks that the phrase used in Irenaeus 'the might of the quiver was captured' is the translator's attempt to make sense of the problematic δοριαλωτος in the Justinian text, and, with the exception of the insertion 'the Romans' for the 'you' of the direct address to the Romans in Justin Martyr, this episode recounting the state of the Jewish nation at the time of Christ, is lifted word for word by Irenaeus from *Apology* I. I do not see the phrase 'the might of the quiver' as problematic in this way. Rather it is more likely to be a reference to *Isaiah* XLIX:2 – 'in his quiver hath he kept me close', referring as this does to Israel as a servant in whom God would be glorified, and whom God had called from the womb. Isaiah, it is noteworthy, introduces this by calling 'peoples from afar' to listen regarding this standing of Israel as the chosen servant and glorification of God. It is this 'might' which is powerless and under foreign subjugation. Again it is significant that Isaiah notes the vain labouring and the spending of strength of Israel, but sees the bringing again 'of Jacob' to God to restore the 'preserved of Israel . . . for a light to the Gentiles . . . a servant of rulers' whom 'kings shall see and arise'. It would seem to me that far from being a translator's problem, the phrase indicates Irenaeus using his own initiative in the interpretation of the matter here via Isaiah, for it fits in exactly with the whole context of his emphasis and aim in these sections. Not only this, but Irenaeus is about to stress the natural descent of Jesus from David and the monarchy of Israel in subsequent sections, and this, together with the comments on point 3 above, make a logical reason for the Irenaean text being very much of his own usage rather than a 'pirating' with all the attendant problems of projecting Justin Martyr's particular aims into his own exposition.

5 'The expectation of the Gentiles', notes Armitage Robinson, is applied by both Justin Martyr and Irenaeus to the second coming of Christ, and this is 'surprising'. This 'surprise' can be alleviated, surely, in the context of Irenaeus's constant emphasis on the universal aspect of the fulfilment of redemption. It is the final 'establishment of the kingdom' as opposed to the historical limitations of the monarchy and leadership of Israel into which our Lord was born in 'the dispensation of His coming in the flesh', which sways the reason that this should be mentioned here.

6 The tethering of the ass's colt 'to the vine' we have mentioned already under the comments on point 2. But there is more, for while Irenaeus does not use this phrase here, Armitage Robinson cites his usage of it in *Adversus Haereses*. Here Irenaeus quotes from the Septuagint version of Genesis XLIX:10–12:

> There shall not fail a chief in Judah, nor a leader from his loins, until He is come for whom it is laid up, and He is the very hope of the nations; binding his foal to the vine and His ass's colt to the creeping ivy. He shall wash His stole in wine, and His upper garment in the blood of the grape; His eyes shall be more joyous than wine, and His teeth whiter than milk.[21]

I fail to see how this can be used as evidence that Irenaeus is indebted to Justin Martyr in this section of the *Demonstration*. It is a quotation which is used felicitously in the midst of Irenaeus's observations about the advent and passion of Christ and how as the Word who created all things, He is our 'life . . . hanging before' our 'eyes', with all the attendant signs of his passion prophesied and the meaning of which should be sought out and considered.

7 The identification of 'the robe' with believers in both Justin Martyr and Irenaeus fits in with both their respective aims, and here particularly with Irenaeus's observation that Christ's birth out of its historical and localized fact leads to his status as 'King of all the redeemed'. His garments of majesty are precisely this 'robe' in this significance.

8 The very point raised by Armitage Robinson in stating that Irenaeus adds to the interpretation of 'the blood of the grape', which 'no man maketh', the gladness of those who drink of it – perhaps referring to Psalm CIV:15 – would rather seem to point to Irenaeus not being beholden to Justin's exact text. This is coupled with the fact that the 'blood of the grape' signifies blood not of human, but of divine origin. Here again this fits with Irenaeus's assertion that with regard to the birth of Christ.

> God . . . promised to David . . . an eternal King . . . of the Virgin, herself of the lineage of David . . . excluding all virile influence . . . God giving the sign, man not working it out.[22]

This blood, it will be noted in Irenaeus, is referred to in the context of 'those whom He cleansed, redeeming us by His blood'. The incarnation, in which the Word takes human flesh and blood to Himself, not generated by human process, but by his own creative activity by the Spirit, is fulfilled. It is that blood, which does what other ordinary human blood cannot do, accomplish the redemption of flesh and blood. This does not introduce a docetic note into the interpretation of Christ's humanity: Irenaeus never countenances this in his constant insistence of the identification of the Word in the incarnation with the reality and limitations of Adamic flesh. It does speak first of the extraordinary circumstances and generation of this human birth of the Word, and the efficacy which is God's alone in the fulfilment of that birth in redeeming all. In this sense, and in this sense alone, this blood is 'of God'. It is the way of becoming which is taken at the incarnation, and what is achieved by that human flesh and nature in union with the Word, rather than the quality of the flesh and nature, to which the 'of God' refers.

9 Again there seems to be an argument against itself in Armitage Robinson's noting of Irenaeus's use of Balaam's prophecy. He does not conjoin it with any words of Isaiah or attribute it to Isaiah, writing specifically: 'Moses says . . .' If he does so attribute it to Isaiah in *Adversus Haereses*,[23] as Armitage Robinson claims (Irenaeus certainly makes a false reference to Isaiah in quoting him instead of the psalmist in Psalm LXXXI, as writing 'Let them be confounded, all who blaspheme God, and carve useless things'[24]), then that only serves to indicate that he is not copying Justin's mistake here. Perhaps Rendel Harris's conjecture of a book of testimonies from prophecies containing mistakes which was commonly used, and therefore the mistakes commonly repeated, is a better option when considering mistakenly consigned texts.

Irenaeus ought to be allowed to be his own man in the matter of the way in which he presents the particularity of the place and birthright of the Word made flesh in order to show the reality of this particularity as the centre from which flows the reality of universal redemption. Influenced by Justin Martyr he may well be, but he is not a mere copyist repeating lazily what has already been written in order to save thinking for himself.

The particularity of Christ's birth 'this economy of the dispensation', is that it is 'among the Jews', and in particular 'from Jacob and the tribe of Judah', is stated in Section 58, and immediately linked with the fact that he is 'King of all the redeemed'. Here Irenaeus introduces the Magi, the representatives of the gentile world, who (and here the outward flowing circle from the birth comes back to the centre) come to Bethlehem and 'entered the house wherein was laid the child, wrapped in swaddling-clothes'. Irenaeus has now narrowed the whole significance back to the exact spot where lay the child. This gives him the opportunity in sections 59 and 60 to bring the humanity and the Godhead together.

From an extended quotation from Isaiah XI:1ff, Irenaeus draws several brief points. The virgin's line of descent, from David, Jesse and eventually to Abraham, is remarked by Irenaeus. In the prophecy of Isaiah, he notes, two particular things refer to the one who was born of that virgin. The first is Moses' 'rod', the symbol of his authority and the sign of the 'mighty works' which were accomplished before Pharaoh's eyes. The 'rod is a sign of rule'. Here the theme of the descent of leadership and monarchy is touched again in summing up what Irenaeus has noted before. But the rule, in this instance is exercised because he is 'flesh'. This, according to Irenaeus is indicated by the mention of the 'flower' which, like the 'rod' comes from the root of Jesse. This flesh 'budded forth' from the Spirit – again a reference to the way of becoming of this flesh.

In Section 60, other references in the prophecy are taken and interpreted. The one born of the virgin shall judge 'not according to opinion', and he shall reprove 'not according to speech', and his judgment shall be one for the 'humble' to whom he 'shall show mercy'. This, according to Irenaeus, 'the more establishes and declares His Godhead'. The corresponding passage to this is in *Adversus Haereses* III:9:3. This sets out the activity of the triune God, for Irenaeus elaborates on the unction of Christ by the Spirit from the father, and emphasizes that He upon whom the Spirit descended at his baptism is none other than the Word who had taken upon himself our flesh and is declared to be the Son by the Father. It is this unction which is the ground of our righteousness, for we are saved 'receiving from the abundance of His unction'. Although the Word made flesh is God,

> He did not judge according to glory, nor reprove after the manner of speech. For: He needed not that any should testify to Him of man, for He Himself knew what was in man.[25]

The quality of His judgment is not after the manner of men, though He is man; nor is it after the burning righteousness of the naked glory of God, though He is God. The basis of the quality of His judgment in righteousness is that God has respect for His handiwork and its limitations, and it is this respect whereby He Himself is both God and man and anointed by the Spirit as such, which is the ground of His righteous judgment. In this righteousness we may participate in the Spirit, and find forgiveness and redemption. This instances Irenaeus's bracketing together of incarnation, the eternal Being of God and our redemption, underlining his essentially ontological approach to the matter of our redemption. While, of course, the noetic aspect of redemption – the knowledge of God and of ourselves in the light of that knowledge – is always present with Irenaeus, it is never considered separately. To divorce the noetic from the ontic, would be to open the gates for a gnosticism. The knowledge from on high, so to speak, is firmly anchored in the very being of the Word made flesh, in the reality of his Godness assuming the reality of our stock, and in the living relation of humanity of God in the 'community of union' which he established by the incarnation and the outpouring of the Holy Spirit.

This ontological slant is given further accent in Sections 61–66 with regard to the significance of the places of the Word made flesh. Section 61 seems, at first sight, to be an intrusion in the flow of Irenaeus's thoughts, so sudden is his transition in considering the state of things when Christ comes again 'to reign over all'. In fact he is still commenting on the prophecy from Isaiah XI:1ff regarding the result of the exercise of our Lord's 'own surpassing righteousness' and the godly judgment he will exercise. It appears that he leaps from a consideration of the humanity and divinity of Christ to the quality of creation at the second advent. But he is merely using the movement of the prophecy and following it through scrupulously, so that he draws from it the fact that this coming quality of creation is grounded on the 'name of Christ', that is who and what Christ is, and is the implementing of that righteousness and judgment and truth which are his alone because, as Irenaeus has shown in the preceding sections, that righteousness and judgment and truth are the very Person of Christ. Yet again, but here permitted to do so by the structure of Isaiah's prophecy, he moves out, and here swiftly, from the particular consideration of the Person of Christ, to the wide estimation of the whole transformation of all creation.

Significant, and very Irenaean, is the statement in Section 60 in which he condenses the words of the prophecy

> And: He shall smite the earth with a word: and: slay the impious: with a word only: this belongs to God who worketh all things with a word.

The prophecy reads

> And He shall smite the earth with the word of His mouth, and with the breath of His lips shall He slay the impious man.

What is rendered here as 'with the breath of the lips' is literally 'with spirit through the lips', following the Septuagint. Here Irenaeus – though it might be expected that he would use this as an opportunity to introduce a possible interpretation of the work of the Word ('the word of His mouth') and the Spirit ('the breath of the lips') – applies both to the Word. He is concerned here with the fulfilment of all things which God accomplishes 'with a word' – according to the rendering by Armitage Robinson. The translation by J. Smith is preferable here – 'this is proper to God who works all things whatsoever by His Word' – as it accords with Irenaeus's constant reminder that God works in this way.

It is also a reminder of Irenaeus's way of thinking regarding the exact correspondence of the work with the Person working – God is as He acts and acts as He is; God is Word, λογος, Logos and therefore He creates and acts 'logically', λογικος, rationally: 'Since God is rational, therefore by the Word He created the things that were made'.[26] The judgment which Christ will exercise in his second advent will be strictly in accord with the righteousness, mercy and truth which He both has accomplished and is in Himself. Irenaeus then turns to that state of righteousness and truth.

He writes in Section 61 of the harmony of the creation when Christ comes 'to reign over all – the union and concord and peace of the animals of different kinds, which by nature are opposed and hostile to each other'. For this view of what the state of things will be, he appeals to the tradition handed down, for that it will be thus 'the Elders say so'. He is referring above all to Papias, 'the hearer of John and a companion of Polycarp', as is clear from the equivalent part of *Adversus Haereses* in which he treats of this subject.[27] This is in the context of Irenaeus's millenarian beliefs concerning the state of affairs when Christ will come again to rule. In this context in *Adversus Haereses* we have an example of Irenaeus's quasi-utility of symbolism. He raises the question of symbolic interpretation of Isaiah's prophecies concerning harmony and peace of wild animals in the coming perfect state of creation, in *Adversus Haereses*.[28] They certainly are symbolic as used by the prophet, he writes, of the dispositions of men and women who have come to believe and now act in righteous harmony, and who formerly were of savage and cruel natures. This change, he notes both in *Adversus Haereses* and in the *Demonstration* is proved by the example of those who formerly disbelieved but now believe. This has come to pass already, thereby justifying this interpretation of Isaiah's prophecy. But it is not the whole interpretation, for, he claims, it will be true in reality and actuality in the second advent. The original order, harmony, and tranquillity of creation in the intent of God will be restored in this millennium of the rule of Christ in earth. For Irenaeus, the present harmony of believers in turn symbolizes the coming actual cosmic order and tranquillity of all things – the whole creation transformed. This order is already found in the resurrected Christ, and those who believe in Him are able to live such transformed existences because they have come together 'in one name'. Here Armitage Robinson notes that the Armenian text reads 'in thy name', but by a different division of letters 'in one name' results. This is the more likely reading, though it does not alter the fundamental meaning, for 'Name' to Irenaeus has all the significance of person, act and accomplishment, and it is by participation in that 'name' that is, in their 'community of union' with Christ, that their existences now bear all the hallmarks of having 'been changed, so as to leave no excellency of righteousness undone'. Again we see the ontic emphasis of redemption in Irenaeus's thought in statements such as we have here in Section 61 of the *Demonstration* – 'so great is the transformation which faith in Christ the Son of God effects for those who believe on Him'.

It is the resurrection of Christ which is the declaration, the vindication and the seal of this righteousness which is His and by which He will judge and restore all things. Irenaeus introduces this theme at the end of Section 61 and continues it in the following section. He stresses the physical resurrection of our Lord, that it is the body, or flesh, born of the line of David, which rises, so that 'He is in aspect a man, but in power God'. 'In aspect' certainly does not imply any docetic interpretation of the resurrection; Irenaeus is too insistent on the actuality and reality of the flesh of the Word to ally himself with any such suggestion. It is as this risen God-man that

Christ is 'judge of all the world and as the only worker of righteousness and redeemer'.

This reality of the flesh of the Word is made abundantly clear in the following sections, for Irenaeus comes down again to the particularity of Christ, the place of his birth and the place of his passion. The birth of the Son of God is to be sought not 'among the Gentiles or elsewhere' but 'in Bethlehem of Judea from Abraham and from David's race'. The pressing concern of Irenaeus comes through in Sections 63 and 64 to present the tangibility and historicity of the birth of Christ. Armitage Robinson notes that he appeals to the prophecy of Micah,[29] but in its Matthean form[30] which does not fully accord with the Septuagint rendering, and that he agrees with Codex Bezae in reading της 'Ιουδαιας for γη 'Ιουδα, and μη for οὐδαμως. What may also be noted are the latter two disparities between Justin Martyr's two citings of this text[31] and Irenaeus's version here. Irenaeus is concerned to show the human descent within the race of David, not only because Christ is born of the virgin who is of David's line, but also in Bethlehem 'the native place of David'.

He then quotes the psalm as David's prophecy:

> For David thy servant's sake, turn not away the face of thy Christ. The Lord sware unto David . . . . Of the fruit of thy body will I set upon thy throne: if thy children shall keep my covenant . . . their sons for evermore (shall sit upon thy throne).[32]

The Armenian text does not contain the phrase bracketed above, but ends at 'evermore', and Irenaeus is reading from the Septuagint in copying 'thy servant's sake' for 'my servant's sake'. Irenaeus's argument is that none of the sons of David sat for evermore, nor was their kingdom everlasting since it was destroyed. It is only in Christ that such everlasting things are to be found, and conversely, Christ is only to be found born of 'the race' of David and in 'the place' which is David's native town.

That Christ is king, and born of David, is shown by his progress into Jerusalem, David's capital city, 'where also was His royal seat and the temple of God', acclaimed by the crowds recognizing the prophecy of his mode of entry on an ass's colt. (It may be noted that Irenaeus's use of the account of this entry in Matthew XXI:5, is different from the same quotation which Justin Martyr employs.[33]) The fact that Christ is both God and man, that He was born in a particular place at a particular time and in a particular way and yet is 'the one eternal King', is the substance of the prophet's declarations. In Section 66, Irenaeus states these apparently contrary facts concerning both the Person of Christ and the acts of Christ. 'Sprung from mankind', He is, nevertheless, the healer and the raiser of the dead. He is healer and raiser of the dead yet, paradoxically, is 'hated and despised' and undergoes 'sufferings', was crucified and put to death. It is in these contraries that Irenaeus sees the interaction of the presence of the Word in, and bearing, the realities of creation, with that created dimension in its Adamic estate. They are the inescapable, prophesied reactions in a creation in its disobedience grasped by the Word, by whom all things were made, in his obedience to the Father, and in the constancy of God towards His handiwork. They are the inevitable responses to the presence of the 'one eternal King' who has His names and His places within a wayward creation, and who bears in himself the perversity which has afflicted His own domain.

Notes

1 Cf. Chapters 1, 4 and 7.
2 Irenaeus: *Adversus Haereses* V:Preface.
3 *Ibid.* V:1:1.
4 *Ibid.* IV:11:2.
5 *Ibid.* IV:20:6,7.
6 *Ibid.* IV:33:11.
7 *Ibid.* III:21:6.
8 *Ibid.* III:21:4.
9 *Ibid.* III:21:5–7.
10 Justin Martyr: *Apology* 1:35.
11 Irenaeus: *Adversus Haereses* IV:Preface:4.
12 *Ibid.* IV:20:1; cf. also I:24:1 and I:30:6 for Irenaeus's noting of heretical interpretations of Genesis I:26.
13 *Ibid.* IV:38:1; cf. 38:2 and 3.
14 *Ibid.* V:1:1.
15 Justin Martyr: *Dialogue with Trypho* I:35.
16 Irenaeus: *Adversus Haereses* III:16:3.
17 Irenaeus: *Demonstration* 89.
18 Cf. Justin Martyr: *Dialogue with Trypho* I:32.
19 J. Armitage Robinson: Introduction to the *Demonstration of the Apostolic Preaching*, pp. 6, 7.
20 Clement of Rome: *Epistle* I:43.
21 Irenaeus: *Adversus Haereses* IV:10:2.
22 *Ibid.* III:21:5,6.
23 *Ibid.* III:9:2 – where it may be noted the Edinburgh Edition translation of the Ante-Nicene Fathers gives Balaam as the source and not Isaiah.
24 *Ibid.* III:6:3.
25 *Ibid.* III:9:3.
26 Irenaeus: *Demonstration* 5 (see comments on Sections 5–8, Chapter 5).
27 Irenaeus: *Adversus Haereses* V:33:4 beginning.
28 *Ibid.* V:33:4 end.
29 Micah V:2.
30 Matthew II:6.
31 Justin Martyr: *Apology* I:34; *Dialogue with Trypho* 78.
32 Psalm CII:10ff.
33 Justin Martyr: *Apology* I:35; *Dialogue with Trypho* 53.

Chapter 15

Section 67–82: The Sufferings of the Word in His Obedience (1)

Sections 67–73: The Spirit and the Nature of the Obedience of the Word:

In the teaching of Irenaeus, incarnation and redemption are never separated. The whole life of Christ is bound together from incarnation to ascension and is construed in terms of His obedience by which He reverses and rescinds our disobedience. Our redemption and obedience, as a corollary to this, is realized in our participation of all that He has done and all that He is – in our 'community of union' which He establishes for us by identifying Himself with us in incarnation and by pouring out His Spirit, thus 'imparting indeed God to men by means of the Spirit, and . . . attaching man to God by means of His incarnation'.[1] By His Person and work, Christ is seen to be 'revealing God indeed to men, but presenting man to God'.[2] Again, this anticipates Athanasius's statement on the incarnation that the Word becomes man that 'He might minister the things of God to us, and ours to God'.[3] This should never be forgotten when looking at Irenaeus's doctrine of the atonement. For this ontological bond forged between God and humanity, Creator and creature, at the incarnation, is determinative of his approach to, his setting out of, and his conclusions concerning, the atonement and our redemption – and indeed, the whole aspect of re-creation as viewed by Irenaeus.

In the sections which follow, he is concerned to look at the 'royal exchange' in terms of the obedience of Christ's sufferings, and does so by concentrating on the 'suffering Servant' prophecies of Isaiah. In Section 67, Irenaeus, in speaking of 'His healings', that is the work of the restoration of humanity from its broken and mortal state by the Word, appeals to Isaiah LIII:4 via Matthew VIII:17 – 'He took our infirmities and bare our sicknesses'. At this point Irenaeus takes up the matter of prophecy and its fulfilment. He notes that the prophecy is in the present tense (although in *Adversus Haereses*[4] he quotes it in the future tense). This, he says, is because the decree of God concerning something is such that the event is spoken of as though it were fulfilled. From the side of God it has been fulfilled indeed, and therefore the Spirit, viewing the temporal and spatial nature of creation, and seeing the time within the created order when this should occur and 'the issues of prophecy fulfilled, utters the words (accordingly)'.

Behind this there are two implicit issues, which here are only hinted at, but which became important for later theologians. The first is that God's utterance of decree within the divine existence is, as it were, 'instantly' fulfilled and accomplished. The second, following from this, is that all time is present 'instantaneously' with God. Thus, regarding this latter point, the later Gregory of Nyssa:

> Past and future . . . such accidents are confined to the creation, whose life is divided with time's divisions into memory and hope. But within that transcendent and blessed Power, all things are present equally as in an instant: past and future are within its all-encircling grasp and its comprehensive view.[5]

Irenaeus himself, in *Adversus Haereses*, regarding the first point, more than hints at this 'instantaneous' thought, decree and action in the Being of God. Here he is remarking on God as the sole Creator:

> Let them cease therefore to claim that the world was made by another; for as soon as God formed a conception in His mind, that was done which He had thus mentally conceived.[6]

It may be that the whole insistence in the theology of Irenaeus on the Word 'joining the end to the beginning' and gather up all things in himself, is a particular development of, a striving to express, albeit unaware, an implicit idea of all time and things being 'present' to God in His Word by whom they are created and fulfilled. If so, then the relation between incarnation and creation, certainly interlocked in Irenaean thought, may be seen as the two aspects of the one act.

Appealing to Isaiah XXIX:18, XXXV:3ff and XXVI:19, in this order, Irenaeus lists the frailties, infirmities and mortality of humanity which Christ will heal, culminating in the resurrection of the dead. The mode of healing, the way taken by the Son of God, is then set out in Section 68 and expounded and expanded in the sections following thereafter. This way is the vicarious way of Christ in assuming these frailties and limitations and mortality and bearing the reproach, despite any rejection which the disbelief of humanity called forth. Irenaeus uses Isaiah LII:13ff, largely, but also appeals to (possibly, for the parallel is not exact) Psalm XXXVIII:8 (9), Isaiah L:6 and Lamentations III:30. What is to be noted in his deployment of these texts is the way in which Irenaeus emphasizes both the passive and active obedience of Christ in His passion and death. In this active and passive obedience, Christ is obediently ministering the things of humanity to God – presenting humanity in its obedience to the Father through his vicarious obedience. Thus, Irenaeus writes in Section 69: 'by the will of the Father these things occurred to Him for the sake of our salvation'. It is to be noted in these sections that the passive and active aspects of Christ's obedience are never separated.

With regard to the active aspect, this is the fulfilment of His life seen as the positive fulfilment in the flesh of His Sonship, His relation to the Father. He offers total filial obedience from incarnation to ascension and receives and lays hold of the love of the Father in so doing. Irenaeus, in stressing that it is

> by the will of the Father these things occurred to Him for our salvation.[7] . . . That He should endure these things and that too by the will of the Father he [the prophet/psalmist[8]] manifestly declared: for by the will of the Father He was to endure sufferings,[9]

also places side by side with this the active obedience of Christ. Thus it is noted that there is Christ's 'voluntary coming to death', and his positive 'taking away of judgment'.[10] And again, 'who else is perfectly righteous but the Son of God, who makes righteous and perfects them that believe on Him'. The positive side of the obedience of Christ is his πϱοεκοπτε – his 'cutting forward', His growth in favour with God and man, His resolution, His hungering and thirsting in fasting, His weeping, His setting His face to go up to Jerusalem and His cross and passion.

The passive aspect is His submission to the righteous judgment of the righteous Father on the fallen and disobedient flesh and nature which He assumed at the incarnation, standing in our place for our sake, bearing that judgment and bearing it away. Hence: 'In the humiliation his judgment was taken away.' But it is not only the Father's judgment which He bears, but, as Irenaeus so emphatically presents here, the manifestations of the reason why there is judgment by God – the despite, rejection and hatred of humanity for God. So, in Section 79, quoting Isaiah LXV:2: 'I have stretched out my hands all the day long to a disobedient and gainsaying people', the 'stretching out' of the hands is to Irenaeus a prophecy of the cross and Christ's death thereon. The very scorn of humanity directed to Him in His sufferings is this which He also bears in addition to the judgment of the Father on the state of humanity which is characterized by this despite of God. The hatred is directed even against the abject pain and death of Jesus.

This Irenaeus sets out in Section 70 with the prophetic question in Isaiah LIII:8 – 'His generation who shall declare?' – noting that the 'undeclarable generation' of Christ is 'His descent' from his Father, that is, as the Son or Word of the Father. This is said 'to warn us' lest, that in the 'outrage of His sufferings, we should despise Him as a mean and contemptible man'. John Donne's question concerning the cross

> It bore all other sinnes, but is it fit
> That it should bear the sin of scorning it?[11]

would find an answer here in the affirmative. In this way, the Word made flesh penetrates to the very place where Adam's folly resides by making His own and taking to Himself even the scorning by humanity of His submission in the flesh to God's judgment, to bear it away.

The humiliation and abasement on the cross is the way in which judgment is exercised – not only upon Christ, but upon humanity. Irenaeus works this out in considering what is meant by 'the taking away of judgment' in Section 69. He points out that there is a 'taking away for a person' and a 'taking away from a person'. Those 'for whom it is taken away have it unto the torments of their perdition'. That is to say, they still exercise unbelief and are judged by their rejection of the form and significance of this judgment suffered by Christ. These are they who, to use Irenaeus's remarks in Section 70, despise him 'because of the sufferings which for thy sake He of purpose endured', and who do not, in their rejection and scorn of him 'fear Him because of His descent'. They reject him as God, the Son from the Father and therefore fail to appreciate the form and significance of these sufferings and death. As such they are a warning to us. They, Irenaeus in effect says in Section 69, have taken upon themselves to judge him. Disbelief is a participation in that rejection of Christ by those who judged and crucified him. Those 'from whom' the judgment is taken away are those who 'fear Him because of His descent', and therefore see the full significance of what happens on the cross, that this is none other than God undergoing this in the flesh for our sakes.

The passive aspect of Christ's obedience is twofold: it is His submission to the judgment of the Father and to the rejection by humanity.

Further it is to be noted that Christ, for Irenaeus, is not merely the agent, but the form and substance of our redemption and atonement with God. For it is for our sake that he is obedient and we find our obedience in participation through the 'community of union' in his obedience. We may refer back to Sections 31–37 of the *Demonstration* (see Chapter 12) in this respect, and to the comment in *Adversus Haereses*: which is fundamental to Irenaeus's understanding of atonement and redemption:

> For by no other means could we have attained to incorruptibility and immortality unless we had been united to incorruptibility and immortality. But how could we be joined to incorruptibility and immortality unless, first, incorruptibility and immortality had become what we also are, so that the corruptible might be swallowed up in incorruption and the mortal by immortality, that we might receive the adoption of sons?[12]

We see in the theology of Irenaeus the strong coming together of the existence of the Word made flesh, the existence of God and, in that Word made flesh, the existence of humanity. Atonement and redemption are not to be found only in some *gnosis* concerning the Word made flesh, the Son of God born a Son of man, but in the actual participation of the totality of our existence in His, which participation is given in the incarnation and the outpouring of the Spirit. But this participation is in the existence of Christ as the suffering servant, as He obediently both cuts his way forward and subjects himself to the will of the Father and the wrath of man, in the obedience of that cutting forward and cross, and bears away the judgment of God on disobedient humanity and the hatred of that humanity for God, re-creating humanity in Himself.

The totality of the obedience of Christ and the fact that the whole process of atonement and redemption is not only centred on His Person as God and man, but, indeed, is His Person, for He is not merely the agent but the substance of atonement and redemption, rules out any idea in the theology of Irenaeus that there is a decree of God, separate from Christ, which Christ either only reveals as a teacher or only effects as an instrument. Nowhere in the writings of Irenaeus can such notions be found to be lurking. For, everywhere in the works of Irenaeus there is this insistence that the Being of God, human existence, atonement and redemption, knowledge and godliness, are bound inseparably in and as the Person of Christ, the Son of God born a Son of man, the Word made flesh. Nor is atonement and redemption found elsewhere than through participation in Christ, in the 'community of union' with God, of which He is the substance. There is, therefore, in the thought of Irenaeus no *gnosis* by which redemption is perceived to be mere enlightenment of mind by an illuminator-Christ opening up a knowledge beyond Himself to which He only points, nor, on the other hand, an idea of a redemption which is either an external forensic act, a judicial contract whereby the penalty for sin is signed over from the transgressors to the one bearing the transgressions, or a legal and fiscal act of ransom paid to the devil thus freeing humanity from the slavery of sin and the chains of wickedness. In any case, behind such an idea as this last would lurk a dualism which Irenaeus would not countenance, familiar as he was with such gnostic tenets. For in leading captivity captive, Christ denies any such right to the powers of darkness. Creation is God's *own*, and into His own possession he comes to reclaim what is His and which belongs to no other power. Thus Irenaeus in *Adversus Haereses*:

> . . . but His passion gave rise to strength and power. For the Lord, through means of suffering 'ascending into the lofty place, led captivity captive, gave gifts to men', and conferred on those who believe in Him the power 'to tread upon serpents and scorpions, and on all the power of the enemy', that is of the leader of the apostasy. Our Lord also by His passion destroyed death and dispersed error, and put an end to corruption and destroyed ignorance, while He manifested life and revealed truth and bestowed the gift of incorruption.[13]

Redemption and atonement certainly are our knowledge of the invisible reality of the Father, but this depends on the visibility of God the incarnate Word – He is 'the visible of the Father' – and certainly they are the saving union between God and humanity in estrangement and at variance and enmity with God in its disobedience. This depends on the unity of God and man in Christ Himself in His total identification with us and His re-creation of us in Himself as He brings human being into healing and sanctifying union with divine nature and Being.

The whole is summed up in Irenaeus's observations:

> The Word of God, Son of God, Christ Jesus our Lord . . . who was made man among men, visible and tangible, in order to abolish death and show forth life, and produce a community of union between God and man.[14]

This is what lies behind the statements of Irenaeus in Section 71. He begins here with a quotation from the prophet Jeremiah, instancing the Septuagint version of Lamentations IV:20, which he interprets as 'The Spirit of our face, the Lord Christ'. In this section, he links the work of the Spirit and the Word in the dispensation of the incarnation, and the work of the Spirit and the Word in our redemption and regeneration. What requires distinction from the outset in looking at this section is that to which reference has already been made in the comments on Sections 5–8[15] – the necessity of distinguishing between Irenaeus's use of 'Holy Spirit' and 'God as Spirit', that is, the differentiation in the usage of 'Spirit' as the Person of the 'Holy Spirit' on the one hand, and as the nature of God as he exists *in se* – the 'Godness' of God. He uses both throughout his works, and the question is to which he refers in this curious phrase 'The Spirit of our face, the Lord Christ'. Is he writing of the Holy Spirit, or the nature of Christ as God, in relation to 'our face'?

The question is intensified by Irenaeus's declaration later in this section that 'Christ's body was made by His Spirit', and linking this to 'Christ's body' as a 'shadow' (for a body casts a shadow), and is called such 'because the Spirit overshadowed it, as it were, with glory and covered it'. And again 'Christ being (the) Spirit of God was to become a suffering man'. That is, behind this first question as to 'our face' and the Spirit, there is the consideration of the relation of the Spirit (either as 'Holy Spirit' or as 'of the nature of God') to the incarnation and the flesh and human nature of Christ.

The argument concerning 'Spirit', 'shadow' and 'body' here is complex. The 'shadow is made by the body', and this indicates 'the humiliation and contemptibility of His body'. Bodies stand upright: their shadows fall on the ground and are 'trodden upon'. But here Irenaeus points out that it is the 'body of Christ' which falls on the ground and is trodden upon. This is then explained by what follows, namely that the 'Spirit overshadowed it, as it were, with glory and covered it'. This would seem to refer to the 'overshadowing' of the Spirit at the conception, and suggests the relation of the Spirit to the incarnate Word. Christ is anointed with the 'Spirit from the Father'. The Word is in eternal relation to the Father and Spirit, and at the incarnation, this union of the flesh with the Word exhibits that relation in such a way that the flesh becomes a factor within it. Therefore it is 'overshadowed' by the Spirit of the Father and itself, in its 'humiliation and contemptibility', in the very despite of humanity against it, becomes a shadow of that relation which is 'trodden upon'.

The way in which Irenaeus states the relation of the Spirit to the incarnation is parallel to that in which he describes the work of the Word and Spirit in creation and, indeed, parallel to the working out of redemption. All things are made *by the hands of God* – the Word and the Spirit. He

> Establishes all things by His Word and binds them together by His Wisdom[16]
>
> . . . made all things by His Word and adorned them by (His) Wisdom[17]
>
> . . . by the Word and Wisdom created and arranged all things.[18]
>
> . . . by (the) Word He created the things that were made, and God is Spirit, and by (the) Spirit He adorned all things.[19]

Moreover:

> The Word establishes, that is, gives body and grants the reality of being, and the Spirit gives order and form to the diversity of power.[20]

Here then are both the demarcations and the unity of the respective actions and functions of Word and Spirit in creation. In Irenaeus's observations on the incarnation we find much the same. It is the Word who establishes the flesh by taking it into union with Himself, that is, by giving it reality and body, but the Spirit who gives it order and form, binding the flesh to the Word. Here in Section 71, we find that 'Christ's body was made by His Spirit'. Again in Section 51 we have read already that 'the same God forms Him from the womb, that is, of the Spirit of God He should be born'. All 'virile influence' is excluded from the incarnation: it is a work of God, and the Spirit, being God 'forms from the womb'. Creation and incarnation are brought together in *Adversus Haereses*:

> So also in the end, the Word of the Father and the Spirit of God, having become united with the ancient substance of Adam's formation, rendered man living and perfect, receptive of the perfect Father, in order that as in the natural [Adam] we all were dead, so in the spiritual we may all be made alive. For never at any time did Adam escape the hands of God, to whom [these hands] the Father speaking said: Let us make man in our image, after our likeness. And for this reason, in the last time, not by the will of the flesh, nor by

> the will of man, but by the good pleasure of the Father, His hands formed a living man, that Adam might be created after the image and likeness of God.[21]

We have to note that when Irenaeus says that Word and Spirit are 'united with the ancient substance of Adam's formation', this is not referring to the incarnation, but to the redemption of man of which the incarnation is the ground whereby the 'ancient substance of Adam's formation' is assumed by the Word and made adaptable to bear the Holy Spirit as He, the Word, is the bearer of the same Spirit. At the incarnation, the same two 'hands' which formed Adam, formed the flesh of the Word in which Adam is recapitulated and re-created.

I do not think that some commentators (Armitage Robinson included) make a strong enough distinction between the incarnation as a completed act and the working out of the incarnation in the establishing of a 'community of union' between God and humanity. It is in this latter respect that such statements by Irenaeus[22] about the 'intermingling' of the Spirit with 'the formation of God' (that is, the creation which is man) should be understood. Manifestly in *Adversus Haereses* this is so:

> . . . the same Word . . . His advent according to the flesh, by which the intermingling and communion of God and man took place [so that] man having embraced the Spirit of God should be brought to the glory of the Father.[23]

This passage is quite clear that it is the Word who becomes flesh, and that it is on the ground of this that the Spirit is related to humanity in order to bring about the fruition of this relation established by the Word. It is the Spirit who

> furnishes us with a knowledge of the truth, and has set forth the dispensations of the Father and the Son, in virtue of which He dwells with every generation of men, according to the will of the Father.[24]

The equivalent passage to this first part of Section 71 in *Adversus Haereses* appears in the context of 'the new phase' which was entered upon by 'the Word arranging after a new manner the advent in the flesh, that He might win back that man which had departed from God to God', and that the Son of God is 'both called and actually is salvation and saviour and salvation-giving' [salus, salvator and salutare].[25] Here, I believe, Irenaeus links both meanings, the 'nature of God' and 'the Holy Spirit'. In introducing the quotation from Lamentations regarding 'the Spirit of our face', he writes of Christ:

> For He is indeed saviour, as being the Son and Word of God; but salutary since He is Spirit; for he [the prophet] says: The Spirit of our face, the Lord Christ. But (he is also) salvation, as being flesh, for: The Word was made flesh and dwelt among us.[26]

The argument here is that Christ is Himself 'saviour' and 'salvation' – saviour because He is God, and salvation because He, as God, is flesh. But he is 'salvation-giving' because He is 'Spirit'. The language used in this last attribution might suggest a confusion between Word and Spirit. But the distinction is explicitly in the text if Irenaeus's general and constant, double use of 'Spirit' is borne in mind. He has written of the divine nature of Christ, being the Son and Word, and therefore saviour: he has written of the humanity of Christ, and therefore salvation: but the means whereby He, as saviour bestows that salvation which He is as man, is 'Spirit'. This can only refer in some way to the Holy Spirit, for the nature of God has been mentioned already in the divinity of the Word. But clearly it is a reference which is bound closely to the being of the Word made flesh.

As has been noted in the last chapter regarding Section 53, Irenaeus says

> He was named Christ, for through Him the Father anointed and adorned all things; and because in His coming as man He was anointed with the Spirit of God and His Father.

Probably such references as this which might suggest a confusion between Word and Spirit are merely Irenaeus's way of indicating the relation between Word and Spirit in the work of saving. He is the 'Christ' because he is anointed with the Spirit, and as the 'anointed' is 'salvation-giver'.

Here in the phrase 'Spirit of our face', 'Spirit' refers, as we have suggested in the comments on Section 2,[27] to 'the communion of the Spirit', that is, the internal relations of the Godhead, and of the Spirit with humanity as He who brings humanity into a 'community of union' with God through the Word made flesh. It surely should be read here in the understanding of redemption which Irenaeus sets out:

> The mighty Word and very man . . . thus has redeemed us by His blood, giving His soul for our souls, and His flesh for our flesh, and has also poured out the Spirit of the Father for the union and communion of God and man, imparting indeed God to men by means of the Spirit, and, on the other hand, attaching man to God by means of His incarnation, and bestowing upon us at His coming immortality, durably and truly, by means of communion with God.[28]

The phrase 'Spirit of our face' would suggest a relation between the 'Godness' of God and our existence. But the 'Godness' of God is the relational existence of God as Father, Word and Spirit. So we are redeemed, Irenaeus seems to propound here, both by the Holy Spirit and the relation of the Spirit, the Word and the Father, in the creation of a 'community of union' for us – by the fact that we receive from the Word 'from the abundance of His unction',[29] that is, from the Spirit of the Father, from the Spirit who anoints Him in the assumption of our flesh and nature. The Word and the Spirit inhere, and function together, so closely, as they do at creation and incarnation, that the Spirit brings to bear upon us the re-creative work of the Word made flesh in His Person, as He does with the creative work of the Word in creation, 'establishing' it and 'adorning' it. This is surely why there is the choice of words 'our face'. 'Face' in the Hebrew is used for the 'presence of God', and the Greek work for 'face' – πϱοσωπον – for person. Is there not here a double meaning indicated in the choice of this singular phrase, namely that on the one hand the very Person and presence of God is meant, and, on the other, that it is our person, our totality, our identity, which is 'established' and 'adorned' in the Person and work of the Word made flesh as the ground of the Spirit bringing us into a 'community of union' with God?

So it is in Section 72 that Irenaeus states that only the Son of God is 'perfectly righteous', and 'makes righteous and perfects them that believe on Him'. In Irenaeus's view of the relation of the Word and Spirit in all that Christ has accomplished, this 'making righteous and perfecting' is the work of the Spirit relating humanity to all that the Word made flesh has accomplished in Himself. The 'community of union' into which humanity is so brought is a matter of participation, by the Spirit, in the Person and work of Christ. On commenting on Isaiah LVII:1f, Irenaeus picks out the phrase 'Peace shall be his burial' interpreting it not only in terms of Christ's death, but of what the community of union as participation in Christ means for the believer. It is 'the peace of redemption', that is, it is the peace of the redemption which Christ is, for to this end He died. Participation in this means peace in the totality of being for the believer – they believe 'with one accord upon Him': they have the peace of unanimity, of minds centred on Christ; they have common faith in Him: they have the peace of universal amity. The harmony which Christ has established between the being of God and the being of humanity is necessarily imaged within the being of humanity in community of union with God through him. This is made explicit in Section 86:

> The apostles . . . preached in all the world the Son of God, who came to suffer, and endured to the destruction of death and the quickening of the flesh: that by the putting away of enmity towards God which is unrighteousness, we should obtain peace with Him, doing that which is pleasing to Him.[30]

Irenaeus goes on to write of the resurrection. It follows on as the comment on the nature of this peace of Christ. He writes 'He appeared no more after His resurrection' – a rather remarkable statement. But what he is meaning here is that Christ did not appear again in His former unresurrected and dishonoured estate. He has now risen in the flesh and that flesh and nature are immortal. But this immortality is only on the basis that he died first, and it is in that irreversible exchange which Christ wrought that our participation in him grants the peace of redemption. A parallel thought of irreversibility is found in Section 89 concerning the redeeming Christ and the law of Moses:

> . . . He would not send back the redeemed to the law of Moses – for the law was fulfilled in Christ – but would have them live in newness by the Word, through faith in the Son of God and love . . .[31]

Sections 72 and 73 exhibit the clear understanding of Irenaeus that Christ's crucifixion cannot be separated from His resurrection, nor His resurrection from His crucifixion; they are both the one act of redemption which is set out for the partaking of all humanity.

Notes

1 Irenaeus: *Adversus Haereses* V:1:1.
2 *Ibid.* IV:20:7.
3 Athanasius: *Contra Arianos* IV:6.
4 Irenaeus: *Adversus Haereses* IV:32:11.
5 Gregory of Nyssa: *Against Eunomius* I:26.

6 Irenaeus: *Adversus Haereses* II:3:2.
7 Irenaeus: *Demonstration* 7.
8 Psalm LXXXIX:39ff.
9 Irenaeus: *Demonstration* 75.
10 *Ibid.* 69.
11 John Donne: *The Crosse.*
12 Irenaeus: *Adversus Haereses* III:19:1.
13 *Ibid.* II:20:3.
14 Irenaeus: *Demonstration* 6; cf. 31ff.
15 Comments on Sections 5–8, Chapter 5.
16 Irenaeus: *Adversus Haereses* III:24:2.
17 *Ibid.* IV:20:2.
18 *Ibid.* IV:20:4; cf. IV:20:1.
19 Comments on Sections 5–8, Chapter 5.
20 *Ibid.*
21 Irenaeus: *Adversus Haereses* V:1:3.
22 Irenaeus: *Demonstration* 97: cf. *Adversus Haereses* IV:20:4.
23 Irenaeus *Adversus Haereses* IV:20:4.
24 *Ibid.* IV:33:7.
25 *Ibid.* III:10:2.
26 *Ibid.*
27 Comments on Section 2, Chapter 2.
28 Irenaeus: *Adversus Haereses* V:1:1.
29 *Ibid.* III:9:3.
30 Irenaeus: *Demonstration of the Apostolic Preaching* 86.
31 *Ibid.* 89.

Chapter 16

Sections 67–82: The Sufferings of the Word in His Obedience (2)

Sections 74–82: The Nature of the Sufferings of the Word Made Flesh

The pattern of these sections is that Christ suffers and is crucified, gathering round Him (in Section 74) the fear of the Gentiles; (in Section 75) the will of the Father; (in Section 76) the cowardice of the disciples; (in Section 77) the divisive politics of Romans and Jews as exhibited in the enmity of Pilate and Herod; (in Section 78) the necessity of the salvation of those who had previously died. Then Irenaeus moves to the instruments of the humiliation and death of Christ; (in Section 79) the cross itself; (in Section 80) the parting of, and gambling for, his garments; (in Section 81) the money of Judas's betrayal; and (in Section 82) the vinegar and gall of his thirst.

In Section 74, Irenaeus places the passion and crucifixion of Christ in its particular historical context – but here there are displayed some of his idiosyncratic interpretations. What lies behind his assertion that Pontius Pilate was 'the governor of Claudius Caesar' is that claim of his in *Adversus Haereses*[1] that our Lord died at the age of nearly fifty years. The importance of this for Irenaeus is shown in the carefulness of the explanation he sets out. This is in the context of Irenaeus's exposure of the grotesque mathematical interpretations of the gnostic heretics (in this instance particularly the Valentinians) concerning the number of aeons within the pleroma of their divinities being shown by the age in years in which Christ was baptized, namely thirty, and speculation regarding the month in which He was crucified, they claiming that it was the twelfth month and finding significance in the number for they believed that His ministry was that of but one year and this the climax of it. Irenaeus carefully sets out the events of our Lord's life as he sees them in sequence and in the time they occurred.[2] He continues:

> Being thirty years old when He came to be baptized, and then possessing the full age of a Teacher, He came to Jerusalem that He might be acknowledged properly by all as a Teacher.[3]

The importance of this is the age of an acknowledged and officially recognized Master or Teacher, who must have seniority of years. It would seem that Irenaeus believed that the ministry of Christ extended to nearly twenty years, and that he was in at least the fourth decade of age when crucified.

> Now, that the first stage of early life concludes thirty years, and this extends [in fruition] to the fortieth year, all will admit; but from the fortieth and fiftieth year a man begins to

> decline towards old age, which our Lord possessed while He still fulfilled the office of Teacher . . .[4]

These conclusions he deduces in three ways in this section of *Adversus Haereses*. First, his general theological argument: that our Lord recapitulates in Himself every age of human existence, from infancy to advanced years – otherwise these ages of man are not sanctified:

> For He came to save all through means of Himself – all, I say, who through Him are born again to God – infants and children and boys and youths and old men. He therefore passed through every age, becoming an infant for infants, thereby sanctifying infants . . . . So likewise He was an old man for old men, that He might be a perfect Teacher for all, not merely with regards to setting forth the truth, but also as regards age, sanctifying at the same time the aged also, and becoming an example to them likewise.[5]

Irenaeus is insistent that Christ was not 'man in appearance only, but what He was that He also appeared to be', and in so doing makes it clear that he is concerned with the actuality and reality of Christ's humanity. Therefore, if old age is to be sanctified, Christ really took to Himself old age. For Irenaeus, the truth of redemption has to be grounded in that emphasis which foreshadows the later maxim 'not assumed is not healed', but not only in the matter of the totality of human being and nature which the Word assumed at the incarnation, but of all circumstances through which the human being passes.

Second, the scriptural. He bases his observations about the advanced years of Christ on the text of John VIII:56,57, in which the Jews are recorded as saying to Christ that He could not have seen Abraham, He being of an age which was not yet of fifty years. Irenaeus seizes on this as meaning that our Lord was approaching fifty years of age. He argues that if the Jews knew that Christ was in his thirties, then they would have said 'Thou art not yet forty years old', and points out with regard to their observation that he was not yet fifty years old:

> Now such language is applied properly to one who has already passed the age of forty without having as yet reached his fiftieth year, yet is not far from this latter period . . . . For those who wished to convict Him of falsehood would certainly not extend the number of His years far beyond what age they saw He had reached . . . whether they had ascertained this clearly out of the entry in the public register, or simply made a conjecture from what they observed that He was more than forty years old and that He certainly was not one of only thirty years of age. For it is altogether unreasonable to suppose that they were mistaken by twenty years when they wished to prove Him younger than the times of Abraham.[6]

Third, from tradition, Irenaeus cites a tradition which maintained a more advanced age of Christ when he was crucified. He links the reference from John with 'even as the Gospel and all the elders testify; those who were conversant with John, the disciple of the Lord, in Asia, [witnessing] that John conveyed to them that information'.[7] Later in *Adversus Haereses*, regarding other issues, Irenaeus writes in the same vein concerning the tradition he relies upon: 'These things are witnessed to in a writing by Papias, the hearer of John and a companion of Polycarp, in his fourth book; for there were five books composed by him . . .[8]

In *Adversus Haereses* III:3:4, we find Irenaeus recounting a story from Polycarp about St John shunning the heretic Cerinthus. Again the appeal seems to be to the authority of this particular strand and brand of tradition which is seen as descending from St John through Papias and Polycarp, and in which Irenaeus sees himself standing.

Certainly the issue of our Lord's age belongs to this which is perceived to be a legitimate strand of apostolic tradition by Irenaeus in his repeated appeal to 'the elders'. The fullness of what exactly it contained as unique cannot be deduced from what little of anything there is that is either primarily or secondarily extant of the writings of Papias and of Polycarp. It may be that the fragments ascribed to Irenaeus are from this collective tradition, particularly such as those numbered L–LIV.

It is certainly within the awareness of this tradition that his assertion in Section 74 of the *Demonstration*, that Pontius Pilate was 'the governor of Claudius Caesar', is to be understood. This placing of Pilate within that particular Caesar's period of rule would, of course, fit in with Irenaeus's assertion of the age of Christ at his death – leaving the problem that Pontius Pilate was Prefect of Judaea from AD26–36, and Claudius did not become Emperor until AD41.

Whatever the thinking behind the content of the tradition on which Irenaeus leans, his main interest is in the recapitulation of all ages by the Word made flesh, and that the obedience of the Word is that which sanctifies from conception and birth, through infancy and youth, to maturity and old age. Therefore, the Word must be seen to pass through all the stages of human existence in the process of bringing His obedience to bear within them to sanctify them, and in summing them up and redeeming the totality of that existence in Himself. Without knowledge of the content of this tradition of 'the elders' through Papias and Polycarp, to which Irenaeus has recourse, little more can be vouchsafed.

In Section 74, Irenaeus introduces the relationship between 'Herod king of the Jews' and 'Pontius Pilate the governor of Claudius Caesar', upon which he further comments in Section 77. But here he concentrates on the person and attitudes of Herod. This is Herod the tetrarch (Antipas). There may be a hint of unconscious parallelism, perhaps even conscious (this being a characteristic of Irenaeus's mode of thinking and presentation), when he states the reasons for Herod's fear of Jesus – 'as though He were to be an earthly king' – no doubt because of our Lord's words to Pilate:[9] 'my kingdom is not of this world' – bringing to mind the same fear of Herod the king after the birth of Jesus.[10] Is Irenaeus showing the constancy of one dimension of the cause of Christ's sufferings – the threat to Him by the earthly preoccupation and fears and envy of those in authority over the Jews, from His birth to His death? In a sense here the end is joined to the beginning in this phrase, and incarnation and crucifixion seen as linked inextricably.

From the mention of the machinations of those in earthly authority, in Section 75 Irenaeus immediately moves to the reason why Christ 'should endure these things', and that is 'the will of the Father'. This is what lies behind, and is the determinative factor in, the dispensation of the sufferings of the Word made flesh. It is this will of the Father which He, the Son, obeys. It is this will which lies behind the manifestations of the rebellion of humanity against God which, in its various forms and domains, are borne by the Son in order to penetrate to the 'very place' of Adamic sin. In this bearing Christ stands alone as Section 76 makes clear.

In the prophecy from Zephaniah quoted by Irenaeus as the opening of this section, there is an error in the Armenian text similar to that in Section 64. In both, 'my' is read for 'thy' – 'my servant' instead of 'thy servant' as in the Septuagint rendering. Citing Zechariah XIII:7 in the version of codex A of the Septuagint – 'Smite the shepherd and the flock shall be scattered' – Irenaeus notes that even the disciples did not 'steadfastly believe' Him in His humiliation, but forsook Him and fled. They too exhibit 'fear' – in this case 'lest they should die with Him'. What emerges here is that this 'fear', whether it be of rulers for their seats of authority or disciples for their lives, is self-centred, which is the very hallmark of the sin of Adam. It therefore is that which is not only opposite to, but is opposed to, that proper fear of which Irenaeus has spoken previously[11] as the prerequisite of the knowledge of God and the ground of our 'community of union' with Him, the fear of God.

At the end of Section 76 Irenaeus's statement that the disciples did not 'stedfastly believe on Him, until they had seen Him risen from the dead', introduces the note of the recognition of Christ in all His significance which is taken up in Sections 83ff.

The relation between Herod and Pilate is then expounded in Section 77, and is done so in terms of the division and hatred and duplicitous alliance between those two in high authority. This is introduced by a quotation from what Irenaeus calls 'the Twelve Prophets', a phrase he uses in Section 93 and in *Adversus Haereses* IV:17:5, probably meaning a book containing the minor prophets.[12] Here the quotation is from Hosea X:6; in the other two instances noted in the *Demonstration* and in *Adversus Haereses*, the quotations are from Malachi. Irenaeus sees this reference of the prophet – 'and they bound him and brought him as a present to the king' – as foreseeing the bringing of Christ to Herod on the sending of Him there by Pilate. The exploitation of Christ for the ends of political expediency is underlined by Irenaeus; Christ is made a 'convenient occasion' whereby Pilate and Herod may be reconciled in their shared condemnation of him. The same verse from Hosea is cited by Justin Martyr[13] concerning the same occasion of the delivery, by Pilate's order, of Jesus, bound, to Herod. Justin Martyr sees this as Pilate's 'compliment' to Herod on the latter's accession to the seat of Archelaus, but nowhere hints, as Irenaeus clearly does, that this gesture was to bring about reconciliation between the two.

In so mentioning this, Irenaeus is commenting implicitly on the nature of the sufferings and humiliation of Christ – that the One who brings reconciliation and a 'community of union' between God, the Lord of all, and humanity, is despised to the extent that He Himself becomes the means whereby devious machinations in the affairs of human government are effected for despicable designs. Instead of the recognition of His significance as the concourse between God and humanity, Jesus is seen as a convenient pawn in the state of human affairs of state and so used in order to become the means of converse between Herod and Pilate in their variance.

There seems to be in the way in which Irenaeus presents this survey of the sufferings of Christ, the implicit setting out of a underlying activity on the part of Christ's accusers and tormentors and judges, which runs parallel – in the dimension of human wickedness, and therefore exactly contrary – to the dispensation of God. The fear of God is contrasted with the fear of the politicians and the disciples; the reconciliation of God with humanity is contrasted with the convergence of the wicked. It is this contradiction, which is a grotesque caricature of the dispensation of God in humanity's ordering of itself, which has to be borne by Christ if He is to penetrate into the depth of the Adamic rejection of God. It is the will of the Father to which Christ submits that this should be so.

Section 78 quotes a prophecy, here ascribed to Jeremiah, which is not found in any text of the Old Testament. Justin Martyr cites it as being one of the texts removed by the Jews from their scriptures. In response to a request from Trypho – 'We ask you first of all to tell us of some of the scriptures which you allege have been completely cancelled'[14] – Justin Martyr claims that a certain text (Jeremiah XI:19) had been recently removed from the Jewish scriptures, but some copies in the synagogues still retained it. This particular text, appearing in a somewhat different form in this section of the *Demonstration*, and rendered by Justin Martyr as

> The Lord God remembered His dead people of Israel who lay in their graves; and He descended to preach to them His own salvation.

was removed, he claims. Irenaeus quotes it as coming from Jeremiah without any comment of its removal. Indeed, in *Adversus Haereses* he employs it several times, in the first instance[15] ascribing it to Isaiah, in the second to Jeremiah,[16] the third with no ascription,[17] and the fourth merely as to 'the prophet'.[18] Where this text came from cannot be discovered. There is, however, an intriguing comment by Irenaeus in *Adversus Haereses* in the context of the accuracy of the translation of the Hebrew scriptures into the Greek language – that is, the Septuagint – and the propriety of interpretations of scripture. Irenaeus claims that the apostles 'agree with this aforesaid translation' and that this shows the correctness of it, since they pre-dated the heretics with their alleged translations. He then continues:

> the translation harmonizes with the tradition of the apostles. For Peter and John and Matthew and Paul and the rest successively, as well as their followers, set out all prophetical [sayings], just as the interpretation of the elders contains them.[19]

This last observation would seem to suggest that there was a source from 'the elders'. By this, Irenaeus always means the tradition from John through Papias and Polycarp, and therefore is perhaps indicating a written source of collective scriptural sayings and texts or interpretations of such which circulated within that tradition. Such a source – be it of proof texts or of material of broader interest or of authoritative interpretations within that tradition – would well explain a number of perplexing references he makes throughout the scope of his works.

This section, opening with this quotation ascribed here to Jeremiah, deals with the descent of our Lord to the dead. The dead, in the references in *Adversus Haereses* indicated above, are variously described as 'His own dead ones who slept in the dust', 'His dead saints', and 'His dead Israel'. 'Even in' this place of the dead, remarks Irenaeus, Christ 'renders the cause of His death'. It is to be noted that neither here nor in any other reference does Irenaeus equate the 'hell' into which Christ descended, with a place of torment. Here it is used in terms of the place where those of past time have 'fallen asleep in the dust of the earth'. His death is efficacious for human existence of all time, and this does not exclude those who lived in time past. Even there His death works 'the salvation of them that had passed away'.

Irenaeus in this section has passed from the particular historical circumstances of the sufferings and condemnation of Christ considered in previous sections, to the breadth of the scope of the redemption which these sufferings have worked. He then goes on to refer to the crucifixion and the significance of the cross, in Section 79, ending there with the quotation from Deuteronomy XXVIII:66, which for him is the warning of Moses to Israel of old of how the people would not believe 'in thy life', which life, on the cross, 'shall be hanged up before thine eyes'. The indication of the cross, writes Irenaeus, is found in the prophet Isaiah (Isaiah LXV:2) in the 'stretching out of my hands all the day long to a disobedient and gainsaying people'. Then, invoking the Psalms[20] in the Septuagint version, he shows the prophetic description of the crowd gathered round the cross and the depth of the agony of Christ.

The 'life hanging before thine eyes' is a favourite quotation of Irenaeus.[21] In *Adversus Haereses*, he couples it with both the disbelief of Israel, those who would 'not believe thy life', and did not receive Him despite the compulsion of the prophetic dispensation concerning Him, and with those of Israel and of the Gentiles – those who did believe and receive Him and who thus come under the Johannine category of 'as many as received Him, to them He gave power to become sons of God'.[22] The references Irenaeus makes to the dead as God's 'dead saints', 'His dead Israel', 'His own dead ones', in his use throughout *Adversus Haereses* of the text supposedly excised from Jeremiah or attributed to Isaiah, indicate that he is referring in Section 78 to the faithful of the old covenant whom Christ redeemed in his descent into hell.

The cross is Irenaeus's first consideration in these sections as he sets out the nature of the sufferings of the Word in His obedience. His prime consideration, however, both here and in all other writings where he sets out these sufferings, is the person of the Word made flesh. It is this which gives significance to the cross and to the other outward instruments, agents and manifestations of these sufferings. These are but ordained and used in order that the prime reason for the sufferings can work out its dispensation, and this reason is the will of the Father for the redemption of humanity, to which will the Word, in both His active and passive obedience in the working out of that dispensation of salvation, willingly submits as the Son of the Father.

This dispensation is not suddenly introduced at the incarnation: it has a hinterland in which the Word and the Spirit move in accordance with the will of the Father. This is the epic of Israel, the time and place of the old covenant, the substance of which is the incarnation and the redemption achieved thereby to which it prophetically points. There is deliberation and design in this time and place of preparation, and these are determined by the nature of the incarnation and the Person of the One to be incarnate. All the prophetic significance of the old covenant is paradigmatic – thus Irenaeus writes in Section 86:

> If then the prophets prophesied that the Son of God was to appear on earth, and prophesied also where in earth and how and in what manner He should make known His

> appearance, and all these prophecies our Lord took upon Himself; our faith in Him was well-founded, and the tradition of the preaching (is) true: that is to say, the testimony of the apostles, who being sent forth by the Lord preached in all the world the Son of God who came to suffer and endured to the destruction of death and the quickening of the flesh . . . .[23]

The lamentations of Israel, and the whole working out of humanity in proximity to the living, active God in covenant with Him, are taken by the Word, made His own, and transformed through His sufferings into the answers to the questions of all humanity in its relation to the Father/Creator.

In all considerations of the sufferings of the Word made flesh, the Son of God born the Son of man, Irenaeus never departs from their grounding in the nature of the relation between Father and Son and the nature of the union of the Word with the flesh.

Irenaeus completes his comments on the crucifixion with references in Sections 80, 81 and 82 to the garment of Christ and the money paid to Judas and the drink offered to our Lord on the cross. These three subjects he treats factually, as though repeating in summary the Gospel narratives of the crucifixion. It may be remarked that in Section 81, where he reports that Judas 'took the thirty staters of the province, and betrayed Christ unto them', he obviously is reading from the Codex Bezae version of Matthew XXVI:15, where 'thirty staters' (στατηρας) is used instead of 'thirty pieces of silver' (ἀργυρια).

Notes

1 Irenaeus: Adversus Haereses II:22:4–6.
2 *Ibid.* II:22:3.
3 *Ibid.* II:22:4.
4 *Ibid.*
5 *Ibid.* II:22:4-6
6 *Ibid.* II:22:6.
7 *Ibid.* II:22:5.
8 *Ibid.* V:33:4.
9 John XVIII:36.
10 Matthew II:2ff.
11 E.g. Irenaeus: *Demonstration* 2.
12 Cf. the fragment (IV) ascribed to Melito of Sardis, being a letter to Onesimus and containing a list of Old Testament books. There the 'twelve' are mentioned as a single book.
13 Justin Martyr: *Dialogue with Trypho* 103.
14 *Ibid.* 72.
15 Irenaeus: *Adversus Haereses* III:20:4.
16 *Ibid.* IV:22:1.
17 *Ibid.*IV:33:12.
18 *Ibid.* V:31:1.
19 *Ibid.* III:21:3.
20 Psalms XXII:16,14,17,20; CXIX:120; XXII:16, in this order.
21 Irenaeus: cf. *Adversus Haereses* IV:10:2; V:18:3.

22 *Ibid.* V:18:3.
23 Irenaeus: *Demonstration of the Apostolic Preaching* 86.

Chapter 17

Sections 83–88: The Resurrection and Ascension of the Word Made Flesh

The scant reference to the resurrection, and the wealth of observations on the ascension in these sections, might give the impression that Irenaeus is passing over the resurrection as of little import. This is far from so, for the resurrection has great weightiness in Irenaeun thought. He does not, however, consider it as an episode in itself, standing by itself. Resurrection and ascension are together one sweep of significance in the whole coherent and integrated movement of the existence of the Word as flesh from the incarnation onwards right through crucifixion, resurrection and ascension and into His coming again. Indeed, in these sections of the *Demonstration* now under our consideration, it is clear that the ascent of the Word made flesh is to be understood only in terms of the descent of the Word to assume that flesh. None of these episodes from incarnation to ascension is considered in isolation from the others. He expresses this succinctly in *Adversus Haereses*, where his argument is that the heretics' 'doctrine is homicidal' because in the last resort they destroy humanity by denying the sole ground of its true being – which ground is

> Jesus Christ . . . one and the same, to whom the gates of heaven were opened, because of His taking upon Him flesh; who shall also come in the same flesh in which He suffered, revealing the glory of the Father.[1]

Irenaeus, in those sections of *Adversus Haereses*[2] where he treats of the resurrection (again seemingly disproportionately small in comparison with his discursive writing on other issues) is emphatic as to the physical nature both of the resurrection of our Lord and of the general resurrection. In this emphasis, the interlinking of incarnation with crucifixion and resurrection is clear, the argument being that the flesh assumed by the Word is that in which not only is our redemption worked, but is that itself which is redeemed.

Irenaeus is clear as to the significance and potency of the resurrection of our Lord. In *Adversus Haereses* he combines the idea of 'firstfruits' with that of the 'head' and the 'body':

> . . . what was thus born should be 'God with us', and descend to those things which are of the earth beneath, seeking the sheep which had perished, which was indeed His own peculiar handiwork, and ascend to the height above, offering and commending to His Father that human nature which had been found, making in His own Person the firstfruits of the resurrection of man; that as the Head rose from the dead, so also the remaining part of the body – of every man who is found in life – when the time is fulfilled of that condemnation which existed by reason of disobedience, may rise, blended together and

> strengthened through means of joints and bands by the increase of God, each of the members having its own fit and proper position in the body.[3]

The object of redemption is the human being in its totality. To deny the resurrection in the flesh is effectively to deny the reality of the flesh which the Word assumed, Irenaeus argues. In these observations he is combating the dualism of the gnostics particularly over their idea of the separation of body and soul and the disparagement of the physical and corporeal as the handiwork of God. Moreover, the physical resurrection guarantees the redemption of humanity's perishable form of existence. The question as to the nature of this totality, the constitution of the human entity, has been discussed fully in the comments on Section 2 of the *Demonstration* in Chapter 2 above.

In these references to the resurrection in *Adversus Haereses*, and, indeed, in this section of the *Demonstration*, Irenaeus betrays the fact that, like the divinity of the Holy Spirit, the resurrection is assumed as fact. As in what references form his doctrine of the Holy Spirit, so too in the paucity of discussion on the resurrection, he does not see the need for apologetic statements; the fact of the resurrection is assumed as self-evident, beyond dispute and unquestionably accepted in the faith of the church. In *Adversus Haereses* he refers to the proclaimed faith of the universal church which has been received 'from the apostles and their disciples', and in the midst of this reference writes of that article of belief in

> the Holy Spirit, who proclaimed through the prophets the dispensation of God, and the advents and the birth from a virgin, and the passion and the resurrection from the dead, and the ascension into heaven in the flesh of the beloved Christ Jesus our Lord, and His manifestation from heaven in the glory of the Father 'to gather together all things into one', and to raise up anew all flesh of the whole human race . . . in the exercise of His grace confer immortality on the righteous and holy and those who have kept His commandments and have persevered in His love, some from the beginning and others from their repentance, and . . . surround them with everlasting glory.[4]

What interests Irenaeus and prompts him to wider debate than any required of him concerning the undisputed resurrection of Christ, is the significance of the ascension as the 'climax', so to speak, of the resurrection and of the whole life of our Lord as the seal and surety and substance of our redemption.

He again exhibits his interest in the historical and spatial particularity of the saving events of the life of Christ. Here in Section 83, he locates the ascension in its geographical place 'For the Lord, he [David, the Psalmist] says, from Sion ascended up on high'. He is quoting Psalm LXVIII:17f, and, in fact, the psalm does not include any such direct reference. It certainly presupposes Sion, and Irenaeus would therefore seem to equate 'the hill which God desires to dwell in' of the psalm with the Mount of Olives 'over against Jerusalem' – the hill of the ascension. The ascension is seen by Irenaeus in terms of the exaltation of the new man, risen from the dead, with the 'place' of his humanity or the 'room' he has made for his flesh and human nature in the assumption of it, still intact, to the 'place' or 'room' which God makes for the reception of our humanity in the heavenly 'places' in the ascended Christ. The temporal/spatial existence is mentioned in its particularity, then is moved on into that which gives all existence to all temporal/spatial entities.

From the particular Irenaeus broadens out into the consideration of the kingdom of heaven into which Christ ascends. Here he is careful to combine word and deed; Christ assembles His disciples, expounds to them 'the things concerning the kingdom', and then ascends there, the disciples seeing 'how the heavens were opened and received Him'.

The ascension therefore is a matter for intelligible proclamation; it is an article of informed faith; it is not a glissando of existence merging mystically into a higher plane. The emphasis of Irenaeus, that the resurrection and the ascension are a matter of the confirming and sealing of the relation between creature and Creator, humanity and God, wherein that relation is seen to be the affirming of the reality of humanity by God, and a raising and ascension of it into union with the divine life, has its necessary and antecedent counterpart in the reality of the humanity which the Word assumed at His descent at the incarnation.

There is a strong anticipation of the concept of περιχορεσις – God 'making room for' – in later doctrine, here in regard to the 'room' God makes for humanity in the humanity of the Word in its incarnation and ascension, and the 'place' He has established as the 'trysting-place' with humanity in the Person and event of Christ. This is found implicitly too in Irenaeus's doctrine of creation, that the Creator, without inner or outer necessity, creates wholly in love and 'makes room' for creation's existence, its time and place, beside His existence in His utter Self-sufficiency. It is the constant anchoring of the reality of the divine presence and action in the actualities of temporal/spatial concerns, in His insistence on particularities which broaden out and anchor these concerns within the divine presence and activity, which gives Irenaeus this insight. His theology is characterized by his emphasis on relations – either of the Father and Son and Spirit, or of Word and humanity, or of Creator and creation, or even in the sphere of faith and godliness – and this too heightens the implicit 'making room for'.

Here he underlines that the faith is concerned with the affirming of the reality and actuality of both that ascent and that descent, the former being anchored firmly in the latter, in the reality and actuality of the Word in relation to the reality and actuality of the humanity He assumes.

This is brought out in Section 84, which we have considered already in the comments on Section 48 in Chapter 13. Here again 'descent' and 'ascent' are interwoven. The argument is that the Word was invisible in His descent to assume human flesh and nature; therefore the angelic powers did not know Him in His descent. But He is visible in His ascent, for He wears that flesh and nature; therefore the angelic powers recognize Him. But they recognize Him as He passes upwards through their domains, those 'below' and those 'on the firmament, so' that the ones 'below' upon their recognition of Him cry out to those 'on the firmament: Lift up your gates, and be ye lift up ye everlasting doors, that the King of glory may come in', and testify a second time as to his identity, that 'The Lord strong and mighty, he is the King of glory'.

Presumably, the ascension is through the 'seven heavens' by which the 'world is encompassed', and our Lord is acknowledged by 'the powers and angels and archangels, doing service to God, the Almighty and Maker of all things'[5] who are the denizens of these, beginning with the angels who 'are in the world',[6] those who are 'below the firmament', calling out to those above.

Here we have both reality and the recognition of the reality set together in the angelic witness. We have already noted in Section 48 that the recognition of that glory is that it is seen to be 'the exaltation with glory which followed on His humanity and humiliation and ingloriousness', so that for Irenaeus the ascent both gathers up the descent and all that was fulfilled in that abased estate and yet is ascent only on the basis of the descent and its significance and achievement.

It may be remarked that while Irenaeus does not follow Justin Martyr's interpretation of the voice calling our 'Lift up your gates' to be that of the Holy Spirit, there is a possible parallel with the apocryphal second century 'The Ascension of Isaiah' with its account of Isaiah's journey through to the seventh heaven and its note of the prophet seeing Christ's ascension through the six heavens and His enthronement in the seventh 'at the right hand of the great Glory'. Caution again has to be exercised here, for Irenaeus nowhere has the description of the descent of the Word which is found in this work, save the phrase that He is 'unrecognized' – but in this instance in this apocryphal work only from the fifth heaven downwards. Nor is there in this work such a detailed working out of the antiphon of the psalm as applied to the ascent of Christ in Irenaeus. General ideas common to writers are not infallible proofs of specific sources used.

The ascension is the leading of 'captivity captive'. Irenaeus explains what he means by 'captivity', namely the 'rule of the apostate angels' which is now destroyed in Christ's triumph. The question arises as to what he means by 'apostasy' and what the origin and nature of this is. We have already noted that in the *Demonstration*[7] Adam is seen to be the victim of Satan's jealousy over the privileged position that humanity enjoys in its relation to God. He notes in the *Demonstration* that 'the Hebrew word "Satan" signifies Apostate, but he is also called Slanderer',[8] and indeed, Irenaeus lays the blame at Satan's door for humanity's entering into apostasy. Therefore,

> justly is he [Satan] led captive, who had led men unjustly into bondage; while man, who had been led captive in times past, was rescued from the grasp of his possessor . . .[9]

As to the serpent in the garden, he is the form, as it were, of Satan the Slanderer whom 'he carried and conveyed . . . the angel hidden and concealed in him, even . . . Satan.[10]

Satan is 'the angel of apostasy' whose vehicle is the serpent. As such he is 'apostasy' itself, and this consists in pride and envy, according to Section 16, and makes him 'the author and originator of sin'. Irenaeus uses the word 'apostasy' in several different ways in *Adversus Haereses*. Primarily it is applied to Satan; but it is also used of the state of 'departing from God' caused by Satan and his fellow angelic followers, whether that state be of angels or of humanity. It is therefore also applied to heresy. The best summary of his belief in this matter of apostasy is in Section 16 of the *Demonstration*. This gathers up the scattered references throughout *Adversus Haereses* and gives a more coherent view of how he regards the problem of the cause and effect of evil. It also makes sharper the descent of the Word into 'the very place' of Adam's sin, so that humanity, as the captivity of apostasy, should be released and redeemed by the Word. Hence there is the insistence that Adam himself must also be saved by Christ,[11] otherwise the victory is not only not complete but, indeed, is of no effect.

In Section 85 Irenaeus penetrates to the heart of apostasy – 'angels and archangels and powers and thrones who despised the truth'. Apostasy is not confined to human error concerning God, but is of cosmic dimension. It is all that is opposed to, and that which seeks to destroy, the right relation between creature and Creator, humanity and God. The one on who bears this right relationship and is Himself this right relationship, the Word made flesh, is the one who has prevailed against this destructive force, and is therefore the one who will judge it, awaiting 'the time appointed by the Father for judgment, when all enemies shall be put under Him'.

In *Adversus Haereses* the 'apostasy' is likened to the story of the whale swallowing Jonah, and here Irenaeus tackles the question of why God permits the apostasy to so triumph. It is because 'strength was made perfect in weakness [and this] showed the kindness and transcendent power of God'.[12] This is in the context of what has been noted already in the comments on Sections 12–15 in Chapter 8, the relation of incarnation to creation. It seems to me that the whole question of Irenaeus's view of creation's and humanity's freedom over against the omniscience and omnipotence of God can only be resolved when consideration is made of this relation – namely that God, in creating that which is distinct from himself, and therefore different in quality, makes provision for the weakness of creation in the incarnation as the undergirding of the act of creating. As has been noted in commenting upon these earlier sections, incarnation is not only the conclusion of the work of creation, but the very initial purpose of it, the *terminus a quo* and the *terminus ad quem* of creation. It is in Christ that humanity moves forward and advances towards God, and this, as has also been noted already, is irrespective of whether or not there would have been a fall. Man is created as a child with the potential of moving forward, but with freedom. The full implications of this freedom, and its exercise by the man to whatever end, are undergirded and encompassed in the incarnation. It would be tempting to conjecture on this further, but Irenaeus does not provide any added directions for such exploration. This freedom can only be a freedom towards God if man is to be true to the source of his being and therefore to his integrity as human, as God's humanity.

It may be noted here that Irenaeus's theology is basically humanity-affirming and world-affirming. There is no disparagement of creature or creation in his thought. If difficulties regarding the relation between the omnipotence of God and the freedom of humanity arise because of this, then they arise not from any dualistic setting of the one against the other, but from the failure to perceive in the theology of Irenaeus the working out of the extent and implications of the provision which God has made for the dignity of his handiwork.

Man was taught the loving-kindness and transcendence of God, and the glory that would be revealed to him, by the Word walking and talking to the man and instructing him in that paradise.[13] That he should in temptation reject this does not mean that God has rejected him, but rather that such is that loving-kindness of the transcendent God that this rejection is also encompassed within the expression of God's care for His handiwork. Thus

> so the Son of God is truly good and patient, the Word of God the Father having been made the Son of man. For He fought and conquered; for He was the man contending for the fathers, and through obedience doing away with disobedience: for He bound the

> strong man and set free the weak and endowed His own handiwork with salvation by destroying sin. For He is a most holy and merciful Lord, and loves the human race.[14]

This love for the human race is exhibited even in the swallowing up of humanity by apostasy, for it is turned into the realization that humanity is utterly dependent upon God for its proper being and upholding and destiny. The sign of Jonah being swallowed and then regurgitated by the whale is the sign that

> man, receiving an un-hoped for salvation from God, might rise from the dead and glorify God, and repeat that word which was uttered in prophecy by Jonah: I cried by reason of my affliction to the Lord my God, and He heard me out of the belly of hell; and that he might always continue glorifying God and giving thanks for that salvation which he has derived from Him: That no flesh should glory in the Lord's presence; and that man should never adopt an opposite opinion with regard to God, supposing that the incorruptibility which belongs to him is his own naturally, and by thus not holding the truth, should boast with empty superciliousness as if he were by nature like to God. For he [Satan] thus rendered him [man] more ungrateful towards his Creator, obscured the love which God had towards man . . .
>
> This therefore was the long-suffering of God, that man passing through all things, and acquiring the knowledge of moral discipline, then attaining to the resurrection of the dead, and learning by experience what is the source of his deliverance, may always live in a state of gratitude to the Lord, having obtained from Him the gift of incorruptibility, that he might love Him the more, for: 'he to whom more is forgiven, loveth more'; and that he may know himself, how mortal and weak he is; while he also understands respecting God that He is immortal and powerful to such a degree as to confer immortality upon what is mortal and eternity upon what is temporal; and may also understand the other attributes of God displayed towards himself, by means of which being instructed he may think of God in terms of the divine greatness. For the glory of man is God . . . and the receptacle of His wisdom and power is man . . . And therefore Paul declares: For God hath concluded all in unbelief that He may have mercy upon all.[15]

The apostasy is used against itself to instruct man even more deeply in the greatness and the loving-kindness of God. That strategy against apostasy and all its effects, and that instruction positively set out, are the accomplishments of the Word who, in His descent in weakness, shows Himself to be the very power and loving-kindness of God in His ascent.

The corresponding passage to Section 85 in *Adversus Haereses* quotes the same psalm to the same end – the descent and ascent of the Word. But here the ones who 'enjoined the principalities of heaven to open the everlasting doors'[16] are the prophets. This part of *Adversus Haereses* is an extended examination of prophecies concerning the coming Christ, each prophet as a member of the body fulfilling his particular part of prophecy so that the whole dispensation of Christ appears 'shadowed forth beforehand'. Here Irenaeus does not mention the apostasy, but dwells on the extent of the opposition to Christ. Christ's coming again in judgment with 'His mighty angels' will 'shake' the whole earth, for there is 'the movement of the whole earth against the Church'. He cites Psalm XCIX:1 – 'the Lord hath reigned; let the people be enraged: He who sitteth on the cherubim; let the earth be moved' – as 'predicting partly that wrath from all nations which after His ascension came on those who believed in Him'. Antagonism to the faith is universal, but this opposition is judged in its entirety, nothing 'being hid from the heat' of that judgment because of the whole cosmic sweep of the Word made flesh who will be seen to be exalted as head over all things and the totality of creation.[17]

The incarnation and ascension are seen as this triumphant sweep of the existence of the Word made flesh throughout all creation and summing up engulfed humanity in its totality, and this is noted by Irenaeus quoting Psalm XIX:6 in Section 85 in implicit terms of joining the end to the beginning – in this case joining the 'place' of his 'going forth' (his descent at the incarnation) to the same 'place' of 'his cessation even at the end of heaven' (the completed work at the ascension). There is therefore nothing at all which will be hid from the 'heat' of His judgment, since all things have been encompassed and summed up in this activity of the Person of the Word.

In Sections 86 and 87, Irenaeus gives a brief statement as to the content and significance of the faith as 'well-founded'. Here he concentrates all that he has been expounding so comprehensively into a consideration of 'the short word which God has made on the earth in the world'. The idea equivalent to this use of a 'short word' is used by Irenaeus elsewhere. By it he seems to indicate particularity of time, place and thought, summing up a larger consideration. He uses it of the Word who 'furnished us, in a brief comprehensive manner, with salvation'.[18] The Word also appeared to Abraham and conversed with him 'in a very small space'.[19] By these last usages, Irenaeus indicates the Word's taking to Himself the particularities of the realities of creation. It does not suggest that the Word was confined within limits, in any Aristotelian 'container' sense, but rather that it is by such, which the Word is pleased to use, that the reality of the Word is found. So too, in the Word taking flesh to Himself, is the whole of salvation to be found. This salvation is concentrated in the Word made flesh. He, and He alone, is the substance of salvation, and, likewise, the testimony to, and proclamation of, Him is 'the brevity of faith and love'. Here we have an echo of 'faith and godliness'. But the operative word here is 'love', and thus the whole of the realization of salvation is concentrated on the brief word 'love'. Hence, the fulfilling of the law (which law, he notes in Section 89, is fulfilled, and therefore Christ does not send us back to it in all its extensive and detailed demands) is 'love . . . for he who loves God has fulfilled the law'. Love for God is formed by faith, which in turn is evoked by, and grows in, response to the love of God towards humanity which has been demonstrated and personified in Christ. This love is summed up in our Lord's brief comprehension of the law – the first commandment being love of God and the second necessarily following, love of neighbour – and this leads to the summing up of the life of faith as that which is 'godly and righteous and good'. I suggest that 'the short word' which 'God has made on the earth', is, in Irenaeus's thought, primarily the Word made flesh Himself, and secondarily because necessarily dependent upon this, the word of love of faith in Him.

This faith is that which is 'well-founded', for the advent of the Word demonstrates that He has fulfilled all the prophecies which were made concerning Him, according to Section 86. He has summed them up and fulfilled them. In the same way, the preaching of the apostles 'is true', for it witnesses to the One who has so fulfilled these prophecies in His coming, His suffering, His obedience, His death and His 'quickening of the flesh'. This is the new law which is to be preached 'in all the earth'.

The apostles themselves in this task were proclaimed by the prophets – and here Irenaeus appeals to Isaiah LII:7; Romans X:15: 'How beautiful are the feet of them that bring tidings of peace, and of them that bring tidings of good things'.[20] He also appeals to Isaiah II:3, concerning the new law of the apostles going out from Jerusalem to the ends of the earth. There is an extended comment on this in *Adversus Haereses* in which, culminating in a rather strange passage of application of metaphors to Christ, Irenaeus claims that through the preaching of the apostles, there was 'caused such a change in the state of things' that peace did come to nations, these nations changing their weapons of war into 'instruments . . . for peaceful purposes'. But, Irenaeus notes here, it is our Lord who has effected this, for He Himself is the one who 'has made the plough and introduced the pruning-hook' – that is, the creation of man as the fruit of the earth and the reclamation of man by the wood and iron of His cross, and the exhibiting of the pruning-hook as Christ's flesh, 'has reclaimed the savage earth'.

The content of preaching is the 'short word' which primarily is the Word made flesh himself, and all that follows from his Person and acts. For these things which were 'previously declared by the prophets . . . were accomplished in the Lord's person; and the same with regard to us, the body following the example of the Head'. [21] Here again is the juxtaposition of the comprehensive and the particular in Irenaean thought. The preaching is universal, but its content is that 'short word'. It is proclaimed by the prophets and all the apostles,[22] and has extensive repercussions, yet it is the 'short word' of the Word alone.

It is noteworthy that the very particularity of the Word, ascending in the victory of the flesh, is, according to Irenaeus in Section 88, the very thing which makes Him incomparable and unequalled. That He is beyond comparison, with none likened to Him, does not reside in His divinity alone, but in His ascended flesh and the victory which this indicates. Thus it is in 'his name' alone that redemption is to be found, and in Him the blessing of all humanity is brought about by his own Person and blood.

> So then by the new calling a change of heart in the Gentiles came to pass through the Word of God when: He was made flesh and tabernacled with men . . . . Wherefore the Church beareth much fruit of the redeemed: because no longer Moses (as) mediator nor Elijah (as) messenger, but the Lord Himself has redeemed us.[23]

Notes

1 Irenaeus: *Adversus Haereses* III:16:8.
2 *Ibid.* I:10:1; II:33:5; IV:33:2; V:2:3; 9:3; 13:1–5; 15:1; 31:1–2.
3 *Ibid.* III:19:3.
4 *Ibid.* I:10:1.
5 Irenaeus: *Demonstration of the Apostolic Preaching* 9.
6 *Ibid.* 10.
7 Comments on Sections 16 and 17, Chapter 9.
8 Irenaeus: *Demonstration of the Apostolic Preaching* 16; cf. *Adversus Haereses* V:21:2.
9 Irenaeus: *Adversus Haereses* V:21:3.
10 Irenaeus: *Demonstration of the Apostolic Preaching* 16.

11 Irenaeus: *Adversus Haereses* III:23:7,8.
12 *Ibid.* III:20:1.
13 Irenaeus: *Demonstration of the Apostolic Preaching* 12.
14 Irenaeus: *Adversus Haereses* III:18:6.
15 *Ibid.* III:20:1–2.
16 *Ibid.* IV:33:13.
17 *Ibid.* IV:33:9–13.
18 *Ibid.* III:18:1.
19 Irenaeus: *Demonstration of the Apostolic Preaching* 45.
20 *Ibid.* 86.
21 Irenaeus: *Adversus Haereses* IV:34:4.
22 *Ibid.* IV:34:1.
23 Irenaeus: *Demonstration of the Apostolic Preaching* 94.

Chapter 18

Sections 89–100: In Newness of Life

In these concluding sections Irenaeus gathers up, in terms of the Christian life, all that he has demonstrated previously. They are characterized by phrases indicating and underlining 'newness' – 'live in newness', 'new things', 'the new way of godliness', 'newness of the Spirit', 'the new testament', 'a new spirit', 'the new calling' – and by broad strokes depicting the consequences of all this as the truth of the Christian life.

Section 89 encapsulates the tone of this life: it is that Christians now 'live in newness by the Word, through faith in the Son of God and love'. Armitage Robinson points out that the verb 'live' here means more especially 'to live in freedom' – a meaning which is borne out by the first sentence of this section that Christ 'would not send back the redeemed to the legislation of Moses'. That, as has been remarked, is now fulfilled in its transformation in the Word made flesh being born under the law, shouldering its demands and bearing away its condemnation on the cross. This transformation into the new law has two repercussions – that the limited past is over, because it is fulfilled, and that the future opens up to an unrestricted universal perspective.

These are set out in the quotation from Isaiah XLIII:18ff employed by Irenaeus here. This remarks on the necessity of no longer remembering 'the former things', and the extension of this newness brought about by God into 'the wilderness' and 'the waterless place'. These two are interlinked, for the fulfilment of the old law by the Word made flesh means an expansion out from, but including, Israel into the totality of His handiwork.

The equivalent section in *Adversus Haereses* makes it clear that this quotation

> plainly announced that liberty which distinguishes the new covenant, and the new wine which is put into new bottles – the faith which is in Christ, by which He has proclaimed the way of righteousness sprung up in the desert, and the streams of the Holy Spirit in a dry land, to give water to the elect people of God whom He has acquired . . . .[1]

Irenaeus notes that with regard to the places of the Gentiles, the 'Word had not passed through them, nor given them the Holy Spirit to drink'. By this he does not mean the Word as Word, but the Word made flesh. The particularity of the place and time of the Word made flesh is maintained; but this particularity is opened out in the sending of the Spirit. The Holy Spirit is poured out over all the earth. The Word made flesh, 'who fashioned the new way of godliness and righteousness', makes 'copious streams to spring forth, disseminating over the earth the Holy Spirit, even as it had been promised through the prophets'.

The Holy Spirit is constantly linked with 'water' in the writings of Irenaeus. He is, for example identified with 'the voice of many waters' in *Adversus Haereses*,[2] and is described as that water which is 'the fluid' which bestows unity as water binds the dry wheat into dough and a loaf of bread

> . . . the water from heaven . . . that laver which leads to incorruption . . . living water . . . the dew, which is the Spirit of God, who descended upon the Lord [which] should be diffused throughout all the earth.[3]

This linking of the Holy Spirit with water immediately suggests baptism. We have noted already in Sections 6 and 7[4] that we are baptized into Christ's birth, His 'cutting forward' as He moves towards His passion and cross, His death, resurrection and ascension. Our baptism is the seal and sign of the 'community of union' we have with Christ through the humanity the Word assumes from the virgin Mary, which is therefore a 'community of union' with the divine existence of the Triune God. It is the Holy Spirit who brings us to Christ and to incorporation with Him in His Person and His acts, and it is the Son who brings us to the Father.

> The baptism of our regeneration proceeds through these three points: God the Father bestowing on us regeneration through His Son by the Holy Spirit. For as many as carry the Spirit of God are led to the Word, that is, to the Son: and the Son brings them to the Father: and the Father causes them to inherit incorruption.[5]

Baptism is not a stage-by-stage progression through the Persons of the Holy Trinity. Irenaeus never entertains even a suggestion of such implicit subordinationism. The whole Being of the Triune God is involved, for it is the Father who bestows 'on us regeneration through His Son by the Spirit'. Baptism is the way of our incorporation into Christ and into a 'community of union' with God, and it is a way of new birth which is comparable to the way of the Word made flesh who at the sending by the Father takes His flesh in the power of the Spirit from the blessed virgin, and it is a likeness of that birth. It is indeed a matter of being given to share in that birth, as it is of sharing in Christ's baptism, His anointing with the Spirit in His identification with humanity in its need of repentance and the beginning of His ministry in setting His face towards His passion and cross.

Baptism for Irenaeus is the beginning of a life of obedience in Christ in participation in all that He is and does. The birth of Christ itself is not complete redemption, nor is it saving by itself. It is the ground of this, for it is the beginning of the exercise of obedience on the part of the Word made flesh which culminates in, by and through his death, with resurrection and ascension. Thus faith carries baptism throughout our days and in its baptismal beginning and growth is 'the perpetuation of our salvation'.[6]

Baptism in the view of Irenaeus is, in inseparable conjunction with this, our participation in the anointing of Christ by the Holy Spirit – that unction which is the power of the Spirit in which the incarnation of the Word takes place and the descent of the Spirit upon Him in the obedience of His baptism and subsequent 'cutting forward'. It is also therefore participation in the effected and loving will of the Father, for in it the Spirit bestows on us and realizes in us, the filial relation of the Son to the Father. In all this we become party to the concourse and conversation within the Triune Being of God and participate in the knowledge which God has of Himself. Thus:

> The Lord has redeemed us through His own blood, giving His soul for our souls and His flesh for our flesh, and also poured out the Spirit of the Father for the union and communion of God with man, imparting indeed God to man by means of the Spirit, and on the other hand, attaching man to God by His own incarnation, and bestowing upon us at His coming immortality durably and truly, by means of communion with God.[7]

Baptism is our 'seal', as Irenaeus calls it, whereby we are signed over to participate in communion with the very existence of the Triune God. It is our 'regeneration'[8] into God. Thus we are not sent back to the former state of affairs – 'to the legislation of Moses . . . in the oldness of the letter' – for our existence is now 'our calling by newness of the spirit'. This 'calling' is the fulfilment of the blessing of Japheth, 'the enlargement of Japheth in the dwellings of Shem'.[9]

It is the inheritance of the Gentiles, promised in the old covenant and to which the old covenant in its true substance and content looked, pointing to it in and beyond all its restrictions. The 'new testament was opened up' to this wide inheritance, notes Irenaeus in Section 91 quoting Isaiah XVII:7ff. For humanity needs no longer to trust 'in altars, nor in the work of their own hands, which their fingers have made'. This 'opening up' is not a development of which Christ is the agent. He Himself is the entrance of life. Only because of participation in the truth which He is may the church and the church's baptism be called 'the entrance of life'.[10]

The calling of the Gentiles and the removal from former things have a common theme. On the one hand, the Gentiles thus called by God are prophesied by Isaiah, in the passage which Irenaeus quotes in Section 91, as forsaking idols. On the other, according to Section 92, the removal from the former things of the old covenant involves the discarding of 'stony worship'. Irenaeus would seem to be indicating by this juxtaposition that adherence to the letter of the former legislation, written on stones, is of itself a form of idolatry. It is dead and lifeless, and is contrasted as 'a heart of flesh' against 'the stony heart', as 'stony worship' against beholding God by means of faith. The visibility of Gentile idols and Moses's tablets of stone is contrasted with the visibility of the Word.

Even in the time of the old covenant there were those Gentiles who had forsaken their idols and 'believed in God through the Holy One of Israel'. But their hope was firmly in the Christ who was to come in visible form, for 'the Holy One of Israel is Christ'. It was in 'the Holy One of Israel' that their hope was placed, as was the hope of the faith of Abraham.

Irenaeus, in pointing out the necessity of removing to the new covenant, does not indicate that he is advocating the total rejection of the law. In all his arguments on this theme he is careful to preserve the intent of that law and to show its paradigmatic role. There is no gulf between the old and new covenants in respect of their true content – they are one and the same substance in this regard. Indeed, in *Adversus Haereses*, he clearly states

> Preparing man for this life, the Lord Himself did speak in His own Person to all alike the words of the Decalogue; and therefore in like manner they remain with us permanently, receiving, by means of His advent in the flesh, extension and increase, but not abolition.[11]

What remains of value in the law is retained but moulded into that which is greater. The significance of the law was that it pointed to him as its σκοπος, and therefore there are retained and transformed those laws which

> He has increased and widened . . . which are natural and noble and common to all, granting to men largely and without grudging, by means of adoption, to know God the Father and to love Him with the whole heart, and to follow His word unswervingly.[12]

In this section of *Adversus Haereses*, Irenaeus points out that this new law is no easy option. It is clear that no longer need there be slaves to the old law – humanity bound in every deed by its demands – for now there is freedom under the new law. But this new law penetrates to the heart and substance of the old, to the looked for Self-revelation of God, and exhibits clearly the Word made flesh, the looked for Christ. This means that for those under the new law, in their knowledge of God found there, that Christ 'also increased the feeling of reverence; for sons should have more veneration than slaves, and greater love for their father'. This requires that account is made not just of deeds, as though humanity were enslaved by the demands of the law governing and directing its every action, but of thoughts and intents and words, for those 'who have truly received the power of liberty, in which a man is more severely tested whether he will reverence and fear and love the Lord'.[13]

There is a greater severity in the law of liberty, for that law uncovers and unveils what the content of the old law is, namely Christ Himself Personally confronting humanity as their knowledge of God and granting it freedom to be God's humanity, living to Him and not to itself, justified by Him and not by its self-justification in scrupulous observance of the rigorous strictures of the old law. No longer is 'Moses mediator, nor Elijah messenger: but the Lord Himself has redeemed us'. This is succinctly brought to a head in Section 96. But first, in the preceding two sections, Irenaeus lays the ground for this as he contrasts the church with the first synagogue in Section 94, and the failure of those under the first legislation with those who have faith in the Son of God and have thereby learned to love God truly, in Section 95.

In Section 94 he sets out the contrast between the old synagogue and the church in terms of the 'new calling'. This redemption, by reason of its universal call, grants 'many more children to the Church than to the first Synagogue'. Here Irenaeus reverses the states of the old synagogue and the church. He appeals to Isaiah XLIV:1 (Galatians IV:27), with the reference to 'the barren', which Irenaeus interprets as the church 'which never at all in former times presented sons to God'. Yet the first synagogue had every opportunity to do so. But she 'had as a husband the Law'. In other words the law is essentially impotent in and by itself, and it is the old synagogue which is in fact barren as a result.

This barrenness is shown in Section 95, where the contrast is between the love which those under the new law know, and the failure of those under the old law who had forsaken the God of Israel. He does this by a series of counterpoints: they 'forsook the God who is, and worshipped and served gods who are not'; slaying the prophets, they prophesied for Baal; despising and rejecting the Son of God, they chose instead a robber and murderer; 'the eternal King they disavowed' and instead gave their loyalty to Caesar.

Because of this, their inheritance (contrasted with the plight of the poverty of the Gentiles who are no people, much less sons of Abraham their father, who 'were not of the polity of God', and ignorant of God) is given to the Gentiles in the opening out of the covenant of love and faith in the Son of God.

In Section 96, Irenaeus contrasts the demands of the old law and the teachings of the new. There is no need for the law, now, as our 'tutor'. The law is superfluous to those whose heart has been hallowed and who have 'grown strong in all righteousness'. The external prohibitions concerning the malicious behaviour of adultery, killing, coveting and the exacting of like vengeance for wrongs done by an enemy, have no place for those who have, in faith and love, been brought to put the thought and intent of such things away.

The law is no longer necessary as a mediator, for now, since it has been fulfilled and transformed in and by the Word made flesh: 'Behold, with the Father we speak, and in His presence we stand'. This is the urgency, the crisis, the reverence and the immediacy of love which the new law lays before us. This is brought about by 'the name of the Lord'.

Here again we see particularity and universality brought together in Irenaeus's thought. He quotes the prophet Joel: 'whosoever shall call upon the name of the Lord shall be saved';[14] and appeals to the Acts of the Apostles[15] to assist in the identification of this 'name': that there is 'none other name of the Lord given under heaven whereby men are saved', and concludes that this name is not other than 'that of God, which is Jesus Christ the Son of God'.

This particular name, and this alone, is that which has universal effect because of its particularity. Here Armitage Robinson notes that Barthoulout, the Jesuit translator of the Armenian text of the *Demonstration* into French, was of the opinion that the first words of Section 97 have been wrongly separated from the end of the preceding chapter. The removal of these words back to the preceding section changes the translation of what then would be the opening of Section 97. The revised sections, from the end of 96 and the new beginning of 97, would then read:

> And there is none other name of the Lord given under heaven whereby men are saved, save that of God, which is Jesus Christ the Son of God, to which also the demons are subject and evil spirits and all apostate energies by the invocation of the name of Jesus Christ, crucified under Pontius Pilate.
>
> He is separated and withdrawn from among men, and (yet) wheresoever any of those who believe on Him should invoke and call upon Him and do His will, He is near and present, fulfilling the requests of those who with pure hearts call upon Him.

J. Smith's translation[16] has kept to the former division between the sections, but this arrangement suggested by Barthoulout fits better with the flow and the sense of Irenaeus's development of argument here. The invocation of the name of 'Jesus Christ crucified under Pontius Pilate', is also used in *Adversus Haereses* in the same way as this re-ordering suggests, in the context of the gifts received by the disciples whereby they were able to perform miracles, drive out demons, heal the sick and raise up the dead, and of the similar gifts bestowed upon the church by God 'in the name of Jesus Christ who was crucified under Pontius Pilate, and which she exerts day by day for the benefit of the Gentiles'.[17]

Section 97 continues with a declaration of salvation by the grace of God – 'to which we by ourselves could not attain'. This salvation is by 'the great, inscrutable and unsearchable wisdom' of God delivering us, which wisdom is 'the visible coming of our Lord, that is, His living as man'. Salvation for Irenaeus is firmly Christocentric, for it is a matter of the wisdom of God operative for and towards and in His creation. This wisdom is borne by the Son alone, and Irenaeus cites a long passage from Baruch,[18] which he attributes to Jeremiah, regarding the impossibility and futility of the human search for, and finding of, this wisdom. The gist of the quotation as employed by Irenaeus is that God alone knows all things and this knowledge is exhibited in His creation which, in turn, acknowledges Him to be the God without comparison. The underlying implication is that only God knows God, and only God comprehends creation truly in His dispensation of its order. This knowledge *in se* and *ad extra* is bestowed upon the Son, whom Irenaeus, gathering up all that he has set down previously as to the true significance of Israel and the old covenant, identifies with 'Jacob his servant and Israel that is beloved of him'. This knowledge, Irenaeus further notes, is 'power over life', and it is this which the Son, having received it from the Father, brings down at His incarnation and in His conversing with humanity.

Here we must be careful as to Irenaeus's use of 'Spirit'. If this use in the phrase 'mingling and mixing the Spirit of God the Father with the creature formed by God', refers, as we have noted already, that it sometimes can so refer in the thought of Irenaeus to the essential being of God, that is, His 'Godness', and that this phrase is to be read as indicating the incarnation, then it does not refer to the mode of the incarnation, as if Christ were a *tertium quid*, a 'third thing', between God and humanity, a compound of both, but to His presence in the flesh as God amongst humanity. That is, the Son of God, as God in all His Godness, is with us, in His concourse and conversation with humanity at His incarnation.

We have commented already, for example on the content of Section 31, as to Irenaeus's scrupulous insistence as to the reality, and continuance of that reality, of the human nature of Christ, and the reality and the continuance of that reality of His divine nature, and the mode of union whereby the integrity of both natures is preserved. Here then is a comment, it must be stressed, not on the mode of the incarnation, but of the very presence of God in the midst of, and conversant with, humanity. If, however, it refers to the pouring out of 'the Holy Spirit' (as it more likely does) whereby the 'community of union' established by the incarnation is confirmed, then the same stricture as to the preservation of human nature upon which the Spirit is poured by Christ, and the integrity of the divinity of the Spirit, holds. Humanity is not transformed into something different; it is transformed in its relation to God, in which relation it now really is affirmed in its formerly lost integrity as being 'after the image of God'.[19] 'Mingling and mixing' refers to the relation through the Word made flesh or the Spirit outpoured, of humanity in its integrity as creature, with God in His divine integrity.

The last two sections of the *Demonstration* are warnings and exhortations of Irenaeus that the faith is to be kept in its purity. Here he joins, as it were, the end to the beginning of this work, this *Demonstration* of his. It is noteworthy that he emphasizes the necessity of holding fast to faith in the triune God, 'the three points of our seal', that is, our baptism, with which he began the setting out of this

Demonstration of the content of the Apostolic preaching, underlining that the Creator is Father, that the dispensation of the Son of God in the incarnation is to be kept inviolate, and that the Holy Spirit, who by the prophets laid out this dispensation, and whose outpouring is the fruition of 'life unto God' in that dispensation, is not to be despised.

In *Adversus Haereses*, to give one example of his credal statement of this faith, Irenaeus writes in similar vein regarding the 'spiritual disciple':

> . . . to him all things are consistent: he has a full faith in one God Almighty, of whom are all things; and in the Son of God, Jesus Christ our Lord, by whom are all things, and in the dispensations connected with Him, by means of which the Son of God became man; and a firm belief in the Spirit of God, who furnishes us with a knowledge of the truth, and has set forth the dispensations of the Father and the Son, in virtue of which He dwells with every generation of men, according to thc will of the Father.[20]

In the significant phrases which Irenaeus uses in all these closing sections of his work, his reverential approach to the truth of God, the dispensation of which he has laid out, is clear. He is aware that in that dispensation of the Word made flesh, in which by grace we have been incorporated in 'a community of union with God, behold with the Father we speak and in his presence we stand. This, beloved, is the preaching of the truth, and this is the manner of our redemption, and this is the way of life, which the prophets proclaimed, and Christ established, and the apostles delivered, and the church hands on to her children'. Only in this can we, and Marcianos, 'desire to be well-pleasing to God, and to attain the redemption that is from Him'.

Notes

1 Irenaeus: *Adversus Haereses* IV:33:14.
2 *Ibid.* IV:14:2.
3 *Ibid.* III:17:2,3.
4 Comments on Sections 6 and 7, Chapter 5.
5 Irenaeus: *Demonstration* 7.
6 *Ibid.* 3.
7 Irenaeus: *Adversus Haereses* V:1:1.
8 Irenaeus: *Demonstration* 7.
9 Cf. comments on Section 45, Chapter 13.
10 Irenaeus: *Adversus Haereses* III:4:1.
11 *Ibid.* IV:16:4.
12 *Ibid.* IV:16:5.
13 *Ibid.*
14 Joel II:32.
15 Acts IV:12.
16 J. Smith: *Proof of the Apostolic Preaching*, p. 107.
17 Irenaeus: Adversus Haereses II:32:4.
18 Baruch III:29–IV:1.
19 Cf. comments on Sections 29–42, Chapter 12.
20 Irenaeus: *Adversus Haereses* IV:33:7.

Bibliography

Patristic Sources cited

The patristic texts, unless otherwise noted, are from the nineteenth-century Edinburgh Edition: *The Ante-Nicene Fathers* and *The Nicene and Post-Nicene Fathers*. The footnote references at the end of each chapter are in accordance with the scheme used in each of these volumes.

Athanasius: *De Decretis*; *Contra Arianos*; *De Incarnatione*
Athenagoras: *A Plea for the Christians*
Basil: *Hexaemeron*; *Homilies*
Clement of Alexandria: *Stromata*; *The Instructor*; *Exhortation to the Heathen*
Clement of Rome: *Epistles*
Eusebius: *Ecclesiastical History*
Gregory Nazianzen: *Orationes*
Gregory of Nyssa: *Against Eunomius*
Hermas: *Vision*
Irenaeus: *Adversus Haereses*; *Fragments*
Jerome (and Gennadius): *Lives of Illustrious Men*
Justin Martyr: *Dialogue with Trypho*; *Apology*
Melito of Sardis: *On Pascha and Fragments* (S. G. Hall, Clarendon, 1979)
Papias: *Fragment*
Socrates: *Ecclesiastical History*
Tatian: *Address to the Greeks*
Theoderet: *Dialogues*; *Letters*

Other Sources Cited

Grosseteste, R: *De Cessationne Legalium* (R. C. Dales and E. B. King: Oxford University Press for the British Academy, 1986).
Andrewes, Lancelot: *Sermons of the Nativitie*, 1635 edn.

Translations of the *Demonstration of the Apostolic Preaching*

J. Armitage Robinson: *SPCK*, 1920
J. P. Smith: *Westminster*, 1952

While this Theological Commentary was being completed, a new translation of Irenaeus's *Demonstration* by J. Behr was published (SVS Press).

Index